Economics
as an
Evolutionary
Science

Economics
as an
Evolutionary
Science

From Utility to Fitness

Arthur E. Gandolfi
Anna Sachko Gandolfi
David P. Barash

Routledge
Taylor & Francis Group

LONDON AND NEW YORK

First published 2002 by Transaction Publishers

Published 2017 by Routledge
2 Park Square, Milton Park, Abingdon, Oxon OX14 4RN
711 Third Avenue, New York, NY 10017

First issued in paperback 2018

Routledge is an imprint of the Taylor and Francis Group, an informa business

Library of Congress Catalog Number: 2002028628

Library of Congress Cataloging-in-Publication Data

Gandolfi, Arthur E.
    Economics as an evolutionary science : from utility to fitness / Arthur E. Gandolfi, Anna Sachko Gandolfi, and David P. Barash.
        p. cm.
    Includes bibliographical references and index.
    ISBN 0-7658-0123-X (alk. paper)
        1. Economics. I. Gandolfi, Anna Sachko. II. Barash, David P. III. Title.

HB71 .G298 2002
330—dc21   2002028628

ISBN 13: 978-1-138-50937-5 (pbk)
ISBN 13: 978-0-7658-0123-4 (hbk)

We dedicate this book to our children,

Arthur, Adrienne, and Amy Gandolfi
Ilona, Eva, and Nellie Barash

without whose existence our appreciation of the arguments
presented in this book might not have been possible.

Contents

Figures and Tables

Introduction

"Economics" derives from the Greek words *oiko,* meaning, "house," and *nomos,* "manager." Hence: *oikonomikos,* for "household manager." Traditionally, economics is taken to be the social science concerned with the production, consumption, exchange and distribution of wealth and commodities. Thus, economists carefully track the comings and goings of the human household, whether written small (microeconomics) or large (macroeconomics). They generate models, often of remarkably arcane complexity, attempting to predict future transactions, especially given certain hypothetical perturbations: What will happen to demand or supply if certain prices go up? What if interest rates go down? And so forth.

This is well and good, except that in its concern for modeling and predicting patterns of "household management," economists have by and large stayed remarkably indifferent to the actual characteristics and motivations of their subjects. These "managers," it must be pointed out, are human beings, members of the species *Homo sapiens.* As such, they bring certain traits to their encounter with the economic world, traits that derive from their nature as biological creatures, generated by a process of organic evolution and carrying its stigmata not only in their bodies but also in their minds. By largely ignoring the nature of human nature, economists have found the goal of an explanatory and predictive science to be elusive.

The present book is an ambitious and perhaps immodest attempt to rectify this problem—or at least, to gesture toward a way of doing so. It is based on the presumption that what economics needs is a more direct appreciation of the essence of its subject: human nature in its biological nakedness, as increasingly revealed by advances in evolutionary science. It is an attempt to marry economics and evolution in the hope of producing a productive new framework. In recent decades, these disciplines have been on a parallel if not convergent course, so that only a small shove may be needed to consummate—or at least, initiate—a union.

The result, we believe, could well be a social science that is rigorous, internally coherent, testable, and most important, consistent with the natural sciences. It is noteworthy that Edward O. Wilson, orchestrator of sociobiology (Wilson, 1975)—itself a synthesis of evolutionary genetics, ecology, and ethology—has also emphasized the desirability as well as the feasibility of such a conceptual union or "consilience" among the sciences, if not all fields of human intellectual endeavor (Wilson, 1998).

The present book is also, to some degree, an example of the medium being the message: written by two economists and a biologist/psychologist, it is itself a collaboration across disciplines. Obviously, we hope that it succeeds, with "success" measured by the degree to which it stimulates further thinking and research.

The bulk of our argument is a framework for integrating economics and evolutionary theory in the hope of producing a better structure for analyzing human behavior, in all its manifestations. Although, in a world of post-modernist academic anarchy, we embrace the heretical notion that there is such a thing as objective scientific truth, we are under no illusions that our goal will be easily achieved, in terms of either professional acceptance or empirical validation. Indeed, we are not so naive, or arrogant, to believe that a creature so complex as *Homo sapiens* will succumb to any single explanatory system, even one so embracing as evolution. The question is not whether such a system makes all others obsolete, but whether it significantly advances knowledge about a difficult and elusive subject.

Shortly after the emergence of sociobiology into public consciousness—during the 1970s and early 1980s—many of its practitioners were guilty of a certain *hubris*, not only proclaiming that the social sciences had failed to achieve a coherent understanding of human behavior (something we reiterate unblushingly), but also that any well-trained sociobiologist would be able to "straighten out" such fields as psychology, anthropology, sociology, even political science, if he or she were only given a semester free.

It hasn't quite happened, partly because biology itself is less mature and comprehensive than one might wish, partly because human beings are devilishly complicated creatures, and partly because of the disciplinary limitations of academies and their denizens. The problem is a bit like the famous story of the blind men and the elephant, as told by the nineteenth-century American poet, John Saxe (1892):

It was six men from Industan, to learning much inclined,
Who went to see the elephant (though all of them were blind),
That each by observation might satisfy his mind ...

Not surprisingly, each blind man felt a different part of the elephant, so that the one touching its legs thought they were tree trunks, the one touching its tail thought it was a snake, and so on. By the end, they

Disputed loud and long, each in his opinion stiff and strong,
Though each was partly in the right, and all of them were wrong.

Sociology, anthropology, psychology and—not least—economics have expended enormous intellectual effort, but have not achieved a picture of human beings that is any more comprehensive or consistent. We suggest that just as the elephant, to be appreciated if not fully understood, must be seen in its entirety, the subject of the social sciences must also be seen in its underlying reality, which is no less biological, no less the product of organic evolution, than Saxe's mythical pachyderm.

We do not claim that economists are blind when it comes to perceiving human beings, or at least, they are no more myopic than most of their colleagues. On one hand, economics is a self-contained, internally consistent logical system and is thus an immense intellectual achievement, as impressive in its own right as any philosophic enterprise ever invented. In its own way it parallels modern physics, a discipline that economics has often tried to imitate in style, if not in technological success. But sad to say, the ability of economists to predict the behavior of human beings or even to explain their behavior after the fact is very meager compared with the power of the analytical engine at their disposal.

At the same time, it is noteworthy that there has already been considerable interchange between the sciences of economics and evolution, or, perhaps more accurately, substantial parallelism and convergence. Thus, whereas economists often see people as utility maximizers, biologists identify living things (including human beings) as fitness maximizers. Economists have pioneered cost-benefit analysis, which has also been employed by biologists to analyze trade-offs whereby animals are selected to behave optimally. Indeed, detailed optimality models—developed by biologists to interpret foraging and reproductive strategies in particular—develop parameters with which most economists would be surprisingly familiar: Is a foraging bird, for example, an input (calorie) maximizer, a risk minimizer, a time minimizer, and so on? (See, for example, Stephens and Krebs, 1986.) Another recently developed interest among biologists is the use of game theory models, wherein the optimum payoff for each contestant is crucially influenced by the tactics employed by the other, no less than by one's self (e.g., Maynard Smith, 1988). In these and other considerations, economists and evolutionary biologists already are, if not intentional bedfellows, then at least accidental intellectual soul mates. As Hirshleifer (1977, pp. 1-2), an early pioneer in the integration of economics and biology, has stated, "The fundamental organizing concepts of the dominant analytical structures employed in economics and in sociobiology are strikingly parallel."

This book is a serious attempt to revise and extend current economic theory, for a broad audience, including professional economists but not limited to them. We believe that what we have to say is relevant to anyone concerned with human affairs, and shall therefore attempt to write in an open and non-technical manner. Where we believe a more formal treatment is required, it is placed in a technical appendix. These may be ignored by the general reader.

Economics is at its heart a theory of rational choice. It is perfectly general; as we discuss below, there is nothing inherent in economic theory that either limits or links it exclusively to *human* behavior. This high level of abstraction and generality is at once the source of economics' strength and its weakness. We contend that despite its evident power, economics is incomplete and needlessly self-limiting, and on occasion, at risk of falling into tautology. By connecting economics more directly to the primary concerns and nature of its subjects—human beings—economics can be made stronger.

To be sure, economics (even disconnected from biology) has been a productive enterprise. Many important theorems can be derived from the pure theory of rational choice, and even if all people don't behave as the theory predicts, economists can argue that they should, not as an ethical imperative, but as a hypothetical imperative, that is, if you want to achieve your goals—whatever they may be—you should be rational maximizers. In this sense, economics has had some of its greatest success in the sub-discipline of finance, in which the goal of profit maximization is both concrete and achievable. It is not surprising that a theory of rational choice does best when the goal is simple profit maximization, and when the actors have been trained and selected for their ability to achieve this goal in a rather abstract (non-household) environment.

It is a characteristic of financial markets to exclude participants who fail to play by the rule of profit maximization. This guarantees that economic theory will be relevant to this chosen area of human activity. It also provides an important clue to how the social sciences in general and economics in particular might usefully be reformulated.

But before embarking on that adventure, we note another area in which economics has also been very successful; one that is in many respects the opposite of finance. It deals with more mundane arenas of human behavior such as marriage, child rearing, schooling, and other activities not usually considered the province of economists, and usually left to sociologists and the occasional psychologist. Nobel laureate Gary Becker, holder of a joint chair in economics and sociology at the University of Chicago, is the pioneer and chief exponent of this approach, one that succeeds in large part because he puts severe constraints on the behavior he studies. For example, Becker assumes that all people share identical tastes and values regardless of their age, sex, or culture. Differences in behavior are thought to result from the different constraints people face in achieving their common goals. More of this later.

In our opinion, the current sad state of the social sciences has a common root, namely, an almost complete disregard and in some cases, hostility toward evolution.[1] In the past thirty years, tremendous advances have been made in understanding both the logic of the evolutionary process and how evolution actively shapes the behavior of all living organisms, including human beings. The importance of evolutionary theory is manifold: Notably, it provides a valid theoretical structure that permits one to integrate all aspects of biology within a comparatively simple scientific framework, one that is also compatible with the physical sciences.

It also allows us to convert all behavior into a single currency, namely, reproductive success. This does not imply conscious assessment by those doing the behaving. For example, when psychologist Brian Little (1989) asked people to identify their "personal projects," they responded either with limited goals such as learning to type or to execute a Telemark ski turn, or larger enterprises such as achieving a particular career or even promoting nuclear disarmament. In twenty years of such inquiry, however, Little reports that no one has ever responded: "I'm maximizing my reproductive success." Nonetheless, this does not mean that proximate behaviors are disconnected from their ultimate, biological goal, even if that connection may be roundabout and not immediately accessible to conscious awareness. (People eat, in most cases, because they feel hungry, not because they are intentionally providing caloric input whereby their intracellular metabolism will eventually generate energy via the production of ATP molecules. But the human need for ATP ultimately drives the sensation of hunger, just as reproductive considerations ultimately drive many seemingly non-reproductive activities.)

As we shall see, the measure of reproductive success is simple neither in practice nor in theory. In particular, perhaps the greatest advance in evolutionary biology in recent decades has been the demonstration by William D. Hamilton (1964) that natural selection operates not on bodies but on genes, with the former merely a proxy for the latter. Such a "gene-centered" perspective provides a more inclusive measure of evolutionary success than mere production of offspring. Nonetheless, science generally advances via creative reductionism, and for much of our purpose we can consider that human beings have been under distinct and long-lasting pressure to maximize their reproductive success.

By converting disparate behavior into a single measure of value, we can make specific predictions about behavior that can be tested in quantitative form. We shall also develop a simple model, showing how the evolutionary approach can be used to extend and enrich the economic model of consumer choice. Of all the social sciences, we have chosen economics as the one to integrate into evolutionary theory because it enjoys the most logical and articulated form. Like geometry, economics has a premise-and-theorem structure. It lends itself, therefore, to making changes in certain premises and thereby deriving new and interesting conclusions. The model presented is simple, but (or perhaps, *because* of its simplicity) we believe that it can shed light on the most basic life activities in which individuals engage.

We also extend our model to incorporate sexual reproduction. The existence of two sexes that invest differently in their joint offspring leads to the adoption of differing reproductive strategies within and between the sexes (Barash and Lipton, 1997), which in turn adds complexity to any reproduction-based model. It is especially illuminating to understand the origin and operation of these strategies in light of the revolution that has occurred in families, child rearing, and sexual conduct in the last forty years.

Often people represent the learning process as a straight line, so that in studying any discipline, it is necessary to proceed step by step, ascending a ladder of knowledge. For example, one must "know" arithmetic before tackling algebra, and one must understand algebra before taking on calculus. Although this metaphor may hold for self-contained disciplines such as mathematics, we do not believe that it applies to wider, less bounded fields of inquiry. This is especially true when confronting something as complicated as human behavior, in which the contributions from many disciplines are required.

In such cases, it may be best to adopt a recursive approach to knowledge, in which particular arguments or analytical problems are addressed and the results used to further one's understanding of other distinct, but related areas of inquiry. Eventually the knowledge gained from the latter effort is used to deepen the understanding of the former. Instead of viewing the search for knowledge as a linear structure in which, step by step, one advances understanding of a particular field of inquiry, we prefer to think of the search as a spiral staircase. (It is only coincidence, but this metaphor of the spiral staircase of knowledge closely resembles the double helix in which the human genetic code resides.)

Moving up this staircase, one continually revisits, at higher and higher levels, the same problems and fields of inquiry previously encountered at a lower level of understanding. For example, to understand history, one must have some knowledge of politics, but a full understanding of politics requires some knowledge of history, and so forth.

This is the approach we have adopted in this book. Certain aspects of human behavior are revisited in different ways, and at different times. We hope that each time we deal with one of these issues, we will advance and provoke the reader's understanding of economics as an enterprise engaged in by human beings, living creatures with an evolutionary, biological past, and whose behavior in the present is distinctly influenced by their shared organic nature.

Note

1.   This statement is not meant to disparage or ignore the pioneering work done by Hirshleifer, Tullock, Alchian, Bergstrom, and other economists who have attempted to integrate the concepts of evolution into the discipline of economics. Despite this growing body of work, economics has, by and large, remained immune to its influence.

1

To Measure Man

Physicist and novelist C. P. Snow famously decried the separation of natural science and the humanities into "two cultures" (Snow, 1959). The chasm persists. Indeed, there is also a deep and persistent intellectual divide between the two great branches of scientific knowledge: the so-called natural sciences and those concerned with the study of human behavior. (Should the latter be designated the "unnatural sciences"?) As a matter of principle, any science worthy of the name should be consistent, not only internally but also consistent with every other science.

A strong case has been made that the natural sciences are already mutually consistent, or "conciliate" (Wilson, 1998). Thus, there is nothing in the laws of chemistry or biology that contradicts those of physics and vice versa, even though we have not yet reached the point where "everything" can be expressed according to one set of universal laws.

"A conceptually integrated theory," we learn in a seminal collection of articles devoted to evolutionary psychology, a human-focused incarnation of sociobiology, is one framed so that it is compatible with data and theory from other relevant fields. Chemists do not propose theories that violate the elementary physics principle of conservation of energy. Instead, they use the principle to make sound inferences about chemical processes. (Cosmides, Tooby, and Barkow, 1992, p. 4).

Whereas natural science can be considered a continuous web, the same cannot be said for its social and behavioral counterparts. Not only are they not coherently integrated into the natural sciences, they are not even integrated among—or, worse yet, within—themselves.

1

This failure of the social sciences to integrate with the natural sciences is serious enough to call into question their right to the title "science." In fact they are often called "soft sciences" in recognition that they do not have the same standing that the natural sciences enjoy in the hierarchy of knowledge and of public esteem. Even more than biology or chemistry, they suffer—and rightfully—from "physics envy."

This failing is often excused by pointing to the fact that, in general, the social sciences are younger, don't have the benefit of repeatable experimentation, and are dealing with phenomena that are more complicated. Even if this explains the lack of integration between the natural and social sciences, how does it account for the complete lack of coherence and consistency among the social sciences themselves?

Introductory students in the natural sciences, after being exposed to the neo-classic texts in their fields, such as Richard Feynman's *Lectures on Physics*, or Linus Pauling's *General Chemistry*, cannot avoid appreciating the profound intellectual momentum with which theories are introduced, evaluated, then refuted or carried further, leading to additional theories of even greater explanatory power. Biology, too, enjoys a comparable unification, owing to the organizing principle of organic evolution.

By contrast, the study of human behavior has remained stubbornly balkanized, not only among such fields as anthropology, psychology, sociology, political science, and even economics, but also, within these disciplines. It is significant that the "social sciences" are characterized by various schools of thought, each named for a different individual whose particular approach it represents. Thus, we have Pavlovians, Skinnerians, Freudians, Marxians, Weberians, Comteans, Durkheimians, Boasians, Keynesians, and so forth, stretching to the intellectual horizon in virtually every direction. Allegiance seems more determined by historical accident and emotional attachments rather than by objectively valid criteria. Returning to our blind men and the elephant, there have been devotees of one guru or another,

> each in his opinion stiff and strong,
> Though each was partly in the right, and all of them were wrong.

Scholars in each field can and often do spend their entire professional lives studying human behavior without any reference to or knowledge of any other discipline. It is astonishing and something of an intellectual scandal that at a time when the physical sciences—ranging from geology to chemistry to biology to physics—form a coherent and mutually consistent body of knowledge, there exists such incoherence within the social sciences.

Within the varied and at times confused collection of theories that we call social science there are at least two great philosophical traditions that bear almost no relationship to each other. These both claim to explain human behavior but are based on different assumptions, posit different laws, and come to widely different and often contradictory results and predictions. These two branches are economics and anthropology/sociology/psychology et al.

To some extent, each of these branches of the social sciences occupies its own watertight compartment, with the explanations and predictions of one having little or no bearing on the explanations and predictions of the other. Or, more benevolently, there has existed for some time a live and let live attitude in which economists have dealt only with behavior involved in some way with markets and exchange while anthropologists, psychologists and sociologists have had the rest of the playing field. Even in the past, however, this boundary was never fully respected. In the last forty years, it has increasingly broken down.

The major aggressor was economics. Led by Gary Becker, economists have dared to use their analytical tools to investigate questions such as discrimination, marriage, fertility, and crime, subject matters once firmly under the surveillance of the other disciplines.[1] This encroachment of economics into the preserve of the other social sciences has created occasional crises in these disciplines. They can no longer pretend that the other fields do not exist or that human beings are simply inconsistent, behaving according to one set of laws when engaging in market exchanges and adhering to a wholly different set for every other activity.

Becker's approach entails the rejection of the traditional theoretical framework of sociology and its replacement by an economic model. He attempts to explain such diverse phenomena as crime, fertility and marriage by nothing more or less than basic economic theory. As one would expect, his efforts have not been greeted with open arms by scholars working in the other social sciences. His efforts, along with those of economists moving along similar paths, have often been viewed as a threat, as a form of "economic imperialism," aimed at destroying the independence of these disciplines.

During the same period that Becker and his disciples have been attempting to integrate the social sciences under the theoretical umbrella of economics, there has been another serious assault on the traditional social science framework, from biology. An enormous body of work has been produced by eminent scientists including George C. Williams, William D. Hamilton, Edward O. Wilson, Robert Trivers, and Richard Alexander, who have pioneered the use of evolutionary theory as the most promising conceptual framework to explain human behavior.

It is interesting to note that whereas this literature is generally critical of traditional social science—which emphasizes the role of social rules, learning, and cultural tradition in generating human behavior—it is often complimentary about economics. There seems to be a conscious or even unconscious appreciation that despite surface differences, economics and evolutionary biology share a fundamental kinship, one that runs deeper than the fact that Darwin was inspired to discover natural selection from reading the work of the great classical economist, Malthus.

It is our contention that these two approaches are fundamentally consistent. They both have, at the core of their theories, the concepts of maximization and efficiency. It is the purpose of this book to show and extend this consistency and to outline an initial project of integrating evolutionary biology and economics.

It is as though the remaining social sciences are fighting a two-front war, with economics invading from the north and biology from the south. What is needed, however, is not capitulation, or a treaty dividing up the conquered territory into two zones of occupation, but a new constitution to form an integrated republic for both the natural and social sciences. The result, we hope, will be an internally coherent, fully integrated social science, consistent and compatible with the natural sciences as well.

To some extent, this integration has already begun. Anthropology, because of its broad, species-wide perspective, is well positioned to appreciate the existence of cross-cultural universals in human behavior, indicating the existence of a shared human identity, founded on the biological commonality of all *Homo sapiens*. Indeed, "evolutionary anthropologists" have become an increasingly powerful voice within their discipline (e.g., Chagnon and Irons, 1979). At the same time, "evolutionary psychology" has achieved growing public prominence as well as academic legitimacy, with insights focused especially upon male-female differences, developmental processes, aggression, and issues surrounding kinship (e.g., Buss, 1999). Even sociology (e.g., van den Berghe, 1979) and political science (e.g., Masters, 1989) have gotten into the act, or perhaps they have begun, at last, to "get their act together." In any event, and although they remain minority traditions within their respective disciplines, the increase in biologically oriented, integrated approaches in the social sciences has been perceptible (see Degler, 1991, for a historian's review of the revival of evolutionary approaches in American social thought).

Even as most social sciences—despite their traditional antipathy to evolution as an organizing principle—have begun, however haltingly, to embrace biology, economics has remained largely celibate. This is especially ironic given the intellectual camaraderie that naturally links the two disciplines. Hence this book, in which we hope to "post the banns" for an eventual marriage, or at least establish some common principles for an amicable living-together agreement.

There is an old economist joke that when you ask a question, the number of different opinions is equal to the number of economists plus one. Similarly, President Harry Truman used to complain that what he really needed was a one-handed economist, since whenever he asked his economic advisers about the consequence of a particular course of action, they would give an initial reply, and then add, "but on the other hand ..."

What laymen don't realize (on the other hand) is the degree of uniformity that exists among economists on most theoretical issues. With regard to microeconomics, the study of price theory and of individual choice, there is no serious disagreement. It is, by and large, a settled theory. This makes its presentation in the next chapter fairly non-controversial and straightforward.

But before turning to economics, we shall glance briefly at some of the major efforts by the other social sciences to understand human behavior, emphasizing those that have sought to achieve a larger conceptual framework.

Functionalism

Among the earliest such approaches—and one that still retains vitality today—is "functionalism," a theory holding that the appropriate way to study any institution or social practice is to understand the contribution that it makes to the survival of society as a whole. The chosen metaphor for functionalists is the human body. Analyzing the "functions" of a social practice is like showing how the various organs of the body function together to enhance the overall health and well being of the total organism. In the case of society, functionalism attempts to show how institutions and social practices relate to each other in furthering their ultimate goal, the continued existence of that society.

Social solidarity is essential to the survival of society, which in turn is essential to the survival of each of its members. The classic example provided by Durkheim (who along with Auguste Comte is one of the fathers of functionalism) is the division of labor, specialization into the various subtasks that go into the production of economic goods and services. Durkheim argued that the growing interdependence of workers in the economic process would eventually replace religion as the main basis of social solidarity. However, the question arises whether division of labor occurs because society "needs" a new basis of solidarity or whether division of labor is an unintended consequence of a process driven by individual entrepreneurs and workers each acting in his or her own self interest. Economists give the latter explanation, while sociologists tend toward the former.

Functionalism has two major defects. It elevates the need for social cohesion above all other forces impinging on society. More importantly, it personifies society. Functionalism carries the organic metaphor to the point of attributing to society qualities such as needs and purposes, which only individuals can have. Even if society and its members as a whole would benefit from a social practice that enhances solidarity, it is necessary to show how its members would be motivated to initiate and sustain this practice. There are many good things that would benefit a social group that are never done because they are never in any person's or sub-group's best interest to do them.

This is the classic free-rider problem that economists and game theorists have studied exhaustively, and which has been given additional life by theoretical advances in biology, which emphasize selection operating at the level of the individual—and of the gene—rather than the group (Williams, 1966). Traditional functionalists fell into this logical trap because their methodology is not sufficiently reductionist. That is, in trying to explain human action, they do not start their analysis with the actor. Rather, they have a collective view of what determines human behavior. This point is so important that we will return to it often in the next few chapters. It appears again when we discuss the evolutionary fallacy of group selection.

Functionalism is also, to a large degree, the reigning theory of social anthropology. Modern anthropology began at the end of the 19th century, with the work of such pioneers as Bronislaw Malinowski (1884-1942) and A.R. Radcliffe-Brown (1881-1955), who were tremendously influenced by Durkheim. These researchers specialized in examining the remaining pre-modern societies and believed that a society or culture could only be studied as a whole, if one hoped to understand its structure and institutions and to understand the behavior of its members (Giddens, 1991).

Robert Merton (b. 1910) developed a more sophisticated version of functionalism, which has been immensely influential in sociology. Merton divided functions into two types, manifest and latent (following and paralleling Freud's identification of manifest *versus* latent content in dreams). Manifest social functions are those desired or intended by individuals. For example, Hopi Indians engage in a rain dance that has the manifest function of helping their crops. Latent functions are the unintended consequences of a social activity. The rain dance may have the latent function of promoting social cohesion among the participants. The major objective of sociological study, according to this approach, is to uncover the latent function of social behavior.

Merton's analysis, while introducing the important concept of unintended consequences into sociology, still suffers from the problem of assigning to abstract concepts such as society, attributes such as "needs" and "purposes" that can only be usefully applied to human beings.

For some types of social action, however, the distinction between intended and unintended effects of social activities can be useful as well as meaningful. Take for example, economic exchange. The intended consequence is to make participants in the exchange "better off" by trading goods of lower value for those of higher value. Besides this direct intended consequence of economic exchange, which provides motivation for the behavior, there may well be unintended consequences. Economic exchange may increase economic interdependence as well as social trust between the participants and thereby increase social cohesiveness. But the fact that the spillover effect of economic exchange is positive may be largely fortuitous. It could just as well have been negative, as in the case of pollution being the unintended by-product of economic production. If the unintended effect is negative enough, the activity may ultimately disappear from the social repertoire; in a biological context, we would then say that it had been "selected against." Nonetheless, the mere existence of a social phenomenon does not necessarily indicate that it was functionally generated by society as a whole, any more than a chance mutation—whether adaptive or maladaptive—is functionally generated by an organism's genome.

Economists are very familiar with the concept of spillover effects from individual behavior; they invented it. In economics, these are called externalities, and are a necessary and important concept in social science.

Marxism also has functionalist components. Thus, it asserts that all societies rest upon an economic infrastructure, with all social institutions, including politics, religion, culture, and law constituting an edifice that depends on the underlying form of economic production. For Marxists, social institutions will necessarily reflect the class interest of those owning the means of production. Changes in production give rise to new social classes and set up tensions in existing institutions, which leads to social evolution or revolution.

Marxism suffers from some of the same problems as functionalism, to which it is related. Thus, Marxism deals with large historical forces without paying sufficient attention to the motivation and behavior of the individuals who constitute the society. For example, Marx postulated the existence of class conflict as a major factor promoting social change. But there is no logical reason why inter-class conflict should be more prevalent than intra-class conflict, that is, competition among different capitalists or among workers. (In the biological world, intra-species competition is nearly always more pronounced than its inter-species counterpart.)

Functionalism and Marxism both deal with large-scale social structures and processes at the expense of analyzing individual behavior.

We turn next to the dominant approach that characterizes most current individual-focused thinking in the social sciences.

The "Standard Social Science Model"

The social sciences are not monolithic. Nonetheless, there exists a more or less homogeneous underpinning to the disciplines concerned with human behavior. It derives from many different strands, all of which emphasize the importance of environmental factors—notably learning and culture—in producing human society. Max Weber (1864-1920) was a general social thinker who could be considered as much an economist as a sociologist. He emphasized that ideas and values are as important to social change as are changes in economic structure. With his concern for the importance of ideas and values, Weber was a forerunner of "Symbolic Interactionism," an approach pioneered by George Herbert Mead (1863-1931).

As its name suggests, symbolic interactionism is concerned with the importance of symbols in everyday behavior. According to Mead, language allows us to become self-conscious, to think about ourselves in the first person. Humans live in a rich symbolic universe and virtually all interactions between individuals involve an exchange of symbols. Both the individual's personality and society as a whole are the result of social interactions based on language and other symbols.

But any theory that simply asserts the primacy of culture has contributed little in the way of explaining the behavior of individual human beings. What, for example, determines differences in behavior among various cultures? An answer relying on "differences in the cultures" is really no explanation at all. The natural follow-up question becomes: "What causes these differences in cultures?"

Any human culture can be viewed as the sum total of the behavior of the members of that group. Therefore, the argument that culture determines behavior is essentially another way of saying that behavior determines behavior. A way out of this logical trap is to argue that culture is more than the sum of its behavioral parts, that it has an organic, dynamic quality, changing and evolving over time, in response to emergent forces within its larger whole. This is again the anthropomorphic argument that we encountered in functionalism, attributing qualities possessed only by individual human beings to impersonal entities.

To symbolic interactionism must be added a huge body of psychological thinking that includes behaviorism à la John Watson and B. F. Skinner as well as more complex social learning models currently prevalent in social psychology. The result has been called the Standard Social Science Model, or SSSM, (Tooby and Cosmides, 1992). It has tremendous influence on the way late twentieth century Americans think about social problems. Even those who have never taken a formal course in anthropology, psychology or sociology use some version of it in their thinking. It dominates all the social sciences (except for economics), including history and political science.

According to Tooby and Cosmides, the SSSM gains its persuasive power because it starts with a simple common sense observation: Individuals develop from unformed, helpless infants that appear remarkably similar from culture to culture, into complex, competent adult members of their social groups with all the peculiar habits, rituals, and behaviors unique to their group. It is this development from simplicity and uniformity to complexity and diversity that this approach attempts to explain. It does so by emphasizing the psychic unity of humankind combined with the demonstrable fact that people are strongly influenced by their experiences.

The use of culture to explain all human values, beliefs and behavior is the central approach most prevalent in social science throughout the twentieth century. In it, the individual plays a largely passive role, being exposed to various learning experiences while everything interesting occurs at the higher, almost metaphysical level of cultural roles and social rules. A major problem for economic theory—and of any other coherent theory of human behavior—is that according to the SSSM, there is no core purpose or structure to human behavior, no ego that exists separate and apart from culture. In this view, culture does not result from interactions among individuals who have independent interests and purposes. Rather, culture somehow provides people with these fundamental interests and purposes. Culture is the reality and individuals are merely the physical manifestations necessary to give it substance. Thus, in an immensely influential article published in 1917, anthropologist Alfred Kroeber argued that human culture is a "superorganism" that must be considered in its own terms and not that of its component parts. Another renowned anthropologist, Leslie White, argued that "culture may be regarded as a thing *sui generis*, with a life of its own and its own laws," and Robert Lowie announced that *omnia cultura ex cultura* ("all culture comes from culture").

It would be unfair to suggest that all modern varieties of sociological and anthropological theory accept the dominant and unitary role of culture. There are at least two notable exceptions, cultural materialism and structuralism. The former, as represented by the work of Marvin Harris (1985) attempts to explain patterns in social behavior by studying the material constraints on human existence. These constraints include the need for food, shelter, tools, and reproduction. This theory distinguishes material constraints from those imposed by ideas, values, religion, and other non-material mental states. Cultural evolution is the result of people trying to satisfy their genetically determined needs. Over time, various useful traits are accumulated on a trial and error basis as people innovate with their culture.

Cultural materialism has the advantage of tying culture to objective phenomena. It parallels evolutionary biology in its focus on random variation (a kind of "cultural mutation") combined with selective retention of those innovations that lead to success in particular environments (a kind of "natural selection"), even though cultural materialists generally disavow any direct evolutionary considerations.

Cultural materialism is also relatively congenial to economics. It makes use of the concept of cost/benefit ratios in determining which traits will be adopted and which rejected. All that is missing is the mathematical formalism so prevalent in economics.

As to structuralism, it derives primarily from the work of Claude Lévi-Strauss, who was in turn strongly influenced by so-called structural linguistics. The structuralist school seeks to analyze human customs as representing a kind of "social grammar," by which cultural practices, myths, and even economic exchange reflect fundamental qualities of the human psyche, but to no evident purpose and for no discernible reason.

The task of the rest of this book is to propose a framework for economics in particular and social science more generally, that treats *individuals* as the basic units of analysis and that takes as their primary motivation a consistent, demonstrable, and comprehensible trait, which they share with all other living things, namely the evolutionarily generated propensity to reproduce.

On Politics, Briefly

Before proceeding, we would like to raise a controversial subject: the politics of an evolutionary social science. Sociobiology has been criticized as inherently conservative, supportive of the status quo, and invidious to state-sponsored efforts to achieve social betterment. Indeed, part of the widespread appeal of the SSSM is that by emphasizing human malleability, the SSSM gives greater credence to liberal—if not socialist or communist—schemes for social engineering as well as an ostensibly benevolent welfare state. Hence, to question the SSSM might seem to question progressive political ideals.

Ironically, when *The Origin of Species* was first published, Darwin was pilloried for, among other things, having given aid and comfort to radical forces whose goal was to undermine social stability, including the divine right of kings. (This is because evolution is a doctrine of change, suggesting that everything is in flux and that neither royalty nor species identity is necessarily as God originally made it.) Karl Marx even sought to dedicate *Das Kapital* to Darwin!

The present authors disagree strenuously among themselves about the political implications of the evolutionary approach we jointly espouse. Arthur and Anna Gandolfi, both economists, maintain stoutly that political and even moral implications can—indeed, should—be derived from biological insights, and moreover, that these implications generally favor a conservative, libertarian ideology that celebrates the individual. David Barash, a biologist/psychologist, disputes this with equal vehemence, claiming that such implications are in the mind of the inferrer, and that evolution can only tell us what *is*, not what *ought* to be.

One might argue, for example, that since evolution guarantees that all individuals and subgroups (including members of the government), will act to maximize their own reproductive potential, we have to be aggressively suspicious of any social system that centralizes political or economic power. At the same time, it could also be maintained that since evolution favors rampant selfishness—whether at the level of the individual or the gene—there is all the more reason for a progressive program of governmental oversight and intervention, so as to insure a humane social outcome.

We leave any resolution of this dilemma to the reader, and to the future.

Note

1. In a sense this "imperialism" is not that new. Ludwig von Mises, famous for his proof of the impossibility of rational economic decisions under central planning, argued the primacy of economics in explaining human behavior in his treatise *Human Action* (1966). The very title of this work sets forth his claim for the universal scope of economics in explaining human behavior.

2

The Dismal Science

Open any textbook and you will usually find economics defined "as the study of the use of limited resources for the achievement of alternative ends" (Henderson and Quant, 1958, p. 1). Broadly interpreted, this definition can cover all purposeful human behavior,[1] for every action undertaken is at the expense of numerous alternatives. Nearly everything we can imagine ourselves doing involves material goods and the effort of self and others. This definition covers not only activities customarily considered "economic" such as working, investing, and shopping, but also the complete spectrum of human behaviors studied by other social scientists: marriage, child rearing, education, religion, participation in politics, and even sex, involve choices.

Time and money used in any one of these activities is no longer available to be used in any other activity. While some notable economists such as Ludwig von Mises have taken this broad view of economic analysis, until recently most economists have limited their inquiries to studying only "the actions of individuals in the process of producing, exchanging, and consuming goods and services" (Henderson and Quant, 1958, p.1).

In fact, economics has traditionally been so narrowly focused on markets and exchange that many have questioned whether it should even be considered a part of the social sciences. This view is reinforced by the distinct theoretical structure of economics, which has further set it apart from the other social sciences.

Nonetheless, economics is not only the oldest social science, but over the past two hundred years, it has produced a consistent and convincing explanation to one of the most profound social questions ever to be pondered by the mind of man: How do millions of individuals, each having his or her own special goals, manage, without any central direction, to coordinate their activities so as to produce and distribute the myriad goods and services required to sustain and enhance their lives?

Given that these activities have consumed an immense proportion of human effort, it becomes clear that the above question is crucial to any theory of human behavior. For those of us raised in and enjoying the benefits of a modern market economy, the answer may no longer seem very profound. But it takes a great deal of intellectual sophistication to comprehend how something as complicated as the coordination of millions of individuals, each engaged in hundreds of decisions, could ever occur spontaneously, or with a minimum of planning. The natural response, on discovering any complex mechanism, is to look for the designer. (The Rev. William Paley's renowned clock metaphor, adduced in an effort to support divine creation, comes to mind.)

Adam Smith, the "father" of modern economic inquiry, was one of the first philosophers to give a detailed answer to the problem of social coordination in the absence of centralized planning and control.[2] Smith's contribution, in short, was that the information and incentives provided by a free and competitive market, operating within the institution of private property, produced social coordination. For Smith, the free market was the "invisible hand of God" that directed people, concerned only with their narrow interest, to pursue that interest in a manner ultimately beneficial to all.

The problem of the social coordination of economic processes entails more than just providing market participants with an incentive to produce the right good in the right location, with the right technology and the right labor and raw materials, to be finally delivered to the right customers at the right price and the right time. The problem is far more complicated than the one faced by any one businessman. It is not enough to make the correct decision for a single product. Since one firm's output is another's input, it is necessary to coordinate the activities of all firms. The problem, as F.A. Hayek demonstrated, is one of information. No central planner has access to, or would be able to process in a timely manner, all the knowledge and information required to effectively coordinate the economic activities of even an eighteenth-century, largely agrarian society.

Smith's great insight was that the problem of social coordination was solved by the market. It doesn't require any central planner, any knowledge as to potential beneficiaries on the part of workers or businessmen, and most important, it doesn't require any change in human nature. Workers or business people could be as selfish as they please but as long as they acted in their own self-interest, the forces of the market would push them in the "right" direction.

For Smith, all the information and incentives that the participants require is provided by the price system. When goods of one type are too abundant, their price will fall, signaling to workers and entrepreneurs that their resources could better be employed in other, more lucrative areas, thereby reducing the supply of those goods. At the same time, lower prices provide consumers with an incentive to increase their purchases of the abundant items at the expense of other goods. The self-regulating nature of market prices is a marvel of unintended social coordination. It is so subtle, so intricate, that it is difficult to convince people who have never experienced it to believe that it is possible. We see this in the former Soviet Union and its satellites, in which many people, raised under socialism, have difficulty conceiving how the market can perform all the intricate "planning" needed to run a modern economy.

No other social science can claim an intellectual achievement comparable to the Western economist's description of the social role played by prices and the market. Is it purely coincidence that this insight derived from a focus on the accumulated behavior of individuals?

The Paradox of Value [3]

Any complete description of the market system requires an acceptable theory of how the prices of goods and services are determined. By Adam Smith's time, it was already an established principle that price was determined by the relationship between demand and supply (Stigler 1965, p. 69). The demand for any commodity is inversely related to its price. In other words, if we plot on a graph the relationship between the quantity demanded by consumers against the price of any good, the relationship between the two will have a negative slope. This negatively sloped demand curve, as shown in figure 2.1, is one of the fundamental relationships in economics.

It is one thing, however, to assert an empirical regularity; it is another to develop a theory of behavior that establishes the conditions under which it holds. The problem was that classical economists, including Smith, lacked a coherent theory of value. They couldn't explain why some items such as water, which is so useful

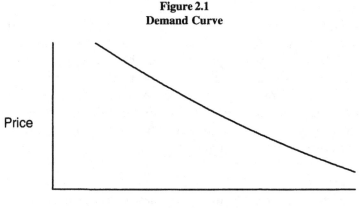

Figure 2.1
Demand Curve

Price

Quantity Demanded

and necessary, have a low price, while other goods such as dia-
monds, which have little practical use, are almost priceless.

To solve this paradox, Smith and his followers made a distinction
between value in use and value in exchange:

> The things which have the greatest value in use have frequently little or no value in
> exchange; and on the contrary, those which have the greatest value in exchange have
> frequently little or no value in use. (Smith, 1976, pp.32-33)

But this is merely a restatement of the problem, which it shoves
onto the buyer. Why is the buyer willing to pay so much for a use-
less good? While classical economists never did solve the paradox
of value, they did develop a theory of relative price determination,
that is, what determines the price of one good relative to that of
another. The solution depends on the classical labor theory of value
and on a theory of agricultural rent. The relative prices of manufactured goods were seen as essentially determined by the relative
amount of labor required to produce them. In any given industry, a
fixed quantity of labor and capital is required to produce a product.
Since capital is produced with past labor, all inputs could, with the
proper accounting, be measured in terms of the common unit, labor.

For example, the relative prices of cloth and shoes depend on
how much labor is required to produce each. If ten hours of "total"
labor is needed to produce a bolt of cloth and five hours to produce
a pair of shoes, then the price of cloth is twice that of shoes. For the
classical economist, the amount of labor needed to produce one unit
of manufactured goods does not depend on the quantity produced.
Scale of production does not affect the cost of production. However,

they also realized that a constant cost of production did not apply to agriculture. With a fixed supply of land, as output expanded, one soon reached a point at which it took increasing inputs of labor for every additional unit of output.

This is the important concept of diminishing returns. If several inputs, such as land and labor, are required to produce an output such as wheat, then, by holding any one factor constant (land, for example), one will, at some point, produce less output for every additional unit of labor applied to the land. Another way of saying this is that as production of wheat is expanded, there comes a point at which the cost of producing each additional unit is higher than the cost of producing the previous one. In other words, the marginal cost of production increases as production rises.

The concept of diminishing returns, and of the equality between marginal cost of production and price, are both important advances, but they do nothing to resolve the paradox of value. For the sake of argument, let us agree that production of the last or marginal pound of gold costs 300 times the cost of the marginal pound of iron. The question that cannot be avoided is why, if iron has more utility than gold, is gold produced at all? There are many potential goods that would be very expensive to produce that are never created. It is not enough to say that the marginal cost of producing gold is 300 times the marginal cost of producing iron. One must explain why people would be willing to buy this less "useful" good at such a high price.

The answer to the paradox of value depends on distinguishing "marginal utility"—that is, the "utility" an individual obtains from consuming an additional unit of something—from the total "utility" the individual receives from his or her total consumption of that good.

Utility Theory

Modern economics comes of age with the development of the theory of utility. After some earlier pioneers, utility theory entered the mainstream of economics due to the independent work of Jevons, Menger, and Walras. Utility theory is very simple in concept. Individuals receive utility or satisfaction from the consumption of goods and services. As they increase their consumption of any given item, the additional utility they receive from it is less than that obtained from consuming the prior unit. This, in a nutshell, is the theory of diminishing marginal utility. It is an intuitive idea derived from our

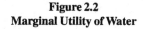

Figure 2.2
Marginal Utility of Water

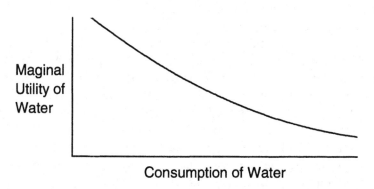

experience with the satiation of biological wants. As shown in figure 2.2, a thirsty man receives more utility from the first pint of water he drinks than from the second, more from the second than from the third, and so on. We all have had this type of experience, so the theory of diminishing marginal utility is easily appreciated by students when introduced to it.

The fundamental assumption of utility theory is that the rational consumer, regardless of income level, selects his or her market basket of goods and services so as to maximize total utility. Combined with the theory of diminishing marginal utility, it produces the necessary conditions that must be satisfied for a consumer to maximize his total utility. The consumer should allocate his income among all goods and services so that the last dollar spent on each item yields the same amount of marginal utility.

If the marginal utility per dollar spent is higher for one good—wine for example—than for others, the consumer can increase total utility by shifting dollars from the consumption of other goods to wine. For each dollar shifted, the consumer gains more utility than he loses. Because marginal utility is negatively related to the quantity of a good consumed, this shift in spending will lower the marginal utility of wine, while raising the marginal utility of all other goods.

The development of the theory of marginal utility solved the paradox of value. The marginal utility of the last dollar spent on gold is equal to the marginal utility of the last dollar spent on iron. This is not inconsistent with the total utility from consuming iron being greater than the total utility from consuming gold. Since, as production expands, gold's marginal cost of production rises far more quickly than iron's and since marginal utility declines as consumption increases, the market will "clear,"—that is, supply will equal demand—at a point where gold is being produced and consumed at a much lower level than iron. At these levels of production, the price of gold will be higher than the price of iron and so will its marginal utility. For example, the market may clear at a price of gold equal to $300 an ounce and a price for iron of $1 an ounce. If the market is in equilibrium with these prices and quantities, we know from consumer utility maximization that the marginal utility (the utility from consuming the last ounce) of gold must be 300 times the marginal utility of iron. The three founders of utility theory treated the utility of any commodity as solely dependent on the quantity consumed. If there are only two goods, say bread and jam, one's total utility is simply one's utility from consuming a given quantity of bread plus that from consuming a given quantity of jam, where the utility derived from one good is independent of the quantity consumed of the other. In mathematical language, utility is a separable "function" of bread and jam. This function is simply a mathematical expression that shows the relationship between the quantities of various goods consumed and the utility obtained from the consumption of those goods.

Separable utility functions have some very nice properties. First, when income increases, the consumer must increase consumption of each good, otherwise the necessary equality between the marginal utilities divided by their prices will not hold. Second and most important, the demand curves for each good must be downward sloping; that is, as the price of any good decreases, the quantity demanded of that good increases.

This type of utility function has another property, this one not so nice: it is totally unrealistic. We used the example of bread and jam deliberately. The utility received from bread is influenced by whether or not there is jam to spread on it. There are many products like this: shoes and shoelaces, tea and sugar, razors and razor blades, and so on. These goods are called complements. According to the formal definition, two or more goods are considered complements if an increase in the consumption of one good raises the marginal utility of the other, increasing the demand for it.

Alternatively, goods can be substitutes such as coffee and tea, beer and wine, Coke and Pepsi. In this case, an increase in the consumption of one lowers the marginal utility of the other, reducing the demand for it.

Edgeworth (see Stigler, 1965, p.98) generalized the utility function so that the quantity of one good could influence the utility derived from another.[4] In his version, total utility is dependent in some unspecified way upon the quantity of bread and jam consumed. Of course, this generalized utility function can contain more than two goods, with a large number of goods that are complementary to each other and many that are substitutes. The condition for consumer maximization of utility presented above still holds. The ratio of marginal utilities of each good to its own price must all be equal for the market basket of goods chosen to be utility maximizing.

So far, we have covered the principal concepts of consumer demand theory, utility functions and demand curves. Now we present a quick overview of the production function.

Production Function

Production functions are to the supply of economic goods what utility functions are to the demand for these goods. They summarize the relationship between the inputs to production (such as labor, land, machines) and the outputs (amount produced) of goods. Just as marginal utility of bread is the change in total utility for an incremental increase in the consumption of bread, the marginal product of labor is the increase in output for an incremental increase in the amount of labor used in production.

One common assumption about the production process is that there are constant returns to scale. This is a very easy concept to understand. The production of shoes depends on several factors of production; for example, labor and capital. If one changes the amount of labor and capital used in production by the same proportion, the output of shoes produced will change by the same proportion. If one doubles the amount of labor and capital used, shoe production doubles. Because the production function has constant returns to scale, the quantity of output is equal to the sum of the marginal product of each factor of production times the quantity of that factor used in the production process. This means that total output can be expressed in terms of the contribution of each factor of production. It can be used to describe the production of a single product, an entire firm, an industry or, with the proper degree of aggregation, the entire output of an economy.

Instead of describing the physical relationship between inputs and outputs, we can transform it into one that is expressed in terms of dollar values. In fact, it can be shown that in any competitive market in which people attempt to maximize profit, the pay of any factor will be equal to the marginal product of the factor times the price of the good produced. Competing producers will bid up the price of any factor until no further profit can be gained by adding an additional unit of the factor. Each factor is paid according to what it produces, not according to its total product—which can't be determined—but rather, according to its marginal product. The question usually asked at this point is, what happens to the rest of the revenue? For a constant returns to scale production function, there is no additional revenue. All revenue is paid out to the factors of production and nothing is left over.

Finally, we wish to emphasize the relationship between marginal cost and marginal productivity. If all factors are increased proportionately, output increases proportionately, and the marginal products of the factors don't change. The marginal product of each factor depends only on the ratio of the quantities of the factors of production used in the production process. If one factor is temporarily held fixed and we attempt to raise production by employing more of the other factor, then by the law of diminishing returns, the marginal product of this variable factor will decrease and the marginal cost of expanding output will rise. As the employment of the variable factor rises, a peculiar thing occurs. The marginal product of the fixed factor rises, and we are no longer in competitive equilibrium. Something has to give. Either we can hire more of the temporarily fixed factor at its old price, which will drive down its marginal product and drive up the marginal product of the variable factor and restore the original relationships, or, in attempting to hire more of the temporarily fixed factor, we raise its price, which restores the relationship that must prevail in a competitive profit maximizing economy.

In general, a combination of hiring additional factors and affecting their prices is what clears the market and satisfies the equilibrium conditions. For this reason, economists usually assume that marginal cost curves, and therefore supply curves, are upward sloping as output expands. Since demand curves slope downward and supply curves slope upward, price and quantity in the market is determined by the intersection of these two curves, as shown in figure 2.3.

Figure 2.3
Demand and Supply

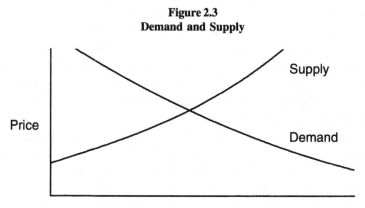

Quantity of Goods Produced and Consumed

General Equilibrium

According to the theory presented above, every individual, given his or her income, chooses that bundle of goods and services that maximizes utility. And every individual, in his or her role as supplier of labor and capital, receives as income, the marginal product of his or her inputs to production. Utility functions determine demand curves and production functions determine supply curves. Utility maximization, profit maximization, and competition guarantee that all markets will clear, that supply will equal demand, and that, for any good or factor of production, all transactions will occur at the same price.

As Adam Smith pointed out, prices perform the function of coordinating the numerous decisions of millions of individuals as producers and consumers. It has been the intellectual mission of economists to describe and analyze the workings of the market system. However, in general, economists have not been satisfied with this type of "positive" investigation. Since the earliest days of Smith and Ricardo, economists have asked "normative" questions about the efficiency and equity of the economic system (Quirk and Saposnik, 1968). The one criterion which economists have settled upon for judging the efficiency of any economic relationship is the concept of Pareto Optimality, named after its originator, the economist Vilfredo Pareto.

Put simply, any situation is Pareto Optimal if it is impossible to make any person better off without making at least one person worse off. Put in terms of the economy, any given set of production and consumption decisions is Pareto Optimal if it is impossible to increase the utility of any person or group of persons without lowering the utility of at least one other person. In such an economy, all mutually beneficial trades have already occurred and all goods are being produced in the most efficient manner at lowest costs. All the conditions of utility maximization and production optimization mentioned earlier in this chapter have been met.

Pareto Optimality is the economist's concept of efficiency. It says nothing about equity, or about the optimal distribution of wealth. It is simply a statement that waste is not desirable, that resources should not be utilized such that there are unrealized opportunities to make at least some people better off without costing the rest anything. Of course, this efficiency rule assumes that envy does not exist. Economists usually assume that the only consumption that affects an individual's utility is his or her own.

Even when economists acknowledge envy, they hold that it is not a "proper" emotion and should not be taken into consideration when judging an economic system. The branch of economics concerned with these issues is called welfare economics. The major conclusion of the work done in this field is that under a broad set of conditions, the competitive market generates Pareto Optimal results.[5] Once the distribution of resources (capital, labor, land) between individuals is determined, the competitive market guarantees an efficient outcome. Change the initial distribution of resources and you will change the outcome, but it too, will be efficient in Pareto's limited sense.[6]

It is easy to give an example of Pareto Optimality. Imagine a prisoner-of-war camp with only two occupants. The Blue prisoner receives eight loaves of bread and one jar of jam every week, the Gold prisoner gets only three loaves of bread, but two jars of jam. The Blue prisoner would gladly trade two loaves of bread for a jar of jam and Gold would gladly trade one jar of jam for two loaves of bread. Since both parties would be made better off by such a trade, the pre-trade situation would not be efficient, that is, not Pareto Optimal. Once they complete the trade, Blue has six loaves and two jams, and Gold has five loaves and one jam, and although both benefit from the trade, Gold is still worse off than Blue and cannot be made better off without making Blue worse off. Nor can Blue be made better off without making Gold worse off. The final distribution of loaves of bread and jars of jam is Pareto-Optimal.

Now let's assume the prison authorities change the initial distribution of food. Gold now gets only two loaves of bread and two jars of jam. Blue receives nine loaves of bread and one jar of jam. The "rich" Blue is able to "take advantage" of Gold's hunger and change the terms of the trade. Instead of trading two loaves of bread for one jar of jam, he wants Gold to give up both of his jars. Bread being more important than jam, Gold agrees. This situation is also Pareto-Optimal since no other trade is possible, even though one party is far worse off than the other. Pareto Optimality says nothing about the "justice" of any outcome, just its efficiency.

Ironically, it was two socialist economists, Abba Lerner (1944) and Oscar Lange (1938) who did some of the pioneering work demonstrating the efficiency of competitive markets. They wished to determine the conditions that made the market work, so as to generate comparable efficiency in a socialist system.[7] Kenneth Arrow, generally considered a liberal economist, completed this proof in the early 1950s. We point to the political orientation of these economists to make the point that in general, when good economists are working within the traditional, theoretical framework, the quality of their work and the conclusions they reach are often independent of their political orientation. Political ax grinding and special pleading does occur in economics, but it has not seriously affected its theoretical foundation, that is, price theory.[8]

We have presented this short course in price theory for two reasons. First, it provides insight into how economists think and the approach they follow. But second, and more important, a passing familiarity with these basic concepts is prerequisite to understanding our approach to the integration of economics and evolutionary theory.

Critique of the Economic Model

The early developers of utility theory conceived of it as reflecting a genuine psychological phenomenon that could potentially be measured and used to make interpersonal comparisons of utility. Jeremy Bentham, originator of the philosophy of Utilitarianism, believed that all human behavior could be explained by the pursuit of pleasure and the avoidance of pain, and that public policy should aim at the maximization of the sum of the utilities of all members of society. His famous saying is that policy should aim at "the greatest happiness of the greatest number" (Bartlett, 1992, p. 305n). This goal, combined with the concept of diminishing marginal utility, inevitably led to a recommendation for income redistribution.

After repeated failures, economics eventually abandoned the search for a utility "yardstick." Nonetheless, the assumption that people consistently strive to maximize their self-interest remains the core concept of economics. Had utility maximization remained defined in terms of some psychological response, then economics would have been made a sub-discipline of psychology. By declaring its independence from psychology, economics also severed its links to the life sciences. What made this separation possible was the discovery that all the theorems of consumer behavior could be proved without assuming a unique index or measure of the utility of goods and services.

The only requirement is that individuals possess a "well-behaved" set of preferences that rank all possible choices. The ability to choose between alternatives is necessary for purposeful activity, and is a basic assumption of economics. By shifting their theoretical focus from quantifiable psychological responses to the existence of ranked alternatives, economists placed the foundation of their discipline at a higher level of abstraction and made it independent of the infant science of psychology.

The irony is that economists, to this day, still speak of utility as if it were a real phenomenon. They can "get away" with this because they have shown it makes no difference. Assume that an individual can rank all goods and combination of goods by his preference for them and that we know these rankings. Now let us devise a mathematical relationship or formula that translates quantities of goods into an index of utility. As long as the values of this index for any two alternative bundles of goods have the same ranking relative to each other as they had in the individual's original ordering, the function can be used to completely explain the individual's consumption decisions.

For example, if someone prefers a car to a boat, and is indifferent between a boat and a motorcycle, then any arbitrary utility function would have to attribute to the car a higher utility value than to the boat, and the same value to the boat and the motorcycle: let's say 100, 50, and 50 utils, respectively. We could also devise a new function that values a car at 1,000 and a boat and motorcycle at 999 utils each. Each mathematical representation of the individual's orderings is equally valid, equally arbitrary, and equally useful. For this reason, and for convenience of exposition, we will continue to use utility as a concept.

In its present form, economics has become the abstract theory of rational action. Utility theory is the pure logic of choice divorced from any assumptions or conclusions that link it uniquely to the human species. Its theorems and conclusions are as valid for humans as they are for any other species, real or imagined, so long as that species acts on the basis of a "well-ordered" and defined set of preferences. Economics, then, is based on presuppositions of rationality and efficiency, divorced from any information about the nature of the individual actor or "its" values. "Modern neoclassical economics has forsworn an attempt to study the source and content of preferences, that is, the goals that motivate men's actions" (Hirshleifer, 1977, p. 17). This is the source of economics' great strength and, as we shall see later, also a great weakness.

To most non-economists, it may be a very unattractive species-portrait to claim that human beings are rational maximizers of their own self-interest, that is, that they always seek utility, and consistently prefer more to less. But the question is not whether this picture flatters the human ego, but rather, whether the economic approach is accurate enough to constitute a sound theoretical framework around which to build a universal science of human behavior. (The "selfish gene" approach of sociobiology has similarly been criticized as reflecting a cynical perspective.)

The standard criticism of economics can be summarized: "People are not like that; they don't really behave the way economists assume." But this kind of comment is too vague to be very useful. Since economics is an axiomatic discipline—that is, its conclusions follow relentlessly from its assumptions—any attack on its conclusions must follow from an attack on those assumptions.

Homo Economicus

Since its beginnings in the late eighteenth century, economics has distinguished itself from the other social sciences by its insistence that human behavior is governed solely by self-interest.[9] When taken literally, this contention seems ridiculous to most people. Everyone can point to hundreds, if not thousands of "selfless" acts, by themselves or others. This does not even include the countless sacrifices parents make for their children. The existence of benevolence has always been something of an embarrassment for economists. (Interestingly, it has long been a similar conundrum for evolutionary biologists, insofar as natural selection is understood to be quintessentially selfish, rewarding traits that contribute to maximum genetic representation in future generations and eliminating altruistic alternatives, which should be—by definition—self limiting.) On the one hand, economists cannot deny the existence of altruism. On the other, altruism or disinterested benevolence toward others makes it impossible to prove that the competitive market is Pareto Optimal. The same goes for envy and disinterested malevolence. Also, it is not only Pareto Optimality that is threatened. Many other results such as downward sloping demand curves are also called into question.

However, the theory of choice holds that people always choose their preferred alternative. Therefore, anything they do, charity included, ostensibly maximizes their self-interest. This approach explains too much and too little at the same time. If every behavior is defined as utility maximizing, then economics is reduced to a near tautology. (Once again, a similar criticism is regularly leveled against the central tenet of evolution: if natural selection means survival of the fittest, it is argued, and only the fittest survive, then what's new or interesting?) Almost no behavior can be ruled out.

Speaking for economists, Samuelson asserts that this approach is not technically meaningless since other assumptions impose at least the requirement of internal consistency on the behavior of individuals (Sen, 1977). Therefore many of the general relationships of demand theory can still be derived. Regardless of what behavior we're talking about—charity, malevolence, or traditional consumption— if someone prefers act A to act B and B to C, then consistency rules out choosing C over A. So, in this sense, the pure theory of choice expanded to include all behavior is refutable and, therefore, scientifically meaningful. But Samuelson's point, while technically valid, is not by itself very useful.

If we observe someone choosing A over B, after which he chooses B over C, we conclude he won't choose C over A. If in fact he later does just this, we can conclude one of two things. Either his behavior is not "rational" and economic theory is wrong, or his preferences have changed and he is behaving consistently with his new preferences. Since economics does not have a theory of what determines preferences, we can't rule this out; so all behavior is potentially consistent with economic theory. The problem exists even when benevolent or malevolent behavior is ruled out. For economic theory to say anything meaningful about human behavior, it must assume that preferences are constant over time: any test of predictions of demand theory is also a test of the stability of preferences. If a prediction is rejected, one cannot be sure if the problem is with the theory or with the assumption that preferences are stable.[10]

Economists also face the problem that preferences or tastes can vary among individuals, no less than within them (if anything, such variation is likely to be even greater in the former case). Although this fact does not disturb economic theory, it does cause a problem in using economics to explain differences in behavior among individuals.

Anyone wanting to undermine the economic approach to explaining human behavior can do no better than to challenge the existence and persistence of rational maximizing behavior. If human beings do not engage in optimizing behavior, if they do not adjust their actions so as to achieve their goals, then there is no point in calculating the conditions under which they maximize their utility. For example, if individual behavior is determined by culturally imposed roles, then even though actions may appear purposeful, the actor is not, strictly speaking, optimizing his behavior.[11] An actor's goal is to perform his or her role properly, not to change the script to maximize the utility of his character. In this regard, the assumption of rationality conflicts with an underlying assumption of the SSSM (see chapter 1); namely, that people respond to their culturally imposed rules and accumulated learning. Although sociologists, for example, don't suggest that human beings are mere automatons reciting their "lines" with blind fidelity, it is difficult to reconcile rational action—economic or otherwise—with the hegemony of culture.

To the extent that the SSSM merely asserts that individuals, in determining which actions will optimize their "utility," must take into consideration the preferences and expectations of those individuals they interact with, there is no problem. To the extent that it asserts there are socially accepted rules that facilitate the coordination of the purposeful actions of individuals, there is also no difficulty. It is only when one argues that roles are acquired unconsciously and determine the sequence of behaviors that are to be followed in any situation that the basic structure of rational behavior is challenged: If people "act out" certain roles without regard to how an alteration in their behavior could improve or worsen their lives, they can't be described as rational maximizers (except perhaps if they are maximizing their adherence to cultural rules, a rather self-referential conclusion).

This is not to argue that economic theory requires that culture not be involved in the determination of individual preferences (utility functions). Economics, as traditionally formulated, says nothing about how preferences are determined; it accepts preferences as a given, not as something to be explained. In fact, we regard this agnosticism about how preferences are determined to be one of the great weaknesses of conventional economic theory.

Another challenge to rationality comes not from denying its existence, which is intuitively difficult, but from the claim that rational behavior is segmented; that is, the assertion that there exists within the human mind separate problem-solving faculties, each with its own capability and value structure. Behavior at any point in time is then governed by the structure that is currently in control. This theory of rational segmentation implies that sexual behavior, for example, is governed by a different value structure and logic than is shopping or hunting.

This argument is destructive of the traditional economic point of view because it denies the unity of the human mind. No longer is it necessary that the utility provided by the marginal dollar spent on beer be equal to that spent on cars or on clothes, and so on. There need be no relation or consistency between activities controlled by these separate faculties. This argument is advanced by evolutionary psychologists. Tooby and Cosmides (1992), for example, maintain not only that this is the way the human mind works, but that it is the *only* way it could work. We consider this view a powerful assault on economic theory because its proponents have a plausible theory as to how and why these separate faculties arose. It also includes a reasonable argument why these faculties are likely to provide solutions to the problems faced by human beings, and why they are superior to those produced by the sort of mind suggested by the unified preference function assumed in economics. The approach taken in this book, like that of economics, rejects the segmented model of the human mind. We believe that a unified model of the human mind is also consistent with evolutionary biology.

If the argument to be presented in the following pages is correct, the economic approach married to evolutionary biology will provide a theoretical framework for understanding human behavior that eluded Bentham, Comte, Marx and others. However, for this framework to generate detailed and powerful explanations of human behavior, not only must the ultimate goals that motivate people be stable over time and fundamentally the same for all individuals, but at some point it is necessary to identify these goals and their relationship to each other.

As long as economists remain ignorant of the ultimate goals that motivate human behavior, our explanations of human behavior must remain tentative. Whenever we encounter a behavior that cannot be explained, the temptation will be to add it to our list of such "goals," just as psychologists in the early twentieth century accumulated a laundry list of human "instincts" that included a parental instinct, gregarious instinct, instincts of acquisition and construction, dominance, companionship, mating, even climbing trees, and this glorious jack-of-all-trades: "purposive striving."

It is the argument of this book that the objective goal(s) of human behavior can in fact be identified, and therefore, powerful explanations and predictions can be generated. Accordingly, we turn next to a brief consideration of the path-breaking work of Gary Becker, the economist whose approach logically precedes our own, in that he presupposes the existence of stable and universal human goals, although, as we shall see, Becker avoids precisely identifying them.

Notes

1. Traditionally economics has dealt only with humans and that definition should be so interpreted. Recently the logic of economic analysis has been applied to non-human animals as well.
2. David Hume and Mandeville are direct precursors to Smith.
3. This section depends heavily on Stigler's *History of Economics*, particularly pp. 66-155.
4. This function is usually written as: $U = f(B, J)$.
5. More formally:
   a. Regardless of the initial distribution of resources, every equilibrium position of the competitive market is Pareto-Optimal.
   b. Every possible Pareto-Optimal situation can be reached in a competitive market equilibrium by appropriate initial distribution of resources.
6. This proof depends on a fair number of assumptions, some already mentioned, like pure self-interest and the absence of monopoly power. Another is that there are no positive or negative externalities. Put simply, this means that activities of consumption and production do not impact on third parties. In other words, there is no pollution, congestion, crime, and so on.
7. What they came up with is called "Market Socialism," an attempt to reproduce through bureaucracy, the functions of the market. This solution failed. Bureaucrats are politicians, not entrepreneurs. Without private property, market participants do not have the correct incentives.
8. Macroeconomics, which is concerned with the business cycle and inflation, has not managed to remain as independent of politics. It deals with issues that are too important to too many people.
9. To demonstrate this, we include two quotes reproduced from Jack Hirshliefer's (1985, p. 54) excellent article on the role of economics in the social sciences. From Adam Smith's *Theory of Moral Sentiments*:

"We are not ready to suspect any person of being defective in selfishness."
And from F.V. Edgeworth's *Mathematical Psychics*:

"The first principle of economics is that every agent is activated only by self-interest."

10. In general, economists rely on the fact that even though individual preferences may change randomly, in the aggregate, these changes cancel out, so economics still has relevant things to say about group behavior.

11. For a discussion of the concept of "role" in sociological analysis, see *Essentials of Sociology*, (Broom, Selznick, and Broom, 1984, pp. 78-82).

3

The New Economic Imperialism
(Becker and Beyond)

At one time there was a live-and-let-live attitude among social scientists. Economists were almost exclusively concerned with behavior directly involved in the production and consumption of market goods and services. Non-market activities ranging from war to politics to marriage were considered the province of political science, sociology, anthropology, or psychology. However, in the last forty years, economists have made a determined effort to expand the reach of their discipline into areas of human behavior that were once considered off limits. It is not clear what motivated this expansionist urge. It would be nice to say that having settled all the questions in their own field, economists went looking for new frontiers to conquer. This is not the case.

Instead, the expansion of economics seems driven by the irresistible power of ideas. The artificial demarcation of human behavior into rational and non-rational areas has been found unsustainable. Either economists are right and their model can be used to explain all behavior, or they are wrong about man being rational and self-interested, in which case even their explanations of market activity are likely incorrect. It became almost a case of expand or die: Either their vision is true and explains everything or it fails and explains nothing. As noted economist Jack Hirshleifer put it, "if the hypothesis of economic man fails in any field of application, the correct scientific response is not modest retreat but an aggressive attempt to produce a better theory" (1985, p.54).

Many economists have pioneered the application of economic theory to other disciplines. Kenneth Boulding (1962) applied economic theory to conflict and war, and became one of the founders of "peace studies" as an organized discipline. James Buchanan and

Gordon Tullock (1962) extended the economic model to politics. Richard Posner (1977) helped develop the economic analysis of legal systems, while Isaac Ehrlich (1973) has applied the economic model to explaining criminal behavior. Jack Hirshleifer (1977), in turn, has engaged in a form of reverse imperialism, introducing concepts from evolutionary biology into economics while Gordon Tullock (1994) has applied economic concepts to biology.

But no one has been more important to this endeavor than Gary Becker. Staying with our military metaphor, he is the field marshal setting the strategy and leading—although not quite orchestrating—the invasion of neighboring disciplines. What makes Becker stand out is not just his technical ability, for there are many technically superb economists who have never contributed anything radically new to the discipline. Becker is unique because of his unqualified belief (perhaps faith is the better word) in the absolute correctness of the economic view of man. "I have come to the position," he writes, "that the economic approach is a comprehensive one that is applicable to all human behavior..." (Becker, 1976, p.8).

Becker's strength is his ability to assume away the nonessential aspects of a problem and concentrate on the core of the behavior under investigation. This is also the most valuable lesson that he teaches his students. The central assumption or simplification at the heart of Becker's approach is the proposition that tastes are stable over time and similar among people. (Note that a universal human nature is key to a sociobiologic conception as well.) In a joint article titled "De Gustibus Non Est Disputandum"[1] (1977), George Stigler and Gary Becker emphasized the centrality of this assumption for using economics to explain human behavior generally.

The key to appreciating Becker's contribution is to understand that for him, the universality and constancy of tastes is not an assumption of convenience, to be adopted when trying to explain one type of behavior and then discarded when no longer useful. This restriction on the utility function is a core principle that characterizes and animates his entire intellectual effort. It is a worldview that on the one hand makes the economist's job more difficult because it limits one's freedom, but on the other, holds out a promise: If successful in explaining behavior without resorting to the crutch of "changes in taste," the economist will likely have uncovered some deep truth about human nature. By making economic theory more specific, Becker hopes, paradoxically, to make it richer and more generalizable, capable of producing testable explanations of why humans *seem* to have such different preferences—but really don't.[2]

The Household Production Function

Universal and stable preferences, combined with utility maximization, have limited explanatory power by themselves. Becker's reformulation of consumer theory contains a second major step, a transformation in the way economists think about consumer behavior. As Stigler and Becker explain it,

> This reformulation transforms the family from a passive maximizer of the utility from market purchases into an active maximizer also engaged in extensive production and investment activities. In traditional theory, households maximize a utility function of the goods and services bought in the marketplace, whereas in the reformulation they maximize a utility function of objects of choice, called commodities, that they produce with market goods, their own time, their skills, training and other human capital, and other inputs (1977, p. 77).

In other words, people do not really value the ordinary goods and services purchased in the market, but rather, certain higher order *results* derived from consuming ordinary products (such as steak, housing, cars, etc.). These higher order results, which Becker terms "commodities," represent general universal requirements of life such as nourishment, shelter, amusement, sex, children, status, and so on. These commodities are produced by the consumer via a range of inputs, including market goods and the consumer's own labor, where the price of these commodities are not observed in any market but are equal to the marginal cost of producing them from their appropriate inputs. It is these ultimate commodities that enter individuals' utility functions. And it is these utility functions that are stable over time and similar across individuals.

As in the traditional case, in which the utility function is defined in terms of market goods, the actual basket of commodities chosen by an individual will depend on his or her income, and the prices of producing those commodities. Utility maximization requires that the utility derived from the last dollar spent on each commodity be equal.

The question raised by Becker's reformulation of consumer behavior is this: If utility functions are identical, what accounts for the observed differences in behavior? Not only are there substantial differences among people in the baskets of goods and services purchased in the market but also differences in other behavior such as career choice, marriage, and number of children, all of which were traditionally considered beyond the purview of economics.

Because utility functions are identical, all differences in behavior must be accounted for by differences in income or in the prices of commodities. Since competition and arbitrage insure that within an economy, the market price for any good or service is roughly the same for all individuals, what could account for differences among individuals in the prices of these commodities?[3]

Remember that according to Becker's theory, commodities are not physical goods and services as conventionally understood. Rather they are best viewed as the ultimate goals that individuals attempt to fulfill. They can't be bought or sold directly in the market but are instead produced by each household, which can be viewed as a little factory or firm whose job is to use market goods and the labor of the members of each household to produce, at minimum cost, the output, that is, commodities demanded by that household's members.[4]

Consider any Beckerian commodity, for example, nourishment. To produce one (arbitrary) unit of it requires a certain quantity of market produce such as meat, vegetables, bread, sugar, salt, and spices, and the use of capital goods such as a stove, sink, refrigerator, and table. Then energy must be expended to shop for the ingredients and to cook the food. Finally, we must take into consideration the time required to prepare and serve it, not to mention the expertise required to do it acceptably, and to clean up afterward. The cost to the household of producing a unit of nourishment will depend, of course, on the market prices of the ingredients, which should be similar for all households in a given locality, but also on the cost of the labor and other materials used in its production.

Consider the simple case in which production requires fixed quantities of each input to generate a given unit of nourishment. Let's say that one unit of nourishment requires a half pound of beef, a pound of potatoes, a half pound of vegetables, and an hour of preparation time. If the price per pound of the ingredients is $4, $1, and $2 respectively and the cost of time as measured by the preparer's market wage rate is $5 per hour, then the cost of a unit of nourishment would be $9.

However, if the preparer's market wage were $10 not $5 per hour, the cost of a unit of nourishment would be $14 rather than $9. Consider two individuals who have the same tastes and the

same income, but one earns a wage of $10 while the other earns
$5. Let us assume for convenience that the lower-wage individual
has a trust fund that makes up the difference. The lower-wage individual can produce a unit of nourishment at a price that is substantially lower than the high-wage neighbor and would be likely
to consume more meals at home rather than buying nourishment
in a restaurant.

The quantity of commodities that households can produce for their
own consumption is limited by their income. But since time must be
allocated between income-producing market activities and non-market production of commodities, the budget constraint facing households must include not only money income but the time used in producing the commodities. To handle this, Becker introduces the concept
of "full income," defined as the sum of property (non-labor) income
plus that which could be earned if the household devoted all of its
time to income generating activity, namely, work.[5]

Many of the differences and changes in people's behavior can be
explained by how the value of time affects the cost of the ultimate
commodities that enter each household's utility function. For example, the rise in wage rates over the past 200 years has dramatically increased the price or cost of any household commodity that
requires substantial time in its production. This effect is offset to
some degree by the rise in income, which should increase the demand for all commodities. But unless the demand for a time-con-
suming activity is very sensitive to income, the net effect of the wage
and income rise will be to reduce the demand for it. There is a whole
range of behavior that fits this prediction, including church atten-
dance, child rearing, home baking, and learning to play musical in-
struments. The time spent on all these activities has declined over
this period (Becker, 1971, p. 42).

Differences among individuals in the cost of time will produce
marked differences in behavior. People with a high wage rate engage in fewer time-intensive activities than do people who place a
lower value on their time because they earn a lower wage rate (Becker,
1971, p. 165).

Human Capital

Differences among individuals in the cost of their time provide a
powerful explanation of differences in behavior. Since the cost of an
individual's time depends on his or her wage rate, we need to ex-

plain the cause of the large and persistent differences in wage rates that we observe in all complex societies. The answer lies in Becker's conception of the household production function and the role that human capital plays in it. Although all utility functions are generally assumed to be identical, the same is certainly not true for the household production function that transforms goods, services, and an individual's time into those commodities that are ultimately valued by people. Differences in this "production technology" are due to the interaction of "biological differences" and the deliberate investment in skills and knowledge (i.e., human capital).

From Becker's perspective, differences in biological endowments not only affect the efficiency of the production function, but such differences also alter the rate of return earned by investment in human capital through training, education, and experience. For example, the rate of return, such as the speed at which a person acquires proficiency in music, will be a great deal less for a tone-deaf person than for one with perfect pitch. It is clear that musical ability has a substantial inherited component: How else can one explain Mozart or other prodigies, not to mention the rest of us, whose aptitudes vary from mediocre to nearly hopeless?

At the same time, even those who emphasize the importance of nature must realize that nature (genotype) only provides potential. Wolfgang Amadeus would never have become "Mozart" if Leopold Mozart, his ambitious father, had not invested so heavily in his son's talent. Moreover, Wolfgang had a sister, who also evidenced great talent, but whose potential was not comparably nurtured and thus, was never realized. (See Virginia Woolf's essay, "A Room of One's Own," for a meditation on what might have befallen a highly talented sister of William Shakespeare.)

In any event, and notwithstanding social pressures that might dictate career paths, rational individuals and their parents should invest resources, that is, education and training, in those skills that potentially offer the highest rate of return. This means that differences in abilities that are observable in small children tend to magnify over time as each child and his or her parents invest more effort and resources in enhancing those talents that offer the greatest promise. The income of individuals will depend on three general factors, the amount of resources invested in them by their parents and others, the efficiency with which that investment is translated into human capital (influenced by their biological potential), and finally, the amount of resources bequeathed or gifted to them.

Variations in human capital can explain differences in behavior that are usually attributed to matters of taste. For starters, people with physical handicaps find the cost of certain activities almost prohibitive. A blind individual will find it cheaper to produce the commodity "entertainment" by attending concerts rather than by frequenting art museums. But even in less extreme cases, much of behavior is influenced by the age, health, and even sex of an individual. Furthermore, not only are household production functions different for different individuals, they are also unstable over time for any one person. Changes in technology can also alter a household's cost of producing commodities as radically as technological change alters prices in the manufacturing sector.

To summarize: for Becker, preferences are identical across individuals and stable over time. Differences in behavior are the result of individual or household differences in the cost of producing the ultimate "commodities." These differences in costs are the result of differences among individuals in their stocks of human capital and differences in biological endowments. Becker has used this approach to extend the range of economic analysis of behavior into areas traditionally not considered the province of economists. In the rest of this chapter, we review some of his contributions, not only to show how economics can be used to explain "non-economic" behavior, but also to lay the groundwork for our discussion of how Becker's approach and evolutionary biology can be merged into a single social science.

Division of Labor

In every society ever studied, there is a division of labor along sexual lines. Certain jobs, such as child rearing, cooking, and maintenance of the home are almost exclusively done by women, while men tend to be involved with occupations that require heavy exertion or prolonged absence from the home, such as hunting large animals and/or making war. In Western societies during the last fifty years, there has been a sudden shift away from this segregation of work by gender. Becker seeks not only to explain why such a division of labor has arisen between the sexes, but also why it is now eroding.

From Adam Smith's famous discussion of specialization in a pin factory, it is generally taken as an article of faith that productivity can be increased by dividing a project into sub-tasks and devoting labor exclusively to each of these. But the reason for such enhanced efficiency is not intuitively obvious. Why don't boredom and the tedium of repetition *reduce* productivity? The answer lies in the theory of human capital. Even without formal training, people learn by doing, gradually increasing their proficiency in any job. For particularly difficult tasks, the advantage to specialization can be enormous.

The return from human capital, like that from passive forms of investment, depends on the rate at which the capital is utilized. Since the return is directly proportional to the amount of time spent at the activity, there is a strong financial incentive to specialize. As with other forms of investment, human capital not employed is wasted. But, unlike passive investments, an individual can participate in only one activity at a time. It is wasteful to acquire a great number of independent skills that have no relationship to each other.

Division of labor occurs not only in the market but also within the household. The household is, in a sense, a small firm that uses goods and services and the time of its members to produce a mix of commodities desired by its members. In order to pay for these goods and services, members of the household sell some of their time in the market in exchange for wages. In the following simplified version of Becker's theory, we assume a traditional household comprised of a husband and wife. If children are present, they do not contribute to either market or household production. They are one of the outputs produced by the household.

There are two types of human capital: market capital, which increases the available wage rate, and household capital, which raises the productivity of time spent in the production of commodities within the household. Each form of human capital is the result of specific investments made in each individual in the form of education, nutrition, and health services.

The market wage rates of husband and wife will depend on the amount of market capital invested in each. Similarly, the marginal product in household production for the husband and wife will depend on the stock of household capital each possesses.[6]

Let us perform the following thought experiment. Assume that both husband and wife enter the marriage with the same amount of market capital so that their market wages are identical. Also assume that both have had the same investment in household capital. Because only women can bear children, the wife has an advantage in household production even if the husband received an equal amount of training in domestic skills. Thus, the wife can be expected to devote relatively more of her time to the production of household commodities and less to earning income, even if the two are equal in earning power.

Recall that the rate of return on human capital is directly related to the time spent employing that capital. Therefore the wife's total return from household capital will be greater than the husband's, just as the husband's total return from market capital will be greater than hers. Insofar as potential investment is limited, it may accordingly be a mistake for the husband to invest heavily in household capital and for the wife to invest heavily in market capital. Both would be better off if they concentrated their investment in the type of human capital that corresponds to the activity in which they will spend the bulk of their time. If they or their parents had so invested, the wage rate of the husband would be higher, while that of the wife would be lower. Conversely, the marginal product of the wife in household production would be raised while that of the husband would be lowered.

This is an important point. Rational men and women making decisions about what form of human capital to accumulate will make choices that tend to magnify any innate difference in comparative advantage. From this type of analysis, Becker proves a number of interesting theorems. Here are two of them:

1. "If all members of an efficient household have different comparative advantages, no more than one member would allocate time to both the market and household sectors" (Becker 1981, p. 17). Consider the two-member household described above. If the family preferences are such that more than one person's time is required in household production, the family's well being would be maximized by the wife devoting all her time to the house, while the husband split his time between the market and the house. If the wife shifted one hour from household to market activity in exchange for the husband shifting one hour from the market to the house, the family would be worse off economically. If wage rates were equal, there would be no loss in earnings but there would be a loss in household production since the husband is less efficient in that sector. Conversely, if the household desires to consume a basket of commodities that requires more market goods as input and less time in household production, a rational household would have the husband specialize completely in market activities while this time the wife splits her time between the market and the home.

2. Because of this, "no more than one member would invest in both market and household capital. Members specializing in the market sector would invest only in market capital, and members specializing in the household sector would invest only in household capital" (Becker 1981, p. 18). This follows directly from theorem 1 and the fact that the return from human capital is directly related to the time spent using it. If an individual is not engaged in an activity, it is wasteful to accumulate capital for it.

These two theorems shed considerable light on one of the most common complaints about modern marriage. At one time, women tended to specialize in household production. As the demand for children has declined and the introduction of household appliances has raised the efficiency of time spent working in the home, wives have increased their participation in the workforce. A frequent complaint is that whereas wives have taken on a greater share of the "burden" of supporting the family, husbands haven't responded by increasing their share of housework. This is widely regarded as a failure of the husband to do his "fair share," and as an indication that he is shirking his responsibilities (Ehrenreich, 1984).

Becker would view the situation differently. Given Becker's analysis, it would be irrational for the husband to respond to his wife's shift of her time from household to market activity by shifting his from the market back to the household. If the family needed more time spent in the household, the wife never should have shifted her time to begin with.

A word of caution is required, however. In the above analysis, Becker assumed that the household is permanent, that people can make their investments in human capital with confidence that their expectations will be fulfilled. Consider a household in which the husband specializes in the market and the wife in household production. Each spouse has also accumulated human capital appropriate to his or her specialty. Now suppose that after their children are grown, they divorce. It may well be difficult for the wife to remarry since she is probably too old to have more children, and the supply of eligible men is relatively smaller at older ages. She is a household specialist without a household of sufficient size to warrant her full attention. She will probably find it necessary to devote the bulk of her time to market activity, but her wage rate will be low because she hasn't accumulated any market capital. Since a great deal of market capital is accumulated not through formal education but by on-the-job experience, the wife is disadvantaged by the very strategy which seemed so optimal when she was married. The husband, with his greater earning power, will find it easier to obtain a new wife. This is reflected, for example, in life insurance ownership: traditionally, men were well insured but women were not (see Gandolfi and Miners, 1996). It was generally assumed that a woman with children would find it hard to replace her husband's income but that a husband could replace his wife's contribution by remarriage (and also, that the wife's contribution was not a significant financial one.)

Severe division of labor within marriage makes economic sense, but over time, it tends to shift the balance of power within the family away from the female and toward the male. Under current law, there is no way for a couple to contract a marriage for life, and alimony settlements have become nonexistent, insufficient, or difficult if not impossible to collect. For this reason, many wives "hedge their bets" by working outside the home, to maintain their professional credentials even when it would make more sense economically for them to shift more time to the household.

An irony is that when women, fearful of being abandoned, reduce their dependence on men by under-specializing in household production, they may in the process reduce the total gain from marriage, so both parties are not much better off than they would be if single—which in turn might reduce the total benefits from marriage, perhaps making divorce more likely! (Becker, 1981, p.251).

Fools Give You Reasons...

No subject seems less amenable to logical analysis than love and marriage. The current Western concept of romantic love seems to place the choice of a mate outside the realm of reason and under the control of our emotions. The conventional argument is that although economic considerations may have played a role in the arranged marriages of traditional societies, modern marriage is an institution whose primary purpose is to produce emotional fulfillment. Becker, by contrast, is not afraid to analyze marriage with the cold calculus of economic formalism. Moreover, he is not just interested in the behavior of households, but also with the process of household formation, asking, for example, "Why do people get married and how do they choose their mates?" We have already seen Becker's answer to the first part of this question: The fundamental reason for marriage is the benefit that both husband and wife receive from the division of labor produced from forming a joint household.[7]

Becker also wants to explain one's choice of a marriage partner. This is a very ambitious goal. For the monogamous marriage that is currently the norm for most of the world's people, there are N! different ways that N men can be paired off with N women. If there are four women and four men in the marriage pool, then any man can marry one of four women, generating twenty-four possible sets of four pairings (4 x 3 x 2 x 1). Each of these sets of pairings differs from every other one by at least two pairings. If there are ten men and ten women, the number of possible outcomes expands to 3,628,800. When the number of men and women are both 100, the number of possible solutions is beyond comprehension.[8] In *The Republic*, Plato assigned his guardians the job of arranging all marriages. Even for a small society comprising only several hundred people in each year's marriage pool, the problem is beyond solution for any group of central planners. This is analogous to the problem of coordinating economic behavior that we discussed in chapter 2. Becker shows how the market solves the marriage problem. Selfish competition for the best mate takes place in the marriage market. This market not only produces a unique sorting of males and females into married couples, but this sorting will also be optimal, in that it is stable and no one could marry someone else without making at least one of them worse off. These pairings also maximize the total productive advantage of all marriages.

For Becker, every individual in the marriage pool has a value of household production that he or she can produce as a single person. For each possible pairing, there also exists a value of production that will, because of the advantage derived from division of labor, exceed the sum of what the partners could produce separately, if they remained single. Each person in the marriage market wants to make the best marriage possible; each acts, in short, to maximize his or her well-being.

We can illustrate Becker's conclusion using the following example. To keep it manageable, let us assume a very small marriage market comprised of only two men and two women, and thus, only two possible pairings. Table 3.1 presents the productivity available from remaining single and from marriage for each possible pair.[9]

The first column and row of table 3.1 represent what males and females can produce if they remain single. The interior cells show

Table 3.1
Productivity of Marriages

		F1 (Female 1)	F2 (Female 2)
		4	1
M1 (Male 1)	2	8	4
M2 (Male 2)	4	9	7

what each of the four possible couplings can produce. For example, Male 1 (M1) can produce two units and Female 2 (F2) one unit if each remains single; but if they marry, they can jointly produce four units. The gain from trade from this marriage is one unit, the difference between the joint production of four units and the sum of the individual production if the participants had remained single.

Becker points out that "although the maximum output of a marriage is produced by a marriage between M2 and F1 (Male 2 and Female 1), the optimal sorting is (a marriage between Male 1 and Female 1 and between Male 2 and Female 2)" (1981, p.69). In this case, the total product for all marriages is fifteen units compared to only thirteen units for the other possible sorting. Notice that the reason why the (M1-F1), (M2-F2) sorting maximizes output is that it maximizes total gains from all marriages. The net gain from marriage produced by the optimal sorting is four, two units from each marriage. The other sorting only produces a net gain of two, one unit from each.

What incentive, however, does each participant have to marry the "right" person? Since each participant wants to maximize his or her utility, how do we know that the optimal sorting does not provide incentives for defection, that is, divorce? To appreciate the logic of this argument, realize that in the "bidding" war for mates, prospective partners negotiate the distribution of the gains from marriage, each hoping to strike the best possible deal. Let's assume that each of the couples in the optimal sorting split the gains from marriage equally between husband and wife. M1 gets three and F1 gets five out of their eight unit joint production. M2 gets five and F2 gets two out of their joint production of seven units. Each participant is one unit better off than when single and there is no other marriage in which husband or wife will be better off. This result may appear trivial when there are only two couples, but the surprising thing is that it holds regardless of the size of the marriage pool.

Becker's proof of the efficiency of the marriage market is a remarkable intellectual achievement. Of course, it depends on a series of simplifying assumptions, such as people having full information about the characteristics of potential partners, including what each of them would contribute to a marriage. But in truth, these assumptions are no more severe than those required for similar proofs about the market economy. As with all models, this one's importance lies not so much in its ability to completely describe reality but in how it changes the way we think about the world. By introducing the concept of a marriage market in which participants, guided by nothing more than self-interest, end up maximizing the total product of all marriages, Becker has, in a sense, shown that Adam Smith's invisible hand operates in the bedroom as well as the boardroom. For those who believe that the greatest achievement in economics is its description of the spontaneous order of the market, extending this analysis to include such social behavior as marriage is a very important development that might be extrapolated to other forms of behavior.

In the real world, people don't have full information about all potential mates and they sometimes make mistakes. After marrying, they may discover that their spouse is not as good as they originally thought, or perhaps a better prospect comes along. But the existence of divorce doesn't invalidate Becker's approach; rather, it simply means that the marriage market operates, like many other markets, by trial and error with its participants forced to act in partial ignorance. Also, as in other markets, all trades do not occur simultaneously. New participants are always entering the pool of eligible, single individuals, while others leave because of marriage, moving, or mortality, as well as by conscious decisions of chastity or monasticism. So even if (M1-F1), (M2-F2) is the best sorting available at a given time, everything is up for grabs once M_n and F_n enter the marriage pool. However, such complications just mean that the model—like any model—is incomplete, not that its basic insight is wrong. In any form of analysis, there is always a tradeoff between completeness and manageability. Despite the intellectual achievement of Becker's marriage model we believe that it is fundamentally flawed. But that discussion will have to wait until we present our model.

Children

Becker's work on the demand for children has special relevance to this book; any theory purporting to shed light on reproduction is pertinent to attempts to incorporate evolution and economics. For simplicity, Becker assumes that the behavior of parents can be explained by a joint household utility function. Utility depends on the number of children, their quality (the amount of human capital invested in them), and the quantity of other commodities consumed by the household. Becker also assumes that all children in the same family are of the same quality. What makes Becker's analysis of the demand for children unique is the manner in which the cost of producing quality and numbers of children interact. Total consumption of commodities and children is constrained by the household's full family income, which consists not only of market income but also of the non-market time and effort by the adult members of the family, valued at market wage rates. The total cost of children is equal to the cost of producing children independent of quality, times the number of desired children, plus the cost of a unit of child quality times the amount of quality desired per child, times the number of children.

Since the household selects the quantity of children (another simplifying assumption!), their quality, and other commodities, so as to maximize its household utility, the usual relationships between the marginal utilities hold. The marginal utility of a dollar spent on any commodity must be equal to that spent on every other commodity, including the marginal utility per dollar spent on number of children and the marginal utility per dollar of raising the quality of any child.

Start from equilibrium, at which the marginal utilities per dollar (marginal utilities divided by their respective prices), on all forms of spending are equal. Now, perform the following thought experiment. Increase the cost of producing a child, independent of its quality. This would depress the ratio of the marginal utility of children to their price and the equilibrium condition would no longer hold; therefore the household would not be maximizing its utility. The household could then increase its utility by transferring resources, by reducing the number of children, increasing their quality and increasing the amount of other commodities consumed. This works because according to the law of diminishing marginal utility, the marginal utility of each commodity including children is inversely related to quantity consumed.

So far, this is exactly the traditional analysis of demand presented in chapter 2. But there is an interesting wrinkle. The total price of quality depends on the number of children.[10] As number of children is reduced, the price of quality falls and the demand for quality increases at the expense of numbers of children and the amount of other commodities. But the full price of children is also dependent on their quality. The increase in demand for quality raises the full cost of having children even more, further depressing the demand for number of children. Finally, demand for number of children will be reduced sufficiently and demand for quality and other commodities will be increased by enough to insure that the marginal utility of each divided by its price will again be equal. At this point, the household is again maximizing its utility. The interaction between the number of children and their quality causes any change in the quality-independent cost of children to have a magnified effect on the ultimate number and quality of children produced.

This analysis is the basis for Becker's explanation of the fall in fertility in modern societies. The demand for children, their quality and all other commodities increases with a rise in income. On this basis, we would expect that consumption of all three would increase along with income. But the growth in income is associated with an increased wage, that is, cost of time, for both men and women. This increases the cost of children and sets in motion the dynamic interaction described above. In the long run, the full price of children rises by more than the amount justified by the change in the wage rate, and the decline in fertility is magnified. As the number of children falls, the full price of quality declines and more is invested in a reduced number of children. At the end of this process, the birth rate tumbles, the quality of children rises, and the demand for other commodities increases relative to numbers of children. Even though the number of desired children has fallen, there is no reason why the total amount spent on children should not also rise since the desired quality of each has risen.

Future of the Family

The American family has undergone tremendous changes since the end of World War II:

> [F]rom 1950 to 1977 the legitimate birth rate declined about one-third, the divorce rate more than doubled, the labor force participation rate of married women with young children more than tripled, and the percent of households headed by women with dependent children also almost tripled. (Becker, 1981, p. 245)

Becker believes that the primary cause of these changes is the growth in the earning power of women, which accompanied American post-war prosperity. Real weekly earnings of women grew by

30 percent between 1950 and 1964 and by 10% from 1964 to 1978. This increase in wages raised women's cost of time, increasing the relative cost of children, thereby reducing demand for them. The rise in wages increases the amount of time women spend in market activities and therefore reduces the gain from division of labor in marriage. The smaller the gain from marriage, the more attractive is divorce.

It appears that increases in women's labor force participation are positively related to subsequent divorce (Michael, 1978). Rising wage rates combined with the resulting increase in labor force participation have a reinforcing effect on the return women receive from investing in market skills. As investment in human capital is shifted away from the household to market activities, women's wages are augmented, further reducing the demand for children and the gains from marriage.

Moreover, insofar as the stigma from divorce is eroded as it becomes more common, single women may be less likely to direct their human capital investment towards specializing in household production, given their well-justified fear that someday they may need market skills to support themselves and their children. This, in turn, would further reduce the gain from marriage.

Value Added

According to Becker's theory of the household production function, the ultimate items valued by individuals are not ordinary economic goods and services but such "commodities" as health, nutrition, children, status, and so on. These are produced by the household using as inputs ordinary economic goods and services, as well as the time of household members. Becker assumes that even though the household production function may vary among individuals and depend on available technology and the stock of human capital, the basic utility function is stable and universal over time.

Recently Becker (1996) has expanded his approach to include the effect of past individual experiences and the role of social forces. With this addition, Becker believes that economic theory will better explain such phenomena as addiction, habit, fads, and fashion, and account more generally for the influence of culture on human behavior. In this effort, Becker introduces two new concepts, personal capital and social capital.

Personal capital represents past individual experiences which influence current behavior. Social capital incorporates past action by other members of the society which affect an individual's behavior. Becker also states that, in a more fundamental sense, personal and social capital should be considered additional inputs to the household production function. For example, if one of the "commodities" valued by an individual is status, that individual could spend resources (economic goods and time) on status enhancing activities. But the amount of status gained by any activity such as buying and driving a Porsche will depend not only on the individual's past behavior but also on how this activity is viewed by other members of society. These two influences on the productivity of Porsches in producing status are captured or represented by personal and social capital respectively.

This approach can help explain many types of behavior. The number of cigarettes a person smokes depends heavily on that person's past consumption of cigarettes. Similarly, the amount of golf a person desires to play will depend on (or at least, be influenced by) the extent to which one's friends and business associates play golf.

Reprise

Gary Becker's contribution to explaining human behavior is original, and of tremendous and continuing importance. (The present chapter reviewed just a small fraction of his work.) We believe that Becker's framework is one of two that offer the best hope of a truly objective science of human behavior. With his assumptions of universality and stability of ultimate goals, Becker has greatly strengthened the predictive power of economics, perhaps taking the strictly economic explanation of human behavior about as far as it can go. The problem lies with economics itself.

As we noted earlier, the generality of the utility function provides economics with a structure that can be applied to all types of behavior. But this comes at a price, namely the lack of specificity in its predictions. Becker has nonetheless retained some of the subjective features of the utility function. He has replaced goods such as pork chops, cars, perfume, etc., as arguments in the utility function with commodities such as nourishment, sex, transportation, etc. But he has not provided a definitive answer to the question of what commodities people value, why they value them, and how come the basic shapes of such preferences are identical for all people?

The use of personal and social capital may help us explain variations in the demand for Porsches (as described earlier), but it does not tell us why people desire status in the first place. Nor does it help us understand the relationship between the things people ultimately value. For example, how do preferences for the various "commodities" relate to each other? How do people trade off health *versus* status, and status versus nutrition, and so on? And why do people have these preferences rather than others?

Becker has at times provided brief hints that he believes in an evolutionary theory of human preferences, that, over time, a common preferences function has evolved under the pressures of natural selection:

> The preferences taken as given by economists and vaguely attributed to "human nature" or something similar - the emphasis on self-interest, altruism toward kin, social distinction, and other enduring aspects of preferences - may be largely explained by the selection over time of traits having greater survival value. (Becker, 1976, p. 294)

But in later writings, he seems to back away from this view and takes a more agnostic approach. After developing a theory of fertility in non-human species in which the goal of behavior is the maximization of genetic fitness (more specifically, the number and quality of offspring) Becker deliberately retreats from applying the same logic to humans:

> ... [T]he economic approach does appear to provide a unified treatment of human and nonhuman behavior while recognizing that cultural forces are major determinants of human behavior and biological forces are decisive determinants of nonhuman behavior. (Becker 1981, pp. 216-217)

Although Becker believes that biological forces play an important role in shaping human preferences, there remains a strong, perhaps predominant, role for culture. It is hard to understand how the uniformity of preferences for all people can be argued if culture is somehow ascendant. Culture is, after all, what is used to describe widely *varying* behaviors among the members of different societies! What is needed is a theory that offers a chance to *explain* culture rather than one that uses culture as an explanation. In our view, such a theory already exists. It is known as evolution, and it offers great opportunities for economics as well, grounded in the premise that basic human preferences are determined by natural selection. As the twenty-first century dawns, there is, if anything, all the more reason to make this assertion, and to do so with enhanced confidence. Recent advances in sociobiology and evolutionary psychology have enhanced understanding of how such preferences have evolved, while enabling better and more precise predictions than ever before.

Notes

1.   A loose translation would be, "You can't argue over tastes," or in vernacular English, "There is no accounting for taste."
2.   Making a theory less general so as to increase its predictive power is often a useful methodological strategy. We shall be attempting something similar in chapter 5.
3.   The equalization of market prices for any goods is known as the law of one price and only holds where there are no impediments to trade. Transportation costs, tariffs, etc. can cause the prices of the same goods to vary.
4.   Even though households usually consist of more than one individual, we will, for the sake of simplicity, assume for now that each household's preferences can be represented by a single utility function.
5.   Some people find it unreasonable to include all time in the definition of full or potential income. After all, a person really can't devote twenty-four hours a day to work. However, sleep and relaxation can be considered commodities to which the household chooses to allocate time.
6.   The time of each member of the household is a perfect substitute for the time of any other member. Household capital just reduces the amount of time required for any task.
7.   There is no inherent reason why a household has to be composed of two members of the opposite sex. However, if one of the desired commodities of both parties is children, then a household composed of one mature male and one or more mature females seems to be the preferred situation.
8.   The answer is approximately 9 followed by 157 zeros.
9.   Of course, the output referred to here is not measured in dollars but refers to the commodities produced by households such as children, sexual satisfaction, and all the other commodities desired by individuals. For the sake of simplicity, Becker assumes they can be measured by a common index.
10. By the price of quality we mean the cost of raising the quality of all children by one unit of quality.

4

God's Sieve

In chapter 2 we described how, beginning with Adam Smith, economics has shown how a market economy coordinates the actions of innumerable individuals in the production, exchange, and consumption of goods and services. The problem of order, arising out of chaos or design without a designer, is not customarily associated with the social sciences. Most of the social sciences have ignored this issue. Even though the concept of spontaneous order can be traced back to Adam Smith, this idea did not achieve scientific prominence until Charles Darwin identified the process of evolution by natural selection in *The Origin of Species*. The problem faced by Darwin was of a different sort than that confronted by economists attempting to explain the order evident in markets. Darwin was attempting to provide a scientific explanation of how the immense complexities of living organisms, each so well adapted to its environment, could have arisen in the absence of purposeful design. In this, he was spectacularly successful.

Darwin also sought to discover the principles that explained the differentiation of life into the specialized plants and animals which inhabit the earth. Biologists term this process "speciation," and in this respect, he was less successful. Thus, *The Origin of Species* actually says very little about the origin of species, but very much about the origin of adaptations, and the organic connectedness of all life.

Darwin faced two problems not confronted by economists. First, he had to discover the principles that account for the evident diversity and complexity that exists among living organisms. Unlike economists, Darwin did not have the advantage of assuming that the minute decisions that shape the phenomena under examination were made by conscious, intelligent agents. Humans can purposely alter their behavior while seeking to maximize their well-being, that is,

55

utility. Plants and animals, however, do not purposely alter their own design while seeking to achieve some objective.[1]

The second problem faced by Darwin was that his explanation ran counter to the strong religious beliefs held by his culture, his class, and even himself. This appears to be why Darwin delayed publication for so many years, thereby running the risk that someone else might discover it independently. This is exactly what happened. In 1858, two decades after Darwin developed his theory of natural selection, he was sent a manuscript by the young naturalist Alfred Russel Wallace, which laid out the essential elements of his own work. Why had Darwin waited so long? The best explanation is that, knowing the hostile reception that earlier theories of evolution had received, he delayed in order to perfect his argument and bring to bear all possible evidence. His caution is understandable: Darwin was directly undermining one of the central pillars of mid-Victorian society, its conception of humanity's relationship to God. In addition, his work threatened notions of aristocratic privilege and the immutability of social and economic institutions. Evolution, after all, is a doctrine of change. If human beings and the rest of the organic world are the result of natural flux, rather than having been created *in situ* by heavenly edict, then who is to say that socio-economic systems (including monarchy and aristocracy) are not also subject to change?

Among Western countries, the United States has been especially resistant to evolutionary science. According to polls, more than one-half the population still considers evolution to be "only a theory." This reveals a fundamentalist streak as well as a deep misunderstanding of the nature of "theory" in science (which includes such unquestioned "truths" as number theory, atomic theory, etc.). Even today, "creation science" contends for equal time in public school classrooms, and some students are still taught that one of the principle proofs for the existence of God is the Argument from Design.

The most brilliant exposition of this "proof" came from the theologian William Paley in 1802. Paley argued that the existence of complex structures and organs, such as the human eye, was evidence of an extremely high level of design, which, in turn, was direct proof of a designer, namely, God. Put another way, the existence of a watch presupposes a watchmaker. Darwin had the temerity to show how natural forces, without the intercession of a supernatural draftsman, could account for all the seemingly miraculous complexities of life. For an accessible yet fastidious account of how Darwinian evolution—operating mindlessly via natural selection—can create masterpieces of design, see Richard Dawkins's book *The Blind Watchmaker*. In fact, the title of our chapter is taken from Dawkins's metaphor of evolution as a sieve. We added the term God to emphasize that natural selection and evolution need not necessarily conflict with a belief in an all-powerful God. It is surely within the capacity of such a deity to make use of natural selection to produce the organic world with all its complexities, human beings included.

It is not widely appreciated that natural selection need not be concerned with living organisms. It can explain the development, or "evolution" of any phenomena that satisfy its three requirements. First, it must be capable of replication. Second, these replications must occasionally occur with some inheritable variations. And third, these entities must be subject to selection, that is, they must have differential rates of reproduction, based on some criteria.

Replication or reproduction is not a property exclusively limited to living organisms. Crystals are inorganic molecules that fit together in a particular manner to form an ordered structure. Given the proper conditions, crystals will reproduce themselves. Drop a seed crystal into a supersaturated solution and it will form a template onto which the dissolved molecules attach themselves, reproducing the molecular structure of the original crystal.

Crystals thereby satisfy the first of the three conditions required for the process of natural selection. What about the second condition? Do mistakes occur? Is there occasionally an error in the structure of a growing crystal and are these variants capable of passing on their structure to succeeding generations of crystals?

"Nearly all naturally occurring crystals have flaws," suggests Dawkins (1987, p. 152). "And once a flaw has appeared, it tends to be copied as subsequent layers of crystals encrust themselves on top of it." So, it appears that crystals satisfy the second condition. But for evolution by natural selection to occur, there must also be selection. The crystals must experience differential survival rates based on their characteristics. Do mutations in crystalline structures influence the ability of these crystals to survive and replicate their mutant structures? If so, then crystals would be subject to all the forces of natural selection and would evolve over time. Is there any evidence for the evolution of crystals?

Not to our knowledge, but Dawkins (1987) speculates on how the crystalline structure of clay may have evolved over time so as to influence the flow of water, so as to produce conditions favorable to the propagation of its own variety of clay. But even if crystals *are* capable of evolution, their ability is obviously limited. The power of natural selection cannot create complex replicating organisms from merely crystalline building blocks.[2]

Fortunately for us and all other forms of life on this planet, certain molecules proved to be far more amenable to the process of natural selection. In a renowned experiment, biochemist Stanley Miller demonstrated in 1953 that a recirculating laboratory set-up containing ammonia, methane, water, and hydrogen gas (likely constituents of the early Earth environment), and receiving electrical discharges (simulating lightning), can produce complex organic molecules, including the building blocks of nucleic acids, the components of life. More recent studies have suggested that abiotically produced RNA may have been the earliest biochemical precursor to life (see Horgan, 1991, for a review of theories).

For our purposes, the precise details of how life arose from nonlife are less important than the specifics of how living things have proceeded to evolve since then. The historical details about life's origin may never be known with any certainty. This does not mean that the origin of life was anything but an entirely natural event. Uncertainty about life's origination does not translate into uncertainty about the evolutionary process whereby living things have transformed themselves ever since.

The key requirement for life, and for subsequent evolution, was the appearance of a molecule capable of making copies of itself, which is not all that difficult or extraordinary. The relative success of various replicating molecules depended on several factors: the length of the molecule's reproductive life, the rate at which it reproduced, and the accuracy of its replication. Every mistake in copying, even if it proved beneficial to the offspring, produced a new line of replicators different from the parent. This reduced the number of replicators in future generations that were identical to the parent. Faithfulness in reproduction, along with fecundity and long length of reproductive life, are characteristics that will be "selected for" in any evolutionary process.

These primitive reproducing molecules were the ancestors of today's genes. Even today, genes replicate themselves, with somatic cells producing identical copies during normal cell division, that is, mitosis—which occurs as part of body growth and tissue replacement—while gonadal cells package copies of themselves into either eggs or sperm (meiosis). But in addition to replication, genes also create bodies for themselves, as information stored in DNA travels via RNA to the cytoplasm, there to oversee the production of suitable proteins. These proteins (which include enzymes as well as structural components), underpin the creation of bodies.

Once again, we do not know the precise details whereby bodies evolved, any more than we know with certainty how life (replicating molecules) first appeared. But we do know that it was a momentous event. Presumably, it took place because naked, unprotected replicating molecules were vulnerable to destruction, including possibly being appropriated ("eaten") by other such molecules, some of which were better protected and thus, more competitive. Insofar as replicating molecules were more successful in projecting copies of themselves into the future when safely ensconced inside larger structures ("bodies"), then selection would have favored those molecules that were capable not only of reproducing but also of generating effective bodies. At this point, we can call these molecules "genes."

The Gene in the Machine

The history of research and analysis in evolutionary biology has seen a steady progression to different "levels of selection," moving from the wider to the narrower, and gaining predictive power with each successive reductionistic refocusing. Thus, the earliest conception—still prevalent among laypersons today—is that natural selection operates for the good of the species. Evolution was thought to act among groups, an approach that is very much in the minority today.

Much of the excitement and intellectual rigor of modern evolutionary biology and sociobiology has come from the recognition that although natural selection may occasionally operate at these levels, it is more cogent when acting on *individuals*, whose reproductive interests may even conflict with those of the larger group (George C. Williams book *Adaptation and Natural Selection*, 1966, is probably the seminal work on this subject).

At about the same time, William D. Hamilton (1964) stunned the biological world when he recognized and demonstrated that even bodies and individuals are, in a sense, subordinate to the interests of the genes that created them. Hamilton pointed out, for example, that even reproduction—previously thought to be the sine qua non of evolutionary success—is merely a special case of the more general phenomenon whereby genes replicate themselves via bodies. When it comes to reproduction, genes within a parent create and (in the case of mammals, for example) nurture bodies that incorporate each parental gene with a probability of 50 percent. But these genes might just as well project themselves into the future via the success of other genes, identical to themselves by descent, that exist in other bodies. These other bodies go by the name of "genetic relatives," with "closer" relatives being those with a higher probability of identical genes.

This perspective has been most effectively popularized by zoologist Richard Dawkins, whose book *The Selfish Gene* makes the case that all living organisms are survival machines that facilitate the propagation of their genetic material:

> We are all survival machines for the same kind of replicator—molecules called DNA—but there are many different ways of making a living in the world, and the replicators have built a vast range of machines to exploit them. A monkey is a machine that preserves genes up trees, a fish is a machine that preserves genes in the water... (Dawkins, 1989, p. 21)

Paradoxically, the "selfishness" of genes is often achieved via a kind of altruism: consider liver cells, which cheerfully undertake the dirty job of detoxifying the blood, while leaving the evolutionarily rewarding task of reproducing to the gonads. But of course, such altruism is really selfishness in disguise, since gonadal cells are identical to liver cells, so that whenever the ovaries or testes produce successful eggs or sperm, the liver cells share equally in their triumph.

Similarly, when a parent sacrifices on behalf of its offspring—including parental care and even the act of reproduction itself—this is not usually seen as either altruistic or selfish, but rather, biologically "normal." Its very normality, however, is due to the fact that it is an efficient way for genes to promote the success of copies of themselves. Under certain circumstances, it may also be effective for genes to promote themselves by inducing their body to behave benevolently toward other bodies that have a sufficient probability of containing the genes in question. Such benevolence is widespread in the animal world. It is also a cross-cultural universal among human beings, often called nepotism.

Hamilton's great insight extended the traditional view of natural selection, adding a more inclusive component to Darwinian or direct fitness, which had traditionally been measured via reproductive success alone. The result, achieved by additional gene success on the part of other relatives who receive assistance, contributes to a total "inclusive fitness," comprising both a direct component (personal reproductive success) and an indirect component (success via nondescendant kin). Hence, Hamiltonian inclusive fitness is often called "kin selection." Although it is a major insight of modern biology, and results in a more complete picture of the unconscious evolutionary striving of genes and individuals, we shall limit most of our analysis to the more traditional measure of personal Darwinian success. We do this in the interest of mathematical tractability, and also because as with all model-building, it seems legitimate to make the simplest initial assumptions, and see how far they get us, even though we realize that reality is more complex. (The great evolutionary biologist J.B.S. Haldane once commented that reality is not only more complex than we imagine, but more complex than we *can* imagine.)

Individuals cannot survive and facilitate the reproduction of their genes unless they are well designed. The survival of genes and their frequency in subsequent generations depends on how efficient their survival machines are at numerous tasks such as acquiring nourishment, avoiding predators, and, in the case of sexual reproduction, acquiring mates, not to mention being successful at producing offspring.

Since genes are not replicated with perfect accuracy, every now and then an offspring will be produced that varies in its design from its parents. Since a random change in the design of any complex organism is unlikely to improve its efficiency (imagine, for example, randomly replacing various components from a personal computer), most mutations are usually deleterious and the mutant organisms are selected against. But every now and then, a mistake in genetic copying will be beneficial, increasing the fitness of the copy. (Terms such as beneficial and deleterious, by the way, have no normative implications. They merely express whether any change helps or hinders the ability of the new design to make copies of itself.)

Even though we observe a world of bodies—eating, sleeping, competing, migrating, courting, caring for young—an important part of the modern evolutionary worldview is that the ultimate beneficiaries, the powers behind the throne, are the genes. As Dawkins (1989) puts it,

> Individuals are not stable things, they are fleeting. Chromosomes too are shuffled into oblivion, like hands of cards soon after they are dealt. But the cards themselves survive the shuffling. The cards are the genes. The genes are not destroyed by crossing-over, they merely change partners and march on.... They are the replicators and we are their survival machines. When we have served our purpose we are cast aside. But genes are denizens of geological time: genes are forever. (p. 35)

But of course genes don't have conscious purposes or intentions, their behavior is simply the result of being selected over thousands of generations for one characteristic, the ability to successfully replicate.

Although it is true that the forces of natural selection operate upon the individual who either succeeds or fails in the struggle to reproduce, the long-term consequence of selection is to change the distribution of genes in a population. When analyzing whether any trait or behavior will spread or recede within a population, we may refer to the reproductive success of the individual, but what really matters is how the reproduction of the underlying genes is affected.

This is not to claim that an individual gene controls the entire design for its body. Creation of a multicellular body—indeed, even a unicellular creature—requires the cooperative interaction of numerous genes, whose contributions are not readily separable. Note, however, that they are nonetheless analytically distinguishable, in that we can specify the fitness of a particular allele by determining its evolutionary success as compared to that of a given alternative. The result is what may be called the fundamental principle of modern evolutionary biology: all other things being equal, living things tend to be composed of and by genes that induce their bodies to behave in a manner that maximizes their inclusive fitness.

The Mikado's Revenge

Notice the phrase "all other things being equal," in the above sentence. It is important, and not simply as a traditional academic caveat. The process of evolution by natural selection is mathematically describable, as is maximization of inclusive fitness, as well as maximizing the difference between benefit and cost for any imaginable behavior. The problem is that there exist many obstacles to optimality.

In Gilbert and Sullivan's operetta *The Mikado*, that royal figure gleefully decrees his punishment for billiard sharps. They are made to play "on a cloth untrue, with a twisted cue, and elliptical billiard balls." Imagine the chaos and consternation as well-planned shots go awry! The real, biological world—as opposed to the ideal one of optimality theory and natural selection—is no less ornery than the Mikado's fiendish scheme. There are, in short, numerous obstacles to optimality. Here are just a few.

Mutations happen. Although the rare mutation contributes positively to fitness, most are deleterious, so that individuals carrying such genes (especially if homozygous) will likely be sub-optimal. In addition, beneficial—fitness enhancing—genes may occur on the same chromosome as other, hurtful genes. As a result of this linkage, selection favoring the beneficial genes may also promote the success of deleterious ones. Moreover, individuals may immigrate into a locally adapted population; these new arrivals are likely to be adapted to a somewhat different environment, and thus, will be less fit in their new surroundings. When populations are small, random effects (known as "genetic drift") may also override the power of selection.

Most important for our purposes, however, is the fact that all organisms have an evolutionary past, which constrains their future prospects and may generate suboptimal performance in the present. Thus, elephants are not only unable to fly (making Dumbo is a fantasy), but are unlikely ever to evolve flight, even though they might be more fit if they could blissfully forage while hovering from the tops of trees. Even when such "phylogenetic inertia" is not necessarily constraining in the long term, it may be overwhelming in the short haul, especially if environments change rapidly. For example, musk ox have for generations responded to their primary predators, wolves, by forming a circle, with the juveniles inside and the adults pointing outward, thereby presenting attackers with a formidable array of sharp horns and thick, bony plates. But the musk ox environment has changed more rapidly than the animals have been able to adapt, such that their primary predators are now hunters with high-powered rifles, riding snowmobiles. Nonetheless, musk ox continue to form their tried-and-true defensive circle, highly adaptive in the past, but lethally inappropriate today.

In much the same way, today's human beings may occasionally find themselves stuck with behavioral tendencies that were fitness-enhancing in an earlier environment, but are outmoded today. We return to this vexing issue in chapter 7; for now, we simply note that even in such cases, analyses based on evolution helps us understand the inclinations of the organisms in question, even if our un-

derstanding reveals that such inclinations are sometimes suboptimal. Also, bear in mind that the bulk of musk ox biology is in fact
adaptive!

This is only a small sampling of the myriad ways evolution double-
crosses its participants, as well as bedeviling those of us who attempt to use natural selection to predict outcomes. But this does not
mean that the usefulness of natural selection, and of its associated
optimality principle, is therefore repealed as a powerful explanatory
mechanism.

In some cases, there are perfectly good biological reasons why
apparent departures from optimality do not seriously "count." For
example, accumulated mutations eventually reach an equilibrium
with back-mutations, and whereas linkage may sometimes give a
temporary benefit to deleterious genes, such linkage is broken up,
over time, by the chromosomal process of "crossing over." More
generally, though, even seemingly intractable problems such as phylogenetic inertia leave adaptive explanations as the best approxima-
tions available.

Think of it this way. Imagine you were at an archery range. The
archers are only moderately skilled, their arrows are imperfectly
feathered and moreover, the wind is blowing. Worse yet, it is gust-
ing unpredictably. Even under these difficult conditions, in which
no one could predict with certainty where the arrows will land, the
worst place to stand would be directly in front of the bull's eye.

Group Selection

In practice, it usually doesn't matter whether we analyze the effect of a trait on the success of the relevant gene or on the individual
that the gene helped generate. Their interests usually coincide, since
in most cases, what is good for the gene is good for the body, and
vice versa. But there are some especially interesting cases in which
body and gene can be expected to conflict just as the interests of the
individual and his or her group can conflict. The proper level of
analysis makes a big difference.

Modern evolutionists are almost unanimous that the forces of natural selection operate primarily at the level of the individual and his
or her genes. Nonetheless, group selection has its devotees, even
today (e.g., Sober and Wilson, 1998). Group selection basically holds
that competition occurs between groups making up a species, not
between the individual members of each group. The groups that

prosper and whose descendants dominate future generations will be the ones whose physical and behavioral traits aid them in competition with other groups. When asking why a certain animal has a particular trait, the group selectionist will answer in terms of how the trait affects the well-being of the group, which in turn is often expanded into "the good (or survival) of the species."

This theory has perpetual appeal because so much of an individual's success depends on the actions of others. The success of an oak tree depends on the amount of sunlight it receives and that, in turn, depends on the height of surrounding oaks. Any inherited trait that matched the rate of reproduction to the availability of resources could be of great help in preventing catastrophic population crashes and group extinction. In fact, individual members of many species do limit the number of their offspring, producing fewer than is biologically possible. The theory of group selection would explain this behavior in terms of what is best for the group: Those groups that failed to control their population experienced severe overcrowding and eventual extinction, compared to groups that practiced some form of population control. If true, this theory could explain a great many phenomena that have longed puzzled evolutionists, such as the existence of self-sacrificing behavior among human beings. The young soldier who dies by throwing himself on a grenade in order to save his comrades is not going to have any more children. The only place he will spread his genes is on the ground. But this sacrifice may be beneficial for his group or nation. A nation of heroes may vanquish the enemy, rape, and impregnate its women, and spread the genes of the group far better than would a nation of selfish cowards.

It seems likely that if individuals took into consideration how their behavior affected their group, everyone would be better off. For example, in many species, there is a tremendous amount of male competition for access to females. But these struggles rarely result in serious injury to either competitor. This non-lethal ritual combat has been interpreted as the result of group selection, in which it is for the benefit of the group that males limit their aggressiveness. Moreover, such competition itself can be seen as a means whereby individuals determine the most fit males, so that they can monopolize reproduction, again, for the benefit of the group, and eventually, the species.

It is a powerful concept, all the more so because it appeals to the human penchant for benevolent socialization. It has been used to explain the origin of everything from ritual combat among stags to seemingly altruistic reproductive restraint among honeybees to the development of morality in humans. There is only one problem with group selection: It is usually not in the interest of selfish genes. Let us grant that some form of altruism, such as reproductive self-restraint or sharing food with other group members, might give that group an advantage in competition with other groups, whose members are largely selfish. The problem is that competition *within* such an altruistic group would inevitably favor individuals—and their genes—that were selfish. (Selfish variants can be expected to arise eventually, whether via mutation or immigration from other groups, whereupon they would have a "field day" among their more altruistic colleagues.)

In order for group selection in favor of altruism to win out over individual and gene selection favoring selfishness, it would be necessary for groups to be very resistant to immigration, and for the differential survival of altruistic groups to be very high, superceding the selective advantage of any selfish individuals and their genes *within* such groups. This is a very demanding condition, and although it is theoretically possible, it appears unreachable in most biological systems.

Consider the following thought experiment. Imagine there exists a species called globs that live in separate herds or tribes. They constitute distinct breeding groups that do not exchange genes and that exploit the same resource base. If one tribe becomes more efficient at finding food or stealing food from its neighbors, it will gain a reproductive advantage and expand at the expense of other tribes. Initially, each member of every tribe is a self-interested maximizer of its own genetic interest. Then one day by chance, a mutant glob is born that possesses a new gene that encourages its owner to put the reproductive interest of its tribe ahead of its own. Upon discovering a new food source, rather than eating its fill, it immediately reports back to the tribe so all can share it. When a conflict breaks out between tribes over food, the holder of this gene will risk its life to save its comrades.

If every member of the tribe possessed this new gene, the tribe as a whole would enjoy a tremendous advantage. Its actions would be more coordinated and disciplined than those of its rivals. Individual globs within such a tribe would be healthier and better fed. The tribe itself would act like one individual, while its competitors were weakened by the self-centered concerns of their members. The problem is that rather than taking over the tribe, this gene is likely to be selected against until it becomes extinct.

Let's add some numbers to the problem. Assume that initially there are N individuals in each tribe and that the gene in question reduces the reproductive fitness of its holder by X offspring and raises the reproductive success of the tribe, including the mutant gene holder, by a total of Y offspring. As long as the expected reproductive gain to the mutant individual from its share of the reproductive gain of the group is less than the reproductive loss suffered as a result of its group-benefiting behavior, the descendants of this mutant gene will decline in every generation until it is extinct. In other words, if Y/N is less than X, the mutant individual and its genes do not get enough benefit from its actions to offset the loss.

For example, if Y is 50 and N is 50 and X is 2, the individual's share of the group benefit of its action is 1 additional child, but its loss is 2 children. The individual will therefore contribute fewer children and genes to the next generation. Even if the loss to the individual was offset by its share of the tribe's gains, that is, Y/N = X, the frequency of the gene (its proportional representative in the gene pool) will decline over time, because the total population of the tribe is growing due to the beneficial action whereas there is not a proportional increase in the descendants of the mutant individual. This point can be generalized. So long as the group-benefiting behavior on average helps other members more than it helps the actor, the frequency of the gene responsible for this behavior will decline over time. For this reason, this gene could never take over and thus, could not determine the way in which the tribe as a whole behaves.

This does not mean that genes benefiting the group could not survive or even come to dominate a group, even as a result of selection acting at the level of groups. All that is necessary would be that the individual receive a sufficiently disproportionate share of the gains to the tribe. Let A be the amount of the total gain accruing to the actor. The net benefit to the individual and the responsible gene is then A minus X (the cost of acting). The benefit left to the rest of the population is (Y-A) and (Y-A)/(N-1) is their average share for all other individuals. If (A-X) is greater than (Y-A)/(N-1), then the frequency of the gene responsible for this beneficial behavior will not only spread but increase in frequency and could eventually dominate the population.

So it is *possible* for group-enhancing traits to evolve as long as the selfish gene gets a big enough share of the bigger pie. This may be part of the reason we reward heroes, giving them medals, parades, and movie contracts, as well as buying their books.

But all is not milk and honey. The same logic applies to selfish, group-damaging behavior. If a new mutant increases the fitness of its bearer relative to others in the group, its frequency will increase even though the group as a whole loses. As the socially destructive gene spreads, the burden on the group increases, further reducing its reproductive capacity. If the negative effect of the behavior is strong enough and if the rest of the population doesn't evolve a defense against the destructive trait, the group faces hard times and possibly, extinction. The relative success of the malevolent gene spells its doom. The gene prospers when it is relatively rare in the population, and it continues to prosper even as it increases in frequency, but as it becomes numerous its destructive behavior imposes a larger and larger burden on every other group member.

The biological effect of individual behavior upon group fitness has a distinct analogy in economic theory. Economists are familiar with the concept of the "free rider," someone who benefits from the actions of someone else without contributing in turn. The classic example involves public goods, those goods and services that yield widespread benefits, regardless of whether the beneficiaries help bear its burdens. For example, spending on national defense is supposed to benefit all citizens. Since it is not practical to defend only those who agree to pay, a selfish individual has an incentive to refrain from contributing. His share, being a small part of the total, will have no significant effect on the level of defense provided. By not paying, he saves money without lowering the amount of protection he receives. So unless there is compulsion, it is hard to see why anyone would pay for defense.

The individual facing the decision to pay or not pay for a public good is in the same position as the "good" gene discussed above. If he pays, he is out the expense and most of the benefits are received by other people. Economists have come to exactly the same conclusion as geneticists: Public goods will not be voluntarily provided by the market unless some way can be found to exclude the free riders, require payment by force, and/or ensure that a disproportionate amount of the benefits go to those who pay. Private companies will not build freeways but will construct toll roads. Like the genes, unless they can get back more than they spend, they eventually go bankrupt.

This analogy also holds for behavior that is socially harmful. Individuals or firms that pollute gain a cost advantage over those who are more socially responsible. Absent any legal restriction, this type of negative behavior will drive non-polluting competitors out of business just as socially harmful genes can take over a population. Whether a society of unrestrained polluters can drive an economy to extinction is an open question.

We believe that the many similarities between economic theory and evolutionary theory are more than coincidental. This is a theme central to this book and the main subject of chapter 5. The logic of maximizing, in the presence of resource constraints, whether by selfish rational agents, as in the case of humans, or by unconscious replicators, as in the case of genes, is inherently the same.

The Facts of Life: 1. Why Sex?

When Lord Chesterfield noted about sex that "the pleasure is momentary, the position ridiculous, and the expense damnable" (Rees, 1998, p. 211) he was more biologically correct than he knew ... at least regarding the matter of "expense." But some explanation is in order.

Given the cogency of fitness maximizing as a natural process, the existence of sex itself is paradoxical. Non-biologists often assume that the adaptive significance of sex is reproduction, but in fact, sex is not only unnecessary for reproduction, it even seems to be a liability. Thus, living things can reproduce asexually, as with amoebas that divide mitotically (and without sex) or strawberries that send out shoots or runners, thereby reproducing "vegetatively." Sexual reproduction, by contrast, is the exchange of genetic material between organisms. It results in the scrambling of genes, analogous to the reshuffling of a deck of cards, which produces a new genetic "hand" for each offspring produced.

The problem is that there are numerous disadvantages attendant on sexual reproduction. For convenience, we can divide them into behavioral/ecological on the one hand, and genetic on the other. As to the former, consider first that an organism intent on reproducing sexually must locate a suitable partner, a process which is not only liable to be time consuming, but potentially risky as well, since individuals typically must advertise at least their presence and receptivity. Advertisements of this sort not only cost precious resources, but may signal one's whereabouts to potential predators. In one species of frog, for example, males have the unenviable task of choosing between remaining silent and thus unmated, or vocalizing, and increasing the chance that they will be overheard by bats, which eat them (Ryan, 1985). Moreover, among some species, such as Indonesian rhinos and perhaps blue whales, sheer rarity makes it difficult to find a partner. It would be much easier if each of these creatures could simply split in two, or develop its eggs parthenogenetically.

When it comes to the biological woes imposed by sex, this is only the beginning. Even if a suitable partner is located, the exchange of genetic material requires a more or less intimate physical association, which renders one or both individuals vulnerable to injury by the other, not to mention to risks of sexually transmitted diseases (which are not limited to human beings). In addition, copulating individuals are often especially prone to being attacked by others—whether predators or competitors—who are not similarly preoccupied. And finally, bear in mind that each prospective parent is only selected to be interested in its long-term evolutionary success, not in that of its partner. The door is thus opened to a range of manipulative strategies and counter-strategies among sexual "partners" (e.g., Rice, 1996) as well as costly competitive interactions even between parent and offspring (e.g., Trivers, 1974).

As if these liabilities weren't enough, the strictly genetic cost of sexual reproduction appears to be even greater. Every sexually reproducing individual has a 50 percent probability that any of his or her genes will appear in the offspring. By contrast, an asexually reproducing individual would enjoy certainty of genetic representation. In electing for 50 percent rather than 100 percent, sexual reproducers are paying a 50 percent tariff. Why?

The short answer is that no one knows. Some biologists, including the highly respected George Williams, even conclude glumly that sexual reproduction may be maladaptive, a historical accident that probably benefited individuals with a very high reproductive rate—such as elm trees and barnacles—but that is disadvantageous for nearly all vertebrates (Williams, 1975).

On the other hand, an alternative consensus has more recently been forming. It recognizes the manifold costs of sex but also acknowledges its benefit: the generation of genetic diversity. Note that it is very easy to slip into a group- or species-selection argument here, presuming that sex has evolved despite its liabilities, because by creating new generations of diverse individuals, it opens new evolutionary opportunities for the group or the species. Our previous discussion should alert the reader that living things should not engage in anything if it is more costly than beneficial to its individual practitioners, even if as a result, the group or species is able to evolve more effectively, or more quickly, etc.

The compensating benefit of sex—assuming there is one—must reside in its ability to produce vast amounts of genetic diversity. Indeed, it has long been known that species that experience temporary situations in which there is a predominant payoff for extremely rapid reproduction and little advantage to the generation of diversity, such as daphnia inhabiting a largely vacant puddle or aphids on an empty rosebush, tend to reproduce asexually, at least until the population increases and the environment becomes less readily exploitable. Then a bout of sexual reproduction typically ensues.

The advantage of sexual reproduction seems to be that by producing a large number of genetically different offspring, parents are able to hedge their bets, increasing the chance that if and when their environment changes, they will have produced at least some winners. In this sense, sex is analogous to buying multiple lottery tickets instead of simply purchasing many copies of the same number.

A particularly cogent addition to this theory has been the apparent role of parasites and disease organisms. These abundant, debilitating, and potentially lethal creatures are also very small, which means that they are nearly always capable of out-reproducing their host/victim. Pathogens therefore experience an immense evolutionary advantage, which, in turn, may well have selected for hosts/victims that are capable of generating a bewildering variety of offspring. The idea is that diverse offspring, produced by sexual recombination, confront potential pathogens with a constantly moving target, making it impossible for the latter to specialize on a particular genotype. This, in turn, would confer a potentially large benefit to parents who reproduce in this manner (Hamilton, 1980).

The Facts of Life: 2. Why Two Sexes?

A second question then arises: Why are there two distinct sexes? After all, sexual reproduction simply implies the swapping of genetic material, not the existence of males and females. There is no reason why two fundamentally similar individuals couldn't exchange genes, or why there couldn't be a dozen or even a thousand mating types within every species, with the sole requirement being, perhaps, that members of one type must reproduce sexually with members from a different type. In this way, the pool of possible mating partners would be enormously expanded. Something very much like this happens among paramecia, for example, which are "isogamous," producing "identical gametes."

But the great majority of sexually reproducing animals are highly specialized, into males and females. They are "anisogamous," producing "different gametes." Indeed, the differing styles of gamete production constitute the defining traits of males and females. This is why biologists have no difficulty identifying the sex of oysters, for example, or of birds, most of which lack external genitals. Maleness and femaleness does not reside in penises or vaginas, beards or breasts, or physical size or behavioral predispositions, although these various differences derive from maleness and femaleness. Rather, the defining characteristic of males and females are the kinds of gametes they produce. Males make a large number of very small gametes, known as sperm; females produce a relatively small number of large gametes, known as eggs.

Thus, males typically contribute half of the blueprint but none of the raw material required to build a child. The origin of anisogamy is almost as mysterious as the origin of life itself, and indeed, it may have occurred very early in the history of living creatures. Several theories have been proposed. Here are two.

British geneticist Geoffrey Parker and colleagues (Parker et al., 1972) developed a computer simulation beginning with an initial population that was essentially isogamous. Built into their model, however, was some variation in gamete size, with most gametes intermediate and the frequency steadily declining in number among those gametes that were larger and smaller. The result was a normal frequency distribution, or bell-shaped curve. Certain other simple assumptions were also incorporated, notably that larger gametes, once combined, produced offspring that were somewhat more successful (because they had a better nutritional head start) and that smaller gametes were more able to achieve unions with other gametes (because they moved more quickly).

When the simulation was run, an interesting result obtained: The intermediate forms disappeared, replaced by a bimodal distribution consisting of large gametes and small gametes. The survivors were the specialists, either those containing lots of nutrient but little motility (eggs) or lots of motility but little nutrient (sperm). Those that waffled, or stayed on the gametic fence, lost out.

A second possible explanation for the evolution of anisogamy is based on the fact that a fertilized zygote, to be functional, must be a cooperative enterprise. The genes within every cell are not limited to nuclear DNA; there is also DNA in the mitochondria, key to most metabolic processes. One way of preventing debilitating civil war between mitochondrial DNA from two different parents might have been for the competing genetic donors to reach a kind of truce whereby one side would only contribute nuclear genetic material—and no cytoplasmic components—whereas the other would contribute not only its share of nuclear DNA but also all of the metabolic supplies and machinery (Hurst and Hamilton, 1992; Anderson, 1992).

Of course, these two models are not mutually exclusive. And either, or both, would result in the two styles of gamete-makers we currently identify as male and female.

So What?

As we shall see, there are immense implications to this male-female difference, implications that are especially important to any attempt at developing a theory of human behavior that hinges on evolutionary (that is, reproductive) considerations. It might seem, however, that mammals are exceptions to the egg/sperm dichotomy characteristic of other animals. After all, whereas birds make eggs that are immense relative to avian sperm, mammalian eggs are comparatively small, indeed, barely visible to the unaided eye. From a purely biological point of view, the cost of one sperm to a male is far less than the cost of an egg to a female, but in reality, mammalian sperm are pre-packaged, with several hundred million in a single ejaculate, along with substantial quantities of seminal fluid.

The crucial male-female dichotomy nonetheless persists in mammals, human beings included. Once a woman's egg is fertilized, she is obliged to devote nine months to gestation, followed by an even more calorically expensive obligation to lactate. Admittedly, this presupposes a world without artificial baby formula, but since more than 99 percent of human evolutionary history took place in such a world, it seems reasonable to suppose that it was especially influential in driving our current biological makeup.

For the present, let us also note that because of anisogamy, males and females can be expected to engage in differing reproductive strategies. The key concept is "parental investment," first enunciated by sociobiologist Robert L. Trivers (1972), at the time a graduate student at Harvard University. Trivers defined parental investment as anything—time, resources, risky behavior—expended on behalf of offspring, which increases their chances of survival and ultimately reproduction, and which occurs at the cost of parents' ability to invest similarly in other offspring. He demonstrated that the sex investing more (usually, but not always females) became a limiting resource for the reproductive success of the sex investing less (usually, but not always males).

As a result, males generally tend to compete among themselves for access to females, with such male-male competition often taking aggressive, even violent, turns, since the consequence—to breed or not to breed—is of immense evolutionary significance. In addition, Trivers's parental investment theory suggests that females, as the sex investing more, are often in a position to choose among the eager, competing males. The male-female asymmetry in parental investment allows biologists to make sense of the most common pattern among vertebrates, in which males tend to be aggressive, sexual advertisers and females, coy comparison shoppers. (In chapter 6 we shall return to the biology of male-female differences—including parental investment theory—with special attention to its implications for courting and parental behavior, as well as the question of what is advertised, and what is chosen.)

For now, we note that parental investment has been powerfully confirmed as the prime factor generating intra-sexual competition as well as choosiness. The relatively rare exceptions—in which females are competitive and males, choosy—essentially prove the rule: when sex roles are reversed, so is the partitioning of parental investment. For example, among neotropical waterbirds known as jacanas, females are brightly colored and aggressive, defending territories against other females; males are drab, coy, and unassuming. This reversal of traditional vertebrate sex roles correlates with a reversal of parental investment: males build the nests, incubate eggs, and care for offspring, thereby providing a significant amount of "female-like" parental investment (Jenni and Collier, 1972). Similarly, among certain insects, males provide not only sperm but also a large proteinaceous "spermatophore," which is consumed by the female as part of mating. In such cases, the total male investment exceeds that of females, and, as predicted, males are "female-like," choosing among potential mates, who, in turn, compete for access to them (Gwynne, 1981).

Sex Ratios and Conflicting Realities

What is the optimal percentage of males in a population? By now, the reader should realize that this is a trick question. The answer is, optimal for what? Evolution does not care about what is optimal for the species, just what is optimal for the relevant gene. As the great statistician and evolutionary theorist R. A. Fisher pointed out, the starting point of any discussion of sex ratios is the fact that each sex makes an equal genetic contribution to each offspring (Fisher, 1930). Every baby has both a father and a mother, even though many males never get to breed. When they do, they hit the reproductive jackpot, so that on average, males have as many children as females.

This is true even in a polygynous situation. Imagine a harem-keeping species in which a successful male mates with ten females, leaving nine bachelors. Lets say that every female produces one offspring per year. The average annual fitness of females is therefore one. What about the males? The nine bachelors have a fitness of zero, but the harem-master's fitness is ten; on average, therefore, the annual fitness of males is also one.

Because of this, sex ratios are usually close to unity; there are as many males as females. Any gene, which would push the sex ratio away from unity, would raise the reproductive value of the scarce sex and reduce the reproductive value of the plentiful one. The parents of the scarce sex would now enjoy a genetic advantage. Any genes that encourage the production of the scarce sex would begin to reproduce more rapidly, moving the sex ratio back to unity. This analysis is unaffected by the starting conditions. Thus, it doesn't matter that in our harem example, we began with ten males and ten females; if the initial sex ratio were unbalanced, selection would still equalize that ratio, until at equilibrium, parents producing males were as genetically fit as parents producing females. (Economists might say that at this point, the expected marginal productivity of males equals that of females, even though every female might breed, and only one male in ten.)

It is possible that if parents could vary the amount of resources invested in each child, they would prefer to have fewer sons but invest more in each of them so as to increase their quality and probability of becoming super-studs. (Recall that males are likely to compete among themselves for access to females, so that the payoff to males of being "high quality" is especially great, just as the penalty to being inadequate is correspondingly high.) In any event, strictly speaking, evolutionary theory does not predict that the numbers of each sex will be equal but that in the aggregate, equal resources will be invested in each sex.

But even if true for the population as a whole, it does not necessarily hold for certain sub-groups. Thus, for instance, it is in the interest of high-quality females—those that are socially dominant, unusually healthy, wealthy, and/or genetically well-endowed—to bias the sex ratio of their offspring to favor sons since each one has a better than average chance of becoming a prolific breeder. On the other hand, low-quality females should bias their offspring in favor of daughters since the odds are stacked against their sons ever getting the opportunity to reproduce, and females are a safer investment (Trivers and Willard, 1973). Recall that as the sex investing more, females are the typical objects of male-male competition, so that the variance in female reproductive success is generally low (i.e., most females breed, and unlike the case for males, the difference between the most and the least successful is not terribly great).

Among human beings, quality may, to some extent, be a consequence of genes, but even more, it results from social and economic considerations. Significantly, there is a robust tendency for people—especially those in stratified societies such as traditional Indian Hindu and medieval Chinese—to practice female infanticide (in the case of the upper classes) or to enroll their sons in monasteries or the military (in the case of the lower classes), precisely as evolutionary theory would predict (Dickemann, 1979). Bear in mind that as members of a biologically polygynous species, high-ranking, upper-class men in stratified societies have the potential of marrying numerous women and thereby producing many children, whereas by contrast, high-ranking, upper-class women are biologically limited in the number of potential offspring they can produce. As a result, it makes evolutionary sense for upper-class families to invest preferentially in boys rather than girls. A mirror-image dynamic can be expected to operate among lower-class families, among whom girls are a more effective investment.

So far, we have assumed that males provide only sperm (i.e., genes) to females. In many species, males contribute more substantial resources to their mates and their offspring. Male birds often build nests and help feed their young. This appears to be driven by the exceptionally high metabolic demands of nestlings, which put a premium on domestic labor contributed by males as well as females. Among mammals, males generally provide very little assistance to their offspring, at least in part because female mammals are uniquely equipped to nourish them via lactation.

Although human beings are perfectly good mammals, they are somewhat unusual in the degree of male parental investment that they provide. Thus, men typically work to care for their wives and children. The more hostile the environment, the scarcer the necessary resources, the more necessary is male parental investment. Assuming that income remains constant, the greater the male's contribution to supporting his offspring, the fewer mates he will be able to afford. In the extreme, as with most bird species, the two sexes form monogamous pairs.

In this case, even low-quality males can hope to find mates; thus, monogamy is perhaps the greatest leveler in human history. Low-quality females need—or at minimum, benefit from—the resources that a male can supply, in order to raise their children. From such a woman's point of view, it may be better to take low-quality sperm that accompanies minimum male resources than to get high-quality sperm and no help in raising the kids. This could be especially true because people seem to find it easier to assess quality of resources than genetic quality (at least for variation within normal limits). In this circumstance, there should be a man for every woman and a woman for every man, and we can all live in monogamous bliss.

But wait! There is a snake in the garden (actually, several). For example, there is another, better strategy available to lower quality females. Instead of settling for the low quality mate because she needs his resources, maybe she can have her cake and eat it too. If she can mate with a high-quality male but still convince the low quality male that she is faithful and that he is the father of her children, she gets the best of both worlds, high-quality genes and the resources of a devoted mate. Given that she is low quality (more precisely, lower quality than he can otherwise obtain), a high-quality male would be generally unwilling to provide her with significant resources; however, he can always spare a little sperm for a worthy cause, which is, at least in part, his own.

Of course, this is disastrous for the low-quality male. Not only does he fail to reproduce, but he is spending his surplus energy supporting someone else's kids rather than looking for a new mate. For the victimized male, cuckoldry is genetic murder. Therefore it is not difficult to understand the violent behavior of males on discovering that their mates have cheated on them. Sociologists who view sexual jealousy as simply learned behavior need a broader view of evolution and of life.

There are numerous animal parallels of this situation. For example, male pied flycatchers (a European songbird) establish mateships with a "primary" female, which they assist in the rearing of offspring (Alatalo et al., 1981). But they also frequently maintain another, "secondary" female at some distance from their primary mate. This secondary female does not receive any assistance, and not surprisingly, her reproductive success is significantly lower than that of the primary female. The male, meanwhile, ends up with a higher fitness than if he remained strictly monogamous. As to the secondary female, the situation is more ambiguous: although she is less successful than her primary counterpart, she is certainly more successful than if she had remained unmated. It is unclear whether she is duped by the male, although the fact that a philandering male maintains non-contiguous mating territories suggests that he deceives the females as to whether they are the sole object of his affection, and thus, sole recipient of his subsequent assistance.

Compared to a cuckolded male—and to the possibly deceived female—the high-quality female whose mate "gets a little something on the side" loses little. It is unlikely that he will leave her for this inferior substitute. It makes most sense for him to invest his limited resources in his highest quality offspring. However, if she catches him eyeing a female of higher quality, for example, younger or healthier than herself, she has every genetic reason to be concerned.

Quality versus Quantity

In our discussion of group selection, we emphasized that an individual is not expected to engage in any behavior unless the individual's reproductive gains from that behavior exceed the cost. Otherwise, the genes responsible for such acts would be culled from the gene pool by natural selection. In general, individual organisms face a variety of choices over their lifetime. As with a consumer who spends his income on that bundle of goods that maximizes his utility, natural selection yields the prediction that if the environment is stable enough, organisms will evolve to "choose" those activities that maximize their genetic fitness, projecting the largest possible number of copies of their genes into future generations. The best strategy, however, is not always to produce the greatest number of children. If an individual could choose between producing two low-quality children or one high-quality child, the optimal choice depends on the relationship between quality and the future reproductive efficiency of the children.

To illustrate this point, let's return to the simple asexual world of our original globs. The run-of-the-mill glob can produce two children of which one can be expected to survive. Since this is asexual reproduction, the expected result is that one copy of its genes will be present in all succeeding generations. Now, let's give one mutant glob a choice. It can produce two ordinary children or it can invest all its resources and produce one superchild. Let us assume that the expected survival rate for this superchild is still 50 percent, but if it does survive, that it can produce three children of its own. Initially, having one superchild does not appear to be a very successful strategy. The number of children has been cut in half in the first generation. But if this sole child survives, it will produce three children of its own, of which one and a half, on average, are expected to survive. Therefore, .75 copies of the original parents' genes will likely be present in this generation. Because every generation of superchildren produces three children, of which half survive, the copies of these genes increase by 50 percent in every generation. Eventually as these more fertile globs become more numerous, the population of globs will push up against the available resources and the expected survival rate for all globs will begin to fall. With time, the new, improved, more fertile globs—all descended from the first mutant parent—will take over the population. Each descendant will then produce three children, of which one is expected to survive.

The same situation would occur if the mutation affected not fertility but survival rate. If the original asexual globs produced four children with a survival rate of 25 percent, the genes of a glob that produced only three children would eventually take over the population if their survival rate were greater than one third. If the increase in resources invested in each child raises, by a sufficient degree, the chances that it will get to reproduce, it doesn't make any difference that fertility has been reduced.

The relationship between quality and quantity in biological systems was underscored by the ecologist David L. Lack, who studied clutch size among wild birds. Lack observed that any species in its given environment will have an optimal number of offspring. Each selfish individual chooses the size of its brood so as to maximize the number of children who survive to reproduce. Lack showed clearly that producing an unusually large clutch of eggs did not result in unusually high reproductive success; quite the opposite. By spreading their available parental investment too thinly, such parents actually experienced a *lower* fitness than those whose clutch size was more moderate (Lack, 1968). This does not even consider an additional and potentially important factor: the diminished lifespan—and hence, reduced overall fitness—of females who stress themselves by over-producing eggs in any given season.

Earlier, we reviewed Gary Becker's approach to the demand for children, emphasizing his work on the interaction between quantity and quality. As it happens, biologists have long recognized the crucial trade-off between quality and quantity of offspring in analyzing the reproductive strategies of other species. It is a distinction that also has crucial importance for our efforts to unite economics and evolutionary biology. Biologists have identified two suites of reproductive strategies, which are not so much alternatives as different ends of a continuum.

At one end is so-called "r-selection," which emphasizes quantity. Species that are r-selected generally show the following traits: small body size, high mortality, early age of sexual maturation, large litter or clutch size, comparatively simple social organization, and relatively little parental care overall. By contrast, "K-selected species," occupying the other end of the tactical continuum, are generally large bodied, and have low mortality, later age of sexual maturation, small litters or clutches, comparatively complex social organization, and comparatively well-developed parental care. Mice, for example, are r-selected relative to elephants, but K-selected relative to codfish. Human beings are K-selected compared to most other species.

Generally, r-selection regimes are found when there is a pay-off to producing a large number of offspring, but with relatively little advantage to investing heavily in any one (the "r" in r-selection derives from a term indicating the spontaneous rate of natural population increase, the so-called "Malthusian parameter"). K-selection, by contrast, characterizes parents whose offspring are in a highly competitive situation, so that fitness is greatest when each one is of comparatively high quality (the "K" in K-selection refers to "carrying capacity," referring to conditions in which a population is at or close to its ecological maximum, such that fitness is greatest when the competitive ability of each is as high as possible). To some extent, males—as sperm-makers—are r-selected, whereas females, as egg-makers, are K-selected.

It is important to emphasize that r-selected and K-selected species are both functioning to maximize fitness of their constituent individuals. They are simply employing different routes to the same ultimate end. Although the distinction between r- and K-selection was first made explicit by MacArthur and Wilson (1967), it was actually suggested nearly 20 years previously by the great evolutionary geneticist Theodosius Dobzhansky (1950), who noted that in general, inhabitants of the temperate and arctic zones suffered mortality that was largely independent of their population density, occurring because of large-scale environmental fluctuations such as drought, storms, or sudden influx of predators. In such conditions, mortality is relatively independent of individual characteristics, so parents ensure their reproductive success by generating a large number of offspring, regardless of quality (they tended to be r-selected). By contrast, Dobzhansky emphasized that tropical species competed most intensely with one another rather than with the environment. Their ecologically benign habitat is virtually filled with organisms, so success is not achieved by producing a large number of offspring, but rather, a smaller number of well-endowed descendants, each of which is more likely to survive and reproduce in turn (that is, K-selection.)

We might say that r-selected individuals follow a "wholesale" strategy, reaping a small average profit from each transaction, but making it up in volume, whereas K-selected individuals are "retailers," investing more heavily in every transaction, and thus necessarily having fewer of them.

Whereas species can be characterized by their degree of r- and K-selectedness, in some cases individuals remain constant in their reproductive strategies (e.g., Krebs et al., 1973), whereas in others, individuals vary theirs, depending on ecological circumstances (Cody, 1966; King and Anderson, 1971). It seems clear that human beings are capable of varying their degree of r- versus K- strategy.

Significantly, one of the best-documented demographic phenomena is the "demographic transition," in which industrialization, improved education, and public health systems typically generate a reduction in birth rates among developing countries, along with a corresponding reduction in mortality. This occurs in what might be termed an enhanced competitive environment, in which skills, education, and nonhuman capital contribute more heavily to offspring success, and parents are thus prone to strive for quality rather than quantity. Although this transition is not strictly an evolutionary event, since it readily takes place in a fraction of a generation, it has all the hallmarks of a shift from r-selection to K-selection, demonstrating if nothing else, that human beings have the flexibility to perform a transition that is appropriate and adaptive, whether viewed evolutionarily, ecologically, or economically.

In recent years, biologically oriented anthropologists have turned increasingly to the demographic transition, seeking to understand—from an evolutionary perspective—why improved socioeconomic conditions are so often correlated with reduced birthrate (e.g., Borgerhoff Mulder, 1998). Anthropologist Hillard Kaplan (1996) has even incorporated economic thinking into the problem, interpreting fertility reduction as a specific response to competitive wage and labor markets associated with modern industrial and post-industrial societies. Referring to investment in children as "embodied capital," Kaplan emphasizes that with enhanced competition for potentially high-paying jobs, parents come to appreciate the value of education and specialized job-training, all of which result in higher incomes and greater social as well as biological success for their children, but which also require higher investment in each child. Kaplan argues, however, that in most cases, the greater earning power of such children is not translated into proportionately higher long-term fitness (for either themselves or the parents who produce them). In this view, the "embodied capital" of relatively high-quality offspring simply represent a response to an atypical human environment: the biologically novel competitive wage economy of modern society.

Another anthropologist, Alan Rogers, has presented several mathematical models focused on the important point—which we develop in succeeding pages—that human wealth is typically inherited, and that "by leaving large bequests to offspring, a human parent may substantially increase the expected wealth of grandchildren" (Rogers, 1990; 1995). Implicit in Rogers' bequesting model—which we only

encountered after completing an initial version of the present book—
is that by limiting the production of offspring in a given generation,
parents could increase their prospects of bequeathing valuable resources to these offspring, with the result that ultimately, more descendants can be produced at some future time.

Another recent effort, again by anthropologists, has sought to interpret the phenomenon of reduced fertility in response to improved
socio-economic conditions by invoking this possibility: It might be
an evolved strategy to maximize long-term genetic reproductive
success "in the face of periodic calamities that result in demographic
crashes" (Boone and Kessler, 1999). The argument is essentially
that throughout human evolutionary history, there have been periodic catastrophic events (famines, plagues, dramatic weather
changes), which, although rare, have exacted immense mortality. At
such times, people in the upper socioeconomic classes are likely to
have survived disproportionately, and ultimately, to have enjoyed
enhanced fitness by virtue of their situation. Boone and Kessler further maintain that the acquisition of high status typically requires the
expenditure of wealth, which in turn requires that they be careful
about "wasting" such resources on their current generation of offspring.

There is some evidence to support this contention. Thus, a survey
of eighty die-offs of large mammals (especially herbivores, carni-
vores, and primates), found a modal reduction in population numbers in the range of 70 to 90 percent (Young, 1993). Although such
events appear to have been infrequent, their evolutionary significance would necessarily be considerable. Moreover, a glimpse at
human reproductive potential strongly suggests that *Homo sapiens*
has long been capable of far greater rates of population increase
than has actually taken place. Present-day !Kung people, for example, living in an arid foraging environment, have a documented
annual growth rate of .7 percent. Take even this figure—low in comparison to the data for many other pre-contact human groups—and
apply it to a hypothetical starting !Kung population of 10,000 and in
fewer than 2,000 years, the numbers of !Kung would exceed the
present total human population on earth (Boone and Kessler, 1999).
Evidently, there have been intervening periods of reduced population growth, quite possibly dramatic declines on occasion.

Boone and Kessler also cite numerous cross-cultural examples
in which famines and other natural disasters have decimated human

populations; in such cases, it is common for those in the upper socioeconomic classes, and their children, to suffer least. Neurologist Oliver Sacks (1996) also provided a dramatic case, in his account of the unusual genetic pattern found among the surviving inhabitants of Pingelap Island, in the South Pacific. When a typhoon devastated the Caroline Islands in 1775, it killed all but about twenty persons out of Pinegelap's initial population of nearly 1,000. These twenty survivors included the hereditary chief and members of his immediate household.

For an example of catastrophe in a technologic society, consider the sinking of the *Titanic*. This event has been cited in modern folklore as demonstrating the foolishness of technological hubris, as well as a cautionary tale about the limits of elitism, in which the wealthy—despite their wealth—died along with the poor. Data on survivorship as a function of passenger status, however, paints a different picture: 62 percent of first-class passengers were saved, compared to 41 percent of second-class passengers, and 25 percent of those in third class, or "steerage" (Garrett, 1986). All thirty children traveling in first and second class were saved, compared to only twenty-seven out of seventy-nine children traveling in steerage. This example is admittedly idiosyncratic, but nonetheless suggestive. Imagine the likely reproductive situation of a poor family that sent all of its four children, steerage class, on the *Titanic*, compared to a wealthy one that sent its two children first class! These examples all emphasize the importance to living things—people not excepted—of a biological "bottom line," namely, the number of successful offspring produced. We go one step further. We contend that it is not simply the number of offspring—in the case of human beings, children—or even the number of surviving children that matters. What is important is the ratio of the expected number of surviving grandchildren to the expected number of children. Actually, there is no limit, at least in theory, to how far forward in time this approach should be carried: a better measure yet would be a ratio based on the surviving number of great-grandchildren, and so on. But for ease of contemplation, it is probably best to begin with this preliminary, one-generation-removed approach.

If this grandchildren-children ratio is higher than the average ratio for the rest of the population, any gene contributing positively to such a strategy will increase in frequency relative to alternatives that act otherwise. This ratio can be interpreted as the expected return on an investment strategy. Both natural selection and the competitive market favor genes—or firms—with the highest rate of return. Again, note the resemblance between evolution and economics, a resemblance born of the logic and reality of competition.

All in the Family, and the ABCs of ESSs
(Evolutionary Stable Strategies)

Thus far, we have been concerned with reproductive strategies. In our simple world, individuals are only concerned about the reproductive success of their direct descendants. Natural selection will favor those individuals who have the optimum number of children and make the optimum investment in each of them. But in the real world, an individual's universe is filled with more than just children and strangers. He or she is surrounded by relatives, parents, siblings, cousins, aunts, and uncles.

Common sense tells us that these individuals will be of special importance to "ego," and vice versa. Moreover, it is also intuitively obvious that the closer the relation, the greater the importance. (Things of this sort, that are so obvious as to appear almost trivial, are often worth more investigation than they typically receive, because—like Newton's proverbial falling apple—they may well embody important truths.) Try the following thought experiment: Imagine a society in which people interact without regard to their genetic relatedness, in which complete strangers, for example, walk in randomly from the street, whereupon they are as likely as a biological parent to prepare dinner for a young child, and change its diapers. Or try conceiving of a society in which siblings have no particular interest in, or even knowledge about, each other.

Insofar as such a society is almost literally unimaginable—not just because of the chaos that would ensue, but because it would deny something fundamental in human biology—we see the pervasiveness of genes, and the power of William D. Hamilton's insight into inclusive fitness, which we described earlier.

Those relatives that loom so large in the social life of all human beings (and indeed, of most other animals as well), experience a probability of shared genes that is higher than what characterizes the population as a whole. Genes have copies of themselves not only within their own body but also can expect to find them with varying degrees of probability in those other bodies identified as "relatives." Elementary arithmetic allows us to calculate exactly the probability that any gene will find its identical copy in the body of another. In sexually reproducing diploid species, with both parents contributing an equal number of genes, those within an individual have a 50 percent probability of being identical with those of a full sibling, 25 percent with a half-sibling and with one's aunts and uncles, and 12.5 percent with first cousins.

Following the logic of natural selection, it should be in the long-run interest of any gene to assist the replication of these copies of itself. So if a gene must "decide" between the survival of its body and the survival of, say, three of its body's siblings or nine of its first cousins, by choosing self-sacrifice, the gene would cause more copies of itself to survive. Hence, such actions would be favored.

Once again, we emphasize that, of course, genes are not conscious. They do not deliberately choose anything, any more than most flowers choose to bloom in the spring. Suppose that ancestral flowers were equally likely to bloom at any time; those that indulged themselves in the autumn, winter, or even late summer, generally left fewer descendants than those that bloomed at such a time that their seeds were ready for germination when their probability of success was greatest. As a result, flowers "behave" as though they understand the progression of the seasons and its implications for horticultural success, although in fact, they lack a nervous system and are unable to consult a calendar, much less make sense of one. But their behavior is fitness-enhancing nonetheless. There is no reason to think that human capacities for fitness enhancement should be any less well developed.

The concept of inclusive fitness is not as simple as it first appears. For example, in maximizing their inclusive fitness, most living things take into account not only degree of relatedness but also the reproductive potential of any possible beneficiary of aid. Parents are generally more likely to invest in a promising offspring than in any likely to die. Similarly, parents are generally more prone to invest in their offspring than in their own parents (especially if the latter have a low probability of reproducing any more).

Here is yet another complexity: In any relatively small population, there is a high probability that we share many genes with all members of the breeding group. Does this mean that group selection can be resuscitated using the concept of inclusive fitness? Will individuals behave in an altruistic manner toward other members of their breeding group because there is a good chance they are helping copies of their genes? Not at all. Inclusive fitness does not imply diffuse altruism. To understand why, consider the concept of evolutionarily stable strategy, or ESS. This is a very important and elegant idea, borrowed from game theory and developed most cogently by the mathematician and evolutionary theorist John Maynard Smith (1982). It recognizes that the success of any strategy adopted by an individual—or, by implication, a gene—depends on the strategies adopted by other members of its population.

To be an ESS, a strategy must be successful enough to become established as dominant within a population. And once established, it cannot be bettered by an alternative strategy. Getting established and staying established are two different problems and must be distinguished from one another. To establish itself, a strategy must be the best one available at the time, and it must do well when rare, that is, when its primary encounters are with alternative strategies. To stay established, it must be able to do well even when it comes up against itself (which is a necessary consequence of becoming abundant). For example, excessive violence may initially spread in a population insofar as violent individuals do well against their meek alternatives. But as violence spreads, violent individuals are increasingly likely to encounter other violent individuals, as a result of which, meekness may increase. Although in such a situation, the meek might not inherit the earth, depending on the pay-offs for each behavior, it is quite likely that both meek and violent strategies could persist at some equilibrium frequencies.

Return now to the problem of inclusive fitness. It can be shown that a strategy of non-discriminating aid to other individuals' genes is not evolutionarily stable. Imagine a population consisting of genetically identical individuals, all of which possess an altruistic gene that directs each to value the reproductive success of every other individual as highly as it values its own. What happens if a selfish gene enters this altruistic paradise?

The selfish gene is only concerned about replicating itself. If it could recognize other individuals who also contain the mutant gene, it might direct its body to behave altruistically only towards these individuals. Although this is theoretically possible, it is extremely unlikely. How, in the absence of a direct indication of who bears this gene, could the individual favor other carriers? By calculating the degree of relatedness between itself and any other individual, it could estimate the probability of sharing any recently evolved trait. Since the gene is newly evolved, it is relatively rare within the population. Therefore, there is a 50 percent chance that siblings share it, a 25 percent chance that aunts and uncles also have it, and a 12.5 percent probability that any first cousin also carries it, and so forth.

By taking into account these probabilities when engaging in altruistic behavior, the selfish gene accomplishes three things. First, by being altruistic to only a small sub-group, it has a reproductive advantage over a nondiscriminating altruistic gene; by itself, this would enable it to take over the population. Second, by rendering aid strictly in accordance with these probabilities, it is safeguarded against the invasion of any alternative strategy. Third, it is fair to all other genes in the body. By rendering assistance only to close relatives according to their degree of relatedness, other recent mutations get the same benefit, as does the gene that influences this behavior.

Consider a gene that for some reason can identify all other holders of that gene. In the example first introduced by Richard Dawkins, (1989), they all possess a green beard. If this hypothetical gene directs altruistic behavior toward all green-bearded people, it will benefit copies of itself. But such altruism would occur at the expense of the individual who possesses this gene and his or her close relatives. Natural selection would favor any mutation that undermined this favoritism to green-chinned individuals. A mutant gene that directs resources only to its gene holder and close relatives, would promote its own reproductive success. These two genes would be engaged in a civil war, undermining the efficiency of both.

For these reasons, restricting help to close relatives based on the probability that they share a common gene is an evolutionarily stable strategy, precluding the evolution of any gene for diffuse altruism.

Parent-Offspring Conflict

We conclude this chapter with brief mention of another important evolutionary insight with likely consequences for traditional economic thought. Like the original formulation for parental investment theory, this insight is also due to the creative genius of Robert L. Trivers (1971). And like parental investment theory, as well as inclusive fitness theory, it is remarkably simple, even obvious, once someone else has pointed it out!

Most people can be forgiven for assuming that parents and offspring have identical interests. After all, offspring—especially when young—are dependent on resources provided by their parents, including but not limited to time, teaching, and protection, as well as physical resources such as food, clothing, and shelter. Parents, for their part, are equally dependent on their offspring as the primary means of their own fitness maximization. Under this reasonable view, and one that has been reinforced by countless Disney-style "natural history" films, parents and offspring (especially mothers and their children) are the epitome of unconflicted bliss. From an economic perspective, parents should be expected to invest wholeheartedly in their offspring, who should accept gratefully, limited only by a civilized disinclination to take more than their fair share.

Indeed, this has long been the perspective of other social sciences concerned with parent-child interactions, notably sociology and developmental psychology. The evolutionary view is somewhat darker, however, and almost certainly more accurate.

It is essentially a matter of seeing a glass of water—shared genes between parent and child—as half empty no less than half full. Thus, the heart-warming, Madonna-and-child image of unconflicted parental solicitude mixed with childhood gratitude is based on reality: the shared-genes, glass-half-full component. But there is also a glass half-empty. A mother, to be sure, has a 50 percent genetic interest in her child (and correspondingly, a child has a 50 percent genetic interest in its mother). But at the same time, there is the other 50 percent that is *not* shared. Or as Trivers put it, a child is 50 percent related to its mother but 100 percent related to itself, and vice versa.

The behavioral implications are profound. A child, for instance, can be expected to devalue its mother's cost by a factor of two. In modern jargon, it can only feel one-half of its mother's pain, and again, vice versa. For an immediate and practical example, a mother can be expected to discontinue lactation, so as to begin producing and investing in the next child, whenever her benefit in doing so exceeds her cost. The child at her breast, for its part, can be expected to see things differently, discounting the mother's benefit-cost assessment and only acquiescing when the mother's benefit exceeds twice her cost. Until that time, mother and child can be expected to disagree, and in fact, weaning conflict is widely observed throughout the natural world, extending even to analogous struggles between adult birds and their fledglings.

It has even been suggested that this fundamental asymmetry emerges before birth. Thus, evolutionary biologist David Haig (1991) proposes that pregnancy provides an arena for conflict between mother and fetus. High blood pressure and pre-eclampsia, for example, are two common complications of pregnancy, both suffered by the mother. They are caused by fetal hormones that, in a sense, attempt to increase blood flow to the unborn child at the expense of injuring the mother's kidneys.

Blood sugar is another possible battleground. During the final trimester of pregnancy, the placenta (a product of the fetus, not the mother,) secretes a hormone that interferes with the effect of the mother's insulin. The mother, at the same time, is producing ever more insulin. Why this particular tug-of-war? Insulin suppresses blood sugar levels, so by producing it, the mother can be seen as attempting to restrict the amount of sugar—her nutrient—that is made available to the fetus, who in turn responds by trying to get as much as possible. As Haig points out, just as raised voices are a likely sign of human conflict, so are raised hormone levels!

Such competition between parent and child can be expected to continue throughout life, depending on specific circumstances. As a general rule, evolutionary considerations lead to the expectations that although parents are indeed selected to provide resources, offspring are selected to seek more than parents are selected to give. This perspective is dramatically different from that of developmental psychology, for example, or sociology, in which rough spots in the parent-offspring nexus are typically attributed to insufficient socialization on the part of the offspring, who are, after all, new to the world, and readily seen as "gnarly" little barbarians, uncivilized savages who have yet to appreciate where their true interests lie. By contrast, the Trivers-led biological revolution suggests that offspring are full actors in their own right, whose disputatious inclinations are not so much a result of ignorance and inexperience as of the fact that they are following their own evolutionary agenda, one that has many correspondences with that of their parents, but that also stands by and for itself.

From this perspective, parents and offspring can be expected to disagree in many interesting ways, especially when it comes to interactions with other individuals. Consider, for example, a parent with two offspring, which are full sibs. That parent can be expected to encourage altruistic behavior from offspring A toward offspring B whenever the cost incurred by A is less than the benefit derived by B (after all, the parent is equally related to both A and B, and he or she profits whenever the net total of benefit accrued by both is positive). But offspring A—the would-be donor—can be expected to disagree. He should be inclined to behave altruistically toward his full sib only when the benefit derived by B is more than twice A's cost. Otherwise, in the realm where B's benefit is more than A's cost but less than twice that cost, A and A's parent can be expected to disagree, with the parent urging altruism and A resisting.

In a sense, this is a biological perspective on sibling rivalry. It is also something to which all parents (as well as children) can relate. Who cannot remember parents urging children to play "more nicely" than the children are inclined to do? Becker (1981, pp.182-183) presents his own analysis of intra-family competition in his Rotten Kid Theorem. In this analysis, the head of the family behaves altruistically towards all other members of the family, that is, the children, and adjusts contributions to them to equalize their incomes. In so doing, the head of the family not only eliminates the incentive for any family member to behave "badly" to any other but also induces each family member to maximize the total income of the family. Our fundamental disagreement with Becker is over the utility function of the parents. Rather than equalize their children's incomes, we hold that parents will act to maximize their reproductive potential and this may well imply unequal investments in each child. More on this is included in the next chapter in which we lay out in detail our reformulation of the utility function.

A similar pattern should also characterize interactions outside the nuclear family. Genes within a parent have a 25 percent probability of being present within a niece or nephew, for example, whereas cousins have a probable genetic overlap of only 12.5 percent. Once again, parents and offspring can therefore be expected to disagree, with parents inducing cousins to interact more benevolently (also more often) than the cousins would elect if left to their own devices.

There are many implications of this perspective, only a few of which have thus far been elucidated. Here is one, especially relevant for our purposes. The inclination of parents to invest in their children—which we see as crucial to an evolution-based view of economics—should itself be influenced by ongoing power struggles and psychological warfare between parents and children. Thus, parents indeed are selected to invest in their children, since it is their primary (although as we have seen, not their only) route to long-term evolutionary success. They should also be selected to be "in-

telligent" investors, preferentially providing scarce resources to recipients able to provide a good return on such investment.

At the same time, offspring have been selected to appeal maximally to their parents, furthering their own interests by obtaining,
whenever possible, more than their parents are selected to provide.
In doing so, both parents and offspring must walk a fine line. Parents must refrain from being suckered by their offspring, but must
also avoid erring on the side of withholding too stringently. Offspring, for their part, might be expected to solicit parental resources
by exaggerating their neediness, or their potential, since all things
being equal, parental investment would be well spent on behalf of
offspring who might otherwise fail to thrive, as well as those who
might return greater-than-average dividends. One can anticipate a
kind of ontogenetic triage: parents should be disinclined to invest in
offspring likely to fail in any case, or those likely to succeed even
without additional investment, reserving most of their resources for
the in-betweens who will succeed with help but fail without it.

If the offspring go too far in signaling their neediness or their
capacity for independent success, they risk being cut off, either because they may be perceived as hopeless causes, no longer worthy
of parental largesse, or so competent as not to need further investment, which the parents might spend more profitably in other ways.

All this conflict between intimates, the expectation of delicate tight-
rope-walking, and the careful balancing of genetic sharing—not to
mention the delicate balancing between quantity and quality—ensure that even a seemingly "simple" and reductionistic model of
human economic and social motivation (of the sort we present in the
next chapter) is unlikely to be definitive. Indeed, evolutionary analyses
of human behavior in general, and of child-bearing, child-rearing,
and child-investing in particular, promise to be complex enough,
when fully fleshed out, to keep things interesting and worthy of their
subject, for a long time to come.

Notes

1.   A view of evolution called "orthogenesis"—now discredited—was popular among
      early twentieth century biologists; it claimed that evolution is goal-directed.
2.   Dawkins (1987, pp. 150-158) relates the theory of Cairns-Smith who postulates
      that primitive evolution in certain crystals may have assisted in the origin of organic
      life.

5

Synthesis

We have briefly surveyed the two theoretical frameworks that have been, in our opinion, most successful in offering logically coherent explanations of the behavior of living organisms. Economics seeks to establish the laws of rational, self-interested human behavior. It has discovered logical relationships between an individual's values and means of achieving them. Economics is not concerned with *what* people value, but rather with how they expend their resources so as (presumably) to maximize their well-being. To put it simply, economics is not about ends, but about the means chosen to satisfy any arbitrary set of desires.

Evolutionary biology is more ambitious, concerned with both ends and means. Whereas economics has simply assumed self-interest as the motivating force of human behavior, evolution has not only shown that all living organisms must act in their own self-interest, but has identified the nature of that self-interest: maximizing genetic fitness is the goal of all life. Natural selection guarantees that individual organisms that attempt to achieve some other goal will be replaced by their more reproductively self-interested competitors.

Evolutionary biology has another advantage over economics; it is fully integrated with the other natural sciences. When it comes to evolution, there need be no distinction between the social sciences and the natural sciences. There is just science.

It is the central argument of this book that together, economics and evolutionary biology can form the foundation for a productive, scientific study of human behavior. Not only is evolutionary biology consistent with the fundamental logic of economics, it can also provide economics with sound theoretical support for its principal assumptions. Most important, it can give definite meaning and content to the heretofore abstract concept of utility maximization.

To draw his interesting conclusions about human behavior, Becker had to assume that utility functions were not only constant over time, but also identical for all individuals. While he, at times, invoked evolution as a justification for these assumptions, at other times Becker has stated that the role of natural selection in determining simple and identical preferences is limited to non-human species (1981, p. 217). In the absence of a convincing theory of how human preferences are determined, Becker's assumption of constancy over time and universality among all individuals remains just that, an assumption. Since no theory can explain all behavior, there will always be a temptation to resort to "differences in taste," or to expand the list of "goods" contained in the utility function. It is our contention that with regard to the human utility function, Becker has been too cautious. Evolutionary biology not only provides a satisfactory explanation of *why* utility functions are constant and universal among all human beings, it also identifies their content and structure, that is, *how* they work.

If it is true, as we believe, that evolutionary biology has a great deal to offer economics, what does economics have to offer in return? Why not simply scrap economics and build a new science of human behavior based on evolutionary theory alone? The reason is simple: a large part of any new evolutionary science of human behavior would closely replicate modern economic theory. In fact, in the last several decades, biologists have increasingly borrowed the logic and methodology of economics in building their models of the impact of natural selection on the behavior of human and non-human species.

At one level, this borrowing from economics may seem surprising. After all, economics deals with rational behavior. Its theories assume that individuals are aware of the costs and benefits of the alternatives they face and are capable of calculating which, among the numerous alternatives, maximizes their utility. This assumption may be a stretch even for humans, so what justification exists for applying it to non-human species? Yet the movement of concepts from economics to evolutionary biology is reasonable and to be expected. Economics is about optimization, and even though genes do not consciously optimize anything, natural selection chooses those genes that—via their bodies—are best at solving the universal problems of survival and reproduction.

At their core, both economics and evolutionary biology are about efficiency in pursuing given goals. Economics lays out the conditions for the efficient satisfaction of desires. The marginal conditions in consumption and production presented in chapter 2 simply establish the relationships between goals and actions required for the optimum utilization of resources, given any set of goals. Evolution, on the other hand, explains not only what the goal of action must be, but how optimizing behavior would arise in the first place, despite the various obstacles to optimality that we have already described.

Adaptation and Optimization

Just as economics can be accused of relying on a tautological definition of self-interest, evolution has been charged with the same logical offense. Since genetic fitness means no more than passing relatively numerous copies of one's genes on to subsequent generations, evolution has been interpreted as being a tautology, whereby "survival" and "fitness" are interchangeable. But in fact, fitness in the evolutionary sense does not simply refer to the survival of individual bodies, but to long-term evolutionary success, whereby genes survive, or don't.

Over time, in a large-enough population, and if the environment in which a population exists is reasonably stable, the best available options—both of structure and of behavior—will come to dominate the population. When we speak of a species being adapted to its environment, relative terms always apply: it is better adapted than the available alternatives. The longer an environment has been stable, the greater the opportunity for natural selection to refine and optimize the exploitation of any particular ecological niche. Change the environment from the one to which adaptations originally evolved, and traits that were promoting fitness could well have the opposite effect.

Conversely, the more stable the environment, the more specialized the species will become in exploiting it. Just as the worker who spends all his time as a carpenter will invest exclusively in carpentry tools, a species that has "earned its living" in a relatively stable ecology will develop those traits that are highly suited for this environment. But a genetic lineage that has evolved in a highly unstable environment can't afford to be overly specialized. Its structure and behavior must be able to cope with more than one set of problems. If the workman is not a specialist but a neighborhood handyman, he may be called upon to do many jobs. His tool kit will contain a broader range of less specialized tools, enabling him to take advantage of diverse employment opportunities. Performing many types of work or surviving in many different types of environments requires compromises in structure and flexibility in behavior. The great majority of species that have ever existed are now extinct, in most cases because they over-specialized, so that their members were unable to adapt when the environment changed (i.e., their genes were insufficiently flexible). As we saw earlier, it only pays to specialize in one form of human capital if there is a reasonable expectation that one will be able to devote all of one's time to that specialty.

Flexibility in responding to changing circumstances is what human choice is all about. Once choice is admitted into the behavioral repertoire, it is appropriate to examine what determines the choices individuals actually make. To choose between various alternatives requires the individual to rank the various outcomes arising from each choice. This ordering of preferences is exactly what the economist's utility function was designed to describe. So, it is not unreasonable to use the structure and logic of the utility function to describe and analyze choice, even for non-human species. An important question we might ask individual members of any species is this: what is the structure of their utility function, that is, the alternative values among which they must choose, and what determines the ordering of these values?

Reproduction and the Utility Function

In economic theory, it is customary to separate ends from means. Human preferences are taken as given, the result of an indecipherable mix of cultural and biological influences. On the other hand, the means or production functions used to satisfy these preferences are usually assumed to be objectively determined by rational technical considerations. One way to reconcile economic theory and evolutionary biology, then, is to define the economist's utility function so it is concerned with and only with the genetic fitness of the individual. This accomplishes two desirable objectives: it synthesizes the social and natural sciences and also provides an objective explanation for the origin of human preferences. [1] (From here on, when we write "fitness," we mean the biological concept of "genetic fitness," as opposed to mere "physical fitness," "fiscal fitness," and various other pretenders to evolutionary consequence. Moreover, even though as we have seen, evolutionary biologists appreciate the importance of "inclusive fitness" rather than simple reproductive success, we shall for the sake of tractability, limit ourselves to the latter, unless otherwise specified.)

Given the logic of natural selection, it is difficult to conceive how, for any living entity, a preference for maximizing fitness could *fail* to evolve. To illustrate, we constructed the following simulation using a simple spreadsheet. We assumed an initial population of 500 individuals, globs if you will, who had the following simple utility function. They "spend" one half of their surplus resources (for simplicity, it is assumed that individuals require no resources for maintenance) on producing children, the other half on unrelated activities. These may be any sort of resource consuming behavior, ranging from unnecessary leisure to luxuries, to unproductive hobbies. They can even include behavior that was once adaptive but that, due to changes in the environment, no longer contributes to fitness. The only thing these activities have in common is that they do not enhance the individual's reproductive success. Except for the resources consumed, they also don't detract from it.

In this example, even after spending half their resources non-reproductively, the population has enough left to reproduce itself. Now let's add some mutations into the mix. In our example, we assumed a mutation rate that allowed a small percentage of each new generation to devote a slightly higher or smaller proportion of its resources to reproduction. For example, a mutation could cause a glob to vary the amount spent on its offspring by plus or minus ten percentage points from the level spent by its parent. Over time, accumulated mutations can produce individuals who devote anywhere from zero to a hundred percent of surplus resources to reproduction. As the population of individuals who "buy" more children increases, the population grows, increasing competition for resources and reducing the amount of resources each member of the next generation receives. As mutations accumulate and generate mutations of their own, the average percentage devoted to bearing children begins to increase. Table 1 presents the results of 200 generations of such "evolution," assuming a relatively low mutation rate. In every generation, there is a low probability that any individual experiences a mutation that raises or lowers by ten percentage points the proportion of its resources that it devotes to reproduction. The next-to-last column presents the total population, while the last column shows

Table 5.1
Mutation of the Utility Function

Gene-ration	% of Surplus Resources Devoted to Reproduction							Pop.	Avg. Rate
	0.4	0.5	0.6	0.7	0.8	0.9	1.0		
1	0	500	0	0	0	0	0	500	0.50
25	0	500	0	0	0	0	0	500	0.50
50	0	491	11	0	0	0	0	502	0.50
75	0	163	355	56	1	0	0	575	0.58
100	0	0	50	373	274	36	1	734	0.74
125	0	0	0	9	191	473	223	896	0.90
150	0	0	0	0	3	130	852	985	0.99
175	0	0	0	0	0	11	988	999	1.00
200	0	0	0	0	0	1	999	1000	1.00

the average rate of commitment of resources to reproduction. Fractions of children can be produced but are not shown in the table.

In this simulation the mutation rate is so low that it is not until the fiftieth generation that we begin to see any noticeable shift toward higher rates of investment in reproduction. As the population of those who invest more in reproduction grows and competes for resources, the growth rates of those with lower investment rates begin to decline.

By the two-hundredth generation, the transformation is essentially complete. The population has doubled, as all surplus resources are now being devoted to reproduction. Competition by the larger population has cut resources *per capita* in half, but since all resources are devoted to childbearing, the population is nonetheless able to reproduce itself.

The speed at which the utility function evolves is, of course, very sensitive to how the simulation is structured. The point of this exercise is simple: natural selection will severely punish any individuals for whom reproductive success is not the exclusive behavioral goal.

It is our contention that this is as true for humans as for all other forms of life, whether real or simulated: "The biological approach to preferences, to what economists call the utility function, postulates that all such motives or drives or tastes represent proximate aspects of a single underlying goal-fitness" (Hirshleifer, 1977, p.8).

Hobson's Choice

Optimization occurs at multiple levels in evolutionary theory. For example, individual organisms and their genes are selected for or against depending on how well adapted they are to their environment. Optimization occurs because of the differential reproductive success of individuals, and—underlying them—their genes: those best suited to survive and reproduce will eventually come to dominate any population.

For another approach to optimization, consider that all environments are, to a degree, unstable. Thus, evolution rewards the ability of genes and their bodies to alter behavior in response to changes in that environment. When any organism responds to changes in its external world by altering its behavior, it is engaged in choice and optimization. Once an organism and its component genes is involved in such optimization, we can speak of it as maximizing its utility function, and economics and evolution are joined.

To illustrate this, let's revisit our old friends, the globs. To keep it simple we will make them asexual again and give them only one choice: they must decide the optimum trade-off between the quality and quantity of their children so as to maximize the expected number of surviving offspring (recall the biological phenomena of r- and K-selection). During its life, each glob accumulates excess resources, which it then "spends" on children. Every glob bears a fixed cost of giving birth to each child. In addition, every glob can spend some of its accumulated resources on improving the quality of its offspring by providing them with additional nourishment. Higher quality offspring have a higher probability of surviving to reproduce. The number of surviving offspring a glob can expect to produce is equal to the number of children produced times the survival rate of each child. Survival rate increases as additional resources are invested in the quality of each child.

Each glob has limited resources to spend on offspring, and each faces the following budget constraint: Total reproductive resources equals the fixed cost of producing a child times the number of children plus the amount of resources devoted to the quality of each child times the number of children. The higher the quality of each child, the fewer the number of children that can be afforded.

This formulation is, of course, very similar to the standard economic maximization problem that is so often encountered in the economic theory of choice. In fact, this model is a simplified version of one developed by Becker (1981, p. 203) to explain reproduction in non-human species. To maximize the expected number of surviving children, the parent glob must "choose" the appropriate level of quality for its children. Every dollar devoted to increasing the quality and therefore the survival rate of its offspring reduces the amount of resources available to produce additional children. It is thus identical to the evolutionary concept of "parental investment" introduced by evolutionary theorist Robert Trivers in 1972.

As in Becker's analysis of the demand for children, we make the simplifying assumption that an equal amount is invested in every child. The survival rate is positively related to the amount invested in quality, but it is reasonable to expect that after a certain point, there are diminishing returns. This is because regardless of how much is invested in quality, the probability of survival cannot exceed or even equal one. Figure 5.1 graphically relates quality and survival rate.

The relationship between survival rate and the amount invested in quality depicted in figure 5.1 consolidates two determinants of the survival rate. First is the efficiency with which a parent glob can transform its resources into quality offspring. Second is the relationship between quality of offspring and survival. The former is an internal characteristic of the parent, varying with the make-up of each glob, whereas the latter is an element of the world external to each parent, varying, for example, with changes in food resources or in the level of competition from fellow globs or predators.

Solving for the investment in numbers and quality of children that maximizes the expected number of surviving children yields the following relationship. There will be an optimum investment in quality at the point where a line drawn through the origin is tangent to the survival rate function.[2]   Figure 5.1 can be redrawn to show this.

The horizontal axis of figure 5.2 measures the constant cost, C, of producing an additional child plus the variable cost, Q, of investing in quality. The asterisks on Q and Sr indicate that this is the quantity

Figure 5.1
Child Quality and Survival Rate

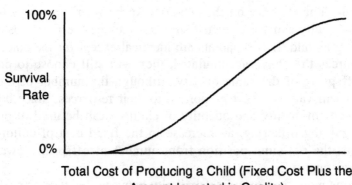

Total Cost of Producing a Child (Fixed Cost Plus the
Amount Invested in Quality)

Figure 5.2
Optimal Investment in Quality

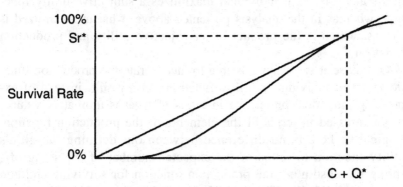

Total Cost of Producing a Child (C + Q)

of Q that produces the optimal value of Sr, that, in turn, maximizes the number of surviving offspring. It is easy to understand why this tangent produces the optimum value for the survival rate: Since this line has the steepest slope of any line through the origin touching or crossing the survival rate function, it is the cheapest attainable way of producing surviving offspring per unit of expenditure. (The mathematical derivation of this result is presented in Technical Appendix 1.)

Once the optimum amount to be spent on quality, Q^*, is determined, the number of children that can be produced is found from the budget constraint. The cost of each child is $C + Q^*$ and the number of children produced is simply the quantity of resources, R, divided by the total cost of producing a child of optimal quality.

This model yields some interesting conclusions. For example, the optimal quality of offspring is independent of the resources of the parent. It depends only on the relationship between resources devoted to quality and the expected survival rate and the fixed cost of producing a child. If two parents are identical except for the amount of resources they have accumulated, they will still choose to produce offspring of the same quality, although the number of their children will vary in direct proportion to their resources. Since both investments in quality and quantity of children can be used to produce surviving offspring, an increase in the fixed cost of children will shift the optimum position from number of offspring toward enhanced quality.

There is more than a surface similarity between this type of analysis and the trade-off between numbers and quality of children as analyzed by Becker (1981, pp. 93-112). The basic difference is that in his analysis, each individual maximizes a subjective utility function, whereas in the analysis presented above, what is maximized is fitness, which is the product of an objective utility and production function.

Of course it is always possible to incorporate the production function into an individual's utility function. As a result, instead of expressing individual preference in terms of what is ultimately valued, it is expressed in terms of the elements of the production function. Logically, there is no difference between our defining the glob's utility function in terms of the expected number of surviving offspring or substituting the production function for surviving children into the glob's utility function. If we did this, the glob's utility function would no longer be a sole function of surviving children but would depend on the arguments of the production function, namely the number of children produced and their quality.

Economists term the results of this kind of substitution a "derived utility function." Since it contains the trade-off between numbers and quality, this derived utility function has the traditional structure of the more familiar utility function. Despite the seeming equivalence between these two formulations, they raise fundamental issues concerning how we analyze both human and non-human behavior.

Becker, in defending his concept of the household production function, stresses the separability of preferences from their means of production: "The utility function should pertain exclusively to preferences," he wrote. "It should deal with the final objects of choice by the consumer unit" (Becker, 1976, p. 146). The survival rate function presented above is a production function and therefore, according to this approach, should not be included in a utility function. The survival rate function may change over time (conditions in the environment alter the relationship between investments in quality and survival rates), and it may differ among individuals, depending on their efficiency in using resources to produce quality offspring. Since a stable and universal utility function is a central requirement in any attempt to use economic theory in explaining behavior, it would seem that the case for a utility function defined solely in terms of long-run genetic fitness is very strong.

If the individual is able to recognize and respond to objective changes in its survival rate function, then we should not use the indirect utility function but instead adopt the approach that separates the varying reproductive production functions from the constant goal represented by the utility function. Given the unvarying goal of maximizing fitness, changes in production technology used to satisfy this goal are subject to objective analysis. If, however, lack of variation in the evolutionary environment resulted in "hard-wiring" of particular solutions to the genetic optimization problem, then a stronger case can be made for using the indirect utility function. This is particularly true if the current environment has changed so much that the behavior in question is no longer adaptive.

We argue that in general, the more flexible the reproductive production function, that is, the more complex the relationships between inputs and fitness, the more justified we are in separating it conceptually from the utility function.

Recalling Becker's admonition that the utility function should be constant and universal, we suggest that a synthesis of economics and evolutionary biology should adopt as its working hypothesis a utility function concerned only with long-run fitness, and a basically flexible production function. As long as individuals are capable of substantial behavioral flexibility, we feel justified in assuming that they are acting to maximize their genetic fitness under constraints imposed by a production function whose character was determined by the laws of nature and past evolutionary history. As long as the behavior chosen produces a higher level of fitness than other available alternatives, it is irrelevant that in some abstract sense, it may not be the "best" behavior imaginable.

Pleistocene People

On the other hand, it is well known that most people have fewer children than they can afford. Becker has been quite explicit on this point. At no point in history, he maintains, has the birth rate reached its biological maximum. Since we have already shown that no organism maximizes its genetic fitness by simply producing the maximum number of possible offspring, we have no dispute. Quality of offspring counts as much as numbers. Even if we had rephrased the question to include the quality of offspring, however, Becker still would likely have rejected the suggestion that human behavior is geared to maximizing genetic fitness:

> Lest I be misunderstood on a highly controversial subject, [he wrote,] let me immediately indicate that the analytical continuity in the behavior of human and other species does not imply that I believe human behavior is primarily biologically determined. Clearly, humans in modern societies do not simply maximize the production of children; they could readily have additional children who would live long and become well educated and prosperous (Becker, 1981, p. 216).

It is not just economists who believe that humans are not optimal maximizers of their genetic fitness. This view is common among some evolutionary theorists as well. The evolutionary argument against the adaptiveness of modern human behavior is as follows: Human evolution proceeds at a very slow rate. The bulk of human evolutionary experience occurred during the Pleistocene Era where humans existed as a small band of hunters and gatherers. It was during this relatively stable evolutionary environment that humans developed their current physical and mental characteristics. One of these developments was language. Language and subsequent cultural developments led to a radical transformation in the environment. We ate the fruit of the tree of knowledge and were expelled from our Pleistocene Garden of Eden. As a result, many of the things we do are today irrelevant to fitness, and perhaps even fitness-reducing.

Another way of saying this: Since human beings evolved in an environment radically different from the one in which we currently find ourselves, much of human behavior is non-adaptive. That is, among the feasible alternatives, humans often fail to choose the behavior that maximizes their fitness. We agree that this is occasionally true. At the same time, however, we point out that human inclinations remain fundamentally adaptive. Just as a falling object is subject to various distracting influences (winds, intervening obstacles, etc.), but nonetheless can be predicted to respond overall to the force of gravity, human behavior is also vulnerable to non-adaptive distractions, but can still be predicted to respond overall to the force of evolution—which is to say, fitness maximization.

For example, human beings, like other animals, desire sexual relations. For *Homo sapiens*, as for most other species, sex has become intimately connected to reproduction (and at least in the human case, to adult social bonding as well). Natural selection has guaranteed that sex will occur by making it pleasurable. Modern birth control has cut the link between sex and reproduction. Nonetheless, people still seek and enjoy sex because that is what their genes "programmed" them to do so as to replicate themselves, despite the fact that this genetic agenda may be short-circuited in favor of pleasure, emotional bonding, and so forth. More than ever before, modern human beings can avoid having children—and to be sure, many do. To some extent, therefore, human consciousness and culture has broken the link between our preferences and our fitness.

Using the notation of economics, the human utility function in the Pleistocene Era looked as follows: $U = P (A, B, C, D, ...)$, where U stands for utility and the other letters stand for preferences such as sex, status, leisure, food, etc., that maximized fitness in that evolutionary environment. If we humans knew enough about the environment in which we evolved, perhaps we could "map out" a precise description of our prehistoric utility function. Because all humans presumably evolved in similar environments, the Pleistocene utility function has the virtue of being both stable and universal. In any event, because the pace of evolution is very slow whereas that of cultural evolution is very rapid, many evolutionary theorists believe that modern humans have a utility function nearly identical to that of their ancestors, but the result is a diverse array of behaviors and resource expenditures that do not advance fitness in today's environment (e.g., Barash, 1986).

We believe, however, that regardless of how slow the speed of biological evolution or how rapid that of cultural evolution, a good case can be made that human behavior remains so flexible that modern humans are still engaging in behavior that is by and large directed at maximizing their genetic fitness. There is undoubtedly much that defies this approach (more of this in chapter 8). But as Einstein once noted, "the grand aim of all science is to cover the greatest number of empirical facts by logical deduction from the smallest possible number of hypotheses." With this in mind, it seems defeatist and a counter-productive self-fulfilling prophecy to assume that long-term fitness maximization necessarily won't work as an analytic and predictive tool, until it is first tried.

This book can be seen as an initial attempt, and a plea for further efforts, to see how far an expanded theory of genetic fitness can take us, assuming that human behavior is essentially adapted to its environment due to a highly flexible reproductive production function.

Investing in Fitness

So far, we have discussed the quantity/quality trade-off in terms of its effect on the survivability of offspring. But survivability is a one-dimensional concept: either a child survives to reproduce or dies without issue. Although this simplification is useful for explaining the basic principles of fertility control, it does not adequately describe the relationship between the quality of a child and its reproductive success. Investments in the quality of children can affect all aspects of their lives, from their efficiency in acquiring food and avoiding predators, to finding mates and investing, in turn, in their own offspring. This is especially true for human beings, in which the returns from parents investing in human capital, that is, quality of their children, are often measured in terms of enhanced earnings.

Even when investment is in non-market related human capital, it is possible to represent the consequence of such an investment as an enhancement of total available resources or wealth. We can rewrite the quality/quantity trade off so that instead of raising the probability of surviving, an increase in resources invested in the quality of each child can be thought of as increasing his or her lifetime earnings.

A portion of these earnings must be spent on the goods and services required to maintain and enhance the individual's earning potential. Obviously, unless resources are spent on food, shelter, clothes, transportation, health, education, and the many other requirements of life, the productive ability of any individual will be curtailed. In a general sense, this is as true for human beings operating in a fully developed market economy as for any organism. Even if the goal of all life (human and otherwise) is to maximize fitness, decisions must be made about how much available resources—money, time, energy, etc.—should be devoted to maintaining the individual, and how much should be devoted directly to reproduction—even assuming the ultimate goal is to maximize the resources available for reproduction.

Total lifetime earnings depend on and are positively related to the amount spent on maintenance. An increase in the amount spent on goods and services necessary to sustain and enhance life will increase health and energy, as well as lifetime earnings. But, as with other processes, there are diminishing returns. After some level of expenditure, every dollar devoted toward maintenance results in smaller increases in total lifetime earnings. For simplicity, we will ignore the time value of money within but not between generations. In addition, for ease of exposition, we will assume that all investments in human capital are done by the parents. This, of course, is not true. Individuals invest in their own human capital. However, this simplification does not affect our analysis.

Net lifetime earnings will be maximized when the marginal contribution of a dollar increase in maintenance produces only a dollar increase in total earnings.[3] This is illustrated in figure 5.3.

M* represents the optimum that should be spent on maintenance in order to maximize the quantity of resources available for reproductive purposes. This occurs where the slope of the maintenance function equals one.[4] A line tangent to this point will intercept the y-axis above zero for an individual that produces more than it consumes. If the intercept is negative, the individual will pass fewer

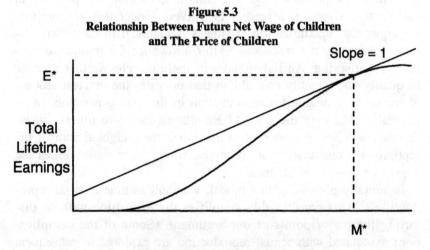

Figure 5.3
Relationship Between Future Net Wage of Children
and The Price of Children

Slope = 1

E*

Total
Lifetime
Earnings

M*

Dollars Spent on Maintenance

resources on to its descendants than it inherited. If this persists across generations, extinction will result for this genetic line.

The problem now facing an individual is how to "spend" his or her net lifetime earnings in a way that optimizes genetic fitness. Maximizing fitness was fairly straightforward when investments in quality only affected offspring survivability, in which case the goal was to choose the combination of quality and quantity that maximized the expected number of surviving children, given the resources available. However, when the parents' reproductive strategy can affect their children's lifetime earnings, it is less clear how to maximize the parents' long-term fitness.

The correct answer depends on the interrelationship between the quality of offspring and their subsequent cost of producing children. By raising the wage rate of children through investment in their human capital, that is, quality, one also increases the value of their time and may therefore increase their cost of producing children. If there are no good substitutes for children's time in the production of grandchildren, a parent will, from a genetic point of view, not get the full benefit, in the next generation, from increasing the earnings of his or her children by investing in their quality. Eventually the higher income will pay its genetic dividend but solving this problem requires a very complicated multi-generational model.

In a simple world in which the cost of producing children is independent of the parent's wage rate and value of time, the problem of maximizing fitness can readily be solved. Under this assumption, we argue that maximization of fitness is identical to the maximization of summed net resources—after allowance for maintenance—of one's offspring. An individual will therefore choose that mixture of quality and quantity of children that provides the greatest amount of resources available for reproduction in the next generation. More generally, following the logic of Hamilton's inclusive fitness, an individual will spend resources to maximize the weighted sum of the reproductive resources of all relatives, where the weights reflect the degree of genetic relatedness.

In initially presenting this model, we shall assume asexual reproduction.[5] This considerably simplifies the exposition without distorting the major points of our argument. (Some of the complications associated with sexual reproduction are explored in subsequent chapters.)

Once an individual has solved the problem of maximizing net earnings, he or she must allocate these resources between quality and quantity of children. In this model, investment in the quality of children does not increase their probability of surviving but rather increases their future wage rate.[6]

Not surprisingly, the solution to this optimization problem is similar to the previous example in which the goal was to maximize survivability. After all, the mathematical formulations are identical. The resources available to the next generation will be maximized when the return from investing in each child's human capital is equal to the return from the only other available investment, an increase in the number of children. The graphic representation of this solution is similar to that presented in figure 5.2.

The optimal level of investment in human capital, Q^*, occurs when the increase in wages due to a dollar increase in human quality is equal to the ratio of the level of net wages to the total price of a child, which is the return from investing in the production of an additional child. In figure 5.4 we see that this occurs when a line drawn from the origin is tangent to the curve describing the relationship between the price of children and their future net wage.

Once the optimum investment in each child is determined, the price of producing each child of such quality is known. It equals the fixed cost of producing each child plus the optimal amount spent on each child's quality: ($P^* = C + Q^*$). Once the parent has determined the optimal quality of her children, the number of offspring produced is simply equal to the number that can be afforded, given the resources available for reproduction and the price of each child. (The mathematical derivation of this result is presented in Appendix 2.)

By maximizing the sum of her children's net wages, a parent is following the optimum strategy for maximizing her long-run fitness. We emphasize once again that the parent is not simply maximizing the number of children. That would be accomplished by producing a large number of low quality children. By maximizing her children's net wage, however, she may well be maximizing the number of her grandchildren. Or, more correctly, as we shall see, she is maximizing her number of potential grandchildren. It is important to understand that even if the parent has a good idea of her children's net wages, the number of grandchildren remains unpredictable. Given changes in the labor market, the optimum quality and therefore the price of producing children in the next generation may change and

Figure 5.4
Relationship Between Future Net Wage of Children and
The Price of Children

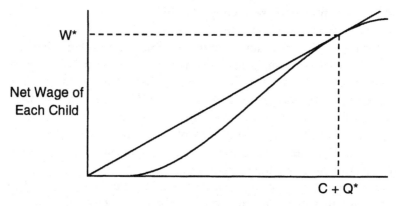

Total Cost of Producing a Child (C+Q)

therefore alter the children's allocation of resources between quality and quantity.

When discussing the evolution of the utility function, we argued that natural selection directs any organism to have, as its ultimate goal, the maximization of its fitness. We did not provide a very detailed description of what such maximizing actually entails. The example presented was limited to considering the impact of not devoting all available resources to the production of offspring. As we have discussed, maximization of fitness sometimes requires a *reduction* in the number of children so as to increase the number of future descendants. In light of this, maximization of fitness cannot be defined by the number of copies of the parent's genes present in the next generation.

It is necessary to take a longer perspective. Therefore, we define fitness maximization as choosing the reproductive strategy that produces the greatest number of descendants in some future generation. How far in the future is indeterminate. For example, suppose our parent chooses to trade off quantity for quality and that all of her descendants produce similarly higher quality offspring. If the advantage produced by making this trade-off is small, it may take many generations for her genetic line to recoup the reduction in numbers required by the original trade-off.

The best way to maximize the number of descendants in any distant future generation is to maximize the reproductive resources available to the previous generation (that is, in the generation antecedent to the one in question). The number of descendants in the next generation is simply equal to the sum of the net resources available to the members of the previous generation divided by the cost of producing children of the desired quality. The way to maximize the net resources of the previous generation is to maximize the net resources of the generation prior to it. By arguing backward in this fashion, it is apparent that the way to maximize the number of descendants in any distant future generation is to maximize the reproductive resources available in each intervening generation.

Any parent can only maximize, by her reproductive decisions, the rate of return on the resources she controls. She cannot control the behavior of her descendants. Rather, she must trust them to make similarly wise reproductive decisions. This is not an unreasonable assumption (even though parents, in every generation, seem prone to think that only *they* are capable of deciding wisely!). After all, insofar as the maximization of fitness is determined by a utility function chosen by natural selection, parents in every generation are equally influenced, and thus, equally likely to choose well.

Whether the future generation is the parent's grandchildren or great great-grandchildren is not important. What matters is that the "next generation" is never the last one. By displacing the final pay-off into the future, a parent is free to engage in an indirect strategy by which the number of descendants in future generations is maximized by restricting to some degree the number of her own children. As we have seen, investing in the quality of children is one way of increasing the resources available to them for producing grandchildren. But as every subsequent generation employs the same indirect strategy, each one chooses to maximize the reproductive resources available to its own children, and its reproductive decisions are never based on merely maximizing the raw number of descendants.

This quality/quantity trade-off is, in principle, no different from the r-K evolutionary decision-making in which all living organisms engage. Human behavior, however, is more complicated. People can and do invest their net resources in more than just children and their human capital. They also receive income from sources other than their own labor. As tool-making animals, they use investments in capital goods as an indirect way of increasing their access to resources. Our central argument and a major contribution of this book is that capital also provides an indirect means of increasing the reproductive resources available to one's children—and to theirs in turn, and so on. Richard Dawkins (1982) has coined the phrase "extended phenotype," referring to the tendency of genes to *extend* their products beyond an organism's body, so as to include inorganic constructs such as bird nests, beaver dams, etc. In that same spirit, we have the temerity to introduce a new term, "extended fitness," to include both genetic fitness in the traditional sense used in biology, and its incorporation into non-human capital, as used in economics.

If the return on non-human capital is high enough, the best way for a parent to maximize the resources available to her children may well involve diverting resources away from the number and quality of her children, and toward other investments. In this way, more resources could be available to produce grandchildren, and so forth. Given this additional option, a parent will attempt to maximize not only the sum of her children's net wages, but the sum of her children's net income including both wages and inheritance of capital. If all children are equal, the sum of her children's net income is equal to the number of children produced times their net wage plus the amount of resources invested by the parent in non-human capital and the return on that capital. In making the allocations of resources between number of children, their quality, and investments in non-human capital, the parent faces a budget constraint: the sum of all expenditures must equal the parent's net income from all sources.

There are three possible investment opportunities available to each parent, namely, number of children, human capital, and non-human capital. As in any investment decision, the parent will maximize the sum of her children's net income when the returns from these three investments are equal. If the return from any one is higher that the others, the parent could increase her children's net income by shifting a portion of her resources from the investment offering a lower return to that providing a higher return.

The optimum investment in human capital occurs when the return from investing an additional dollar in quality is equal to the available return from non-human capital. Figure 5.5 describes the relationship between the investment in human capital and the child's future net wage.

Figure 5.5
Relationship Between Net Wage of Children and Their Price

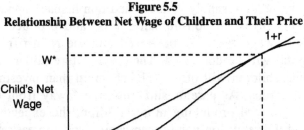

Price of Child (C + Q)

The optimal level of human capital investment, Q*, occurs when the slope of the net wage/quality relationship, (which is the return from investing in human capital), is equal to the return available from investing in non-human capital, (1+r).

The return from producing an additional child of any quality is equal to the future net wage of a child of that quality divided by the price of producing such a child. When all investment markets are in equilibrium, that is, when there are no gains to be had from shifting resources among investments, the return from investing in human capital equals the return from non-human capital, which in turn equals the return from investing in an additional child of optimal quality, W*/(C+Q*). At this point, the optimal number of children of optimal quality will be produced.

Because the price of additional children is unaffected by the number of children already produced, and the return from investing in number of children and non-human capital is equal, there is nothing in this model that uniquely determines the number of children any given parent should choose to have relative to the amount of non-human capital in which she invests. The quality of children and their price is determined, but from the perspective of each parent, children and bequests of non-human capital are perfect substitutes. So long as the parent produces at least one surviving child, the way to maximize the number of descendants in some future generation is to maximize her child's, or children's, net income. If the market is in equilibrium so that the returns from the two investments are equal, any given parent can substitute non-human capital for children with no effect on her next generation's net income.

Of course, parents as a whole do not have such freedom. The wage rate as well as the return from non-human capital is determined by the relative supply of labor and non-human capital. If too many parents invest in non-human capital and produce too few children, the wage rate will be raised and the return from non-human capital will be depressed. Therefore, future dollars invested in additional children will offer a higher return than investments in non-human capital. As parents shift resources away from non-human capital toward producing more children, the expected wage will fall and the return on non-human capital will increase until the market is again in equilibrium. When the return on the optimal quantity of human capital is equal to the return on non-human capital, which in turn equals the return from producing an additional child, the "market" is in equilibrium and all parents are satisfied with their decisions. Similarly, if parents produce too many children the return on the optimal quality child will be below the return on non-human capital and it would then be in the genetic interest of parents to reduce the number of children produced and increase the amount invested in non-human capital until equilibrium is restored. (The mathematical derivation of this result is shown in Appendix 3.)

To summarize, this model describes how a parent can maximize the number of copies of her genes in future generations by engaging in various indirect reproductive strategies. As an alternative to investing her surplus resources in a large number of offspring, a parent can take the indirect approach of limiting offspring number and using the freed-up resources to increase their quality. The rise in quality can increase her children's productivity and thus the resources available to produce grandchildren. We repeat that this strategy is not exclusively human. All living organisms must engage in some form of the quality/quantity trade off; each occupies some place on the r-K continuum. But human beings are unique in some ways. Their final trade off, although biologically influenced, is not biologically determined. Thus, it can be deliberately varied depending on the cost and benefits of investing in human capital—as well as other factors, arrived at through the use of consciousness and that elusive characteristic, free will (see chapter 7 for more). In any event, human beings do not have to wait for the forces of natural selection to adjust their behavior.

Back in the world of evolutionary economics, human beings have yet another arrow in their reproductive quiver, one that is only rarely available to animals: they can invest in non-human capital. Such wealth is, in a sense, potential or "frozen" children, resources that can be turned into children at any time by future descendants.

Inequality

Thus far, we have dealt with representative parents and children, implicitly assuming that all parents and children are equal. But in the real world, they are not. The relationship between the amount of resources invested in human capital and future wages is not necessarily the same for all children, with such differences arising from a number of sources. To begin with, the natural ability of children to convert human capital investments into traits valued by the labor market can vary due to genetic differences, even among siblings. Because of this, it would not be rational, that is, optimal from the viewpoint of fitness, for parents to invest the same amount of human capital in children with different natural abilities. (Recall the phenomenon of parent-offspring conflict, discussed in chapter 4, and the strategic maneuvering with respect to real versus apparent child quality that it can be expected to generate.)

Another source of difference in the return from investment in human capital arises from variations in the efficiency of the investment process. High quality parents have several advantages when investing in their children's human capital. For example, they are likely to be more knowledgeable about how to invest in such aspects of human capital as choice of schools and career paths best suited to their children's talents. More important perhaps, is the direct impact high quality parents predictably have on their children. Parents generally are the primary teachers of their children, especially during the early years. The more intelligent, better educated, and highly motivated a parent is, the more efficient he or she will be in transmitting skills and values likely to increase the future productivity of offspring.

In addition, high-quality parents are likely to associate with other high-quality parents, thereby giving their children increased prospects of "marrying well." The argument can even be made that this is one of the primary reasons why people establish such assortive associations in the first place.

Another advantage generally enjoyed by high-quality parents is possessing sufficient resources to invest the optimal amount in each of their children. Poorer parents, even when they limit the number of their children, may not have sufficient resources to invest in human capital to the point at which the return on this capital is equal to the market return on non-human capital. Poor parents do not leave substantial bequests and may, in fact, have to borrow against the future wages of their children—student loans, for example—to finance investments in human capital. Since loans secured only by future wages are inherently risky, this method of financing human capital is, in the absence of subsidies, inherently expensive.

Sex and Numbers

To keep our model manageable, we have assumed that the cost of children is constant, with no economies or diseconomies of scale in rearing children. This allowed us to demonstrate that by maximizing the next generation's net income, parents were maximizing the number of potential descendants in some future generation. But once again, reality is more complicated. For example, the cost of having children is considerably different for men and women. For a man, the cost of a child equals the fixed cost of finding and courting a suitable willing woman, plus the cost of child support, which sometimes is zero. This description may seem flippant and cynical, but it conveys a fundamental truth: there is no simple biological constraint on the number of children a male can sire and raise. The limit is purely financial and to some extent, social. With sufficient money, a man can attract numerous mates and even pay for substantial schooling and childcare.

For a woman, the situation is different. Given the amount of time and energy that she must invest in every pregnancy, the number of children she can bear in her lifetime is limited. After a certain point, the closer the spacing of her pregnancies, the greater the physical strain on her, and the greater the danger to her and her baby. Therefore, the incremental cost to a woman of having a child increases with the number of children she has already had.

In a perfectly monogamous marriage, the husband's reproductive success is constrained by the physical limitations of his wife. The couple would have an increasing marginal cost of children. Assuming, for the moment, that the parents still desire to maximize the resources of the next generation, the rising cost function of children will alter their demand for children. While the condition for optimal investment in human capital will be the same as described above, parents should no longer be indifferent about whether they invest in children or in non-human capital.

With a rising marginal cost of producing children, there arises an optimal number of children for each parent. The equilibrium condition for investment in human capital remains the same, the return on human capital must be equal to the return on non-human capital, and the equilibrium condition for numbers of children still occurs, at the point such that the optimal wage of a child divided by its price equals the return on non-human capital. However, the price of children is no longer constant but rather increases with each additional child. The cost of investing in the optimal quantity of human capital remains the same for identical children but the fixed cost per child now increases with each pregnancy. (For a mathematical derivation of this result, see Technical Appendix 4.)

Figure 5.6 shows the demand and supply for children in graphical terms. The equilibrium relationship for children, that is, $W/P = 1 + r$, can be written so that the future wages discounted by the return on non-human capital is equal to the cost of producing the marginal child.

For those children whose marginal cost is less than $W*/(1 + r)$, parents earn a higher-than-market return. The optimum number of children, $N*$, occurs when marginal cost equals marginal revenue. Only those resources that remain after the optimum quantity of children has been produced will be invested in non-human capital, to be gifted or bequeathed to the next generation.

If the cost of producing a child of optimal quality is not constant, then it is no longer true that maximization of the next generation's net income is equivalent to maximizing the number of future descendants. Maximizing fitness then becomes a more complicated problem, the solution of which would involve a level of mathemati-

Figure 5.6
Demand and Supply of Children

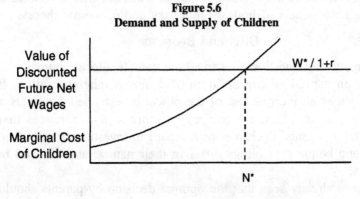

Value of Discounted Future Net Wages

Marginal Cost of Children

$W* / 1+r$

$N*$

Number of Children

cal sophistication beyond this book. But the need for a complicated solution does not undermine the relevance of the concept of extended genetic fitness to these issues. It is still true that humans can use the indirect strategy of investing in non-human capital to boost the reproductive potential of their future descendants, even if the equilibrium relationships are not as simple or as concise as the ones we have presented.[7]

In any case, we believe that our formulation is a good approximation for promiscuous or polygynous males, and (as we develop later in this chapter) it is not surprising that large inheritances have historically been concentrated in sons. We guess that the longer the parent's time horizon—that is, the larger the number of intermediate generations between the parent and the generation in which the parent aims to maximize the number of his or her descendants—the more likely the parent's goal will be to maximize the net resources of the next generation rather than maximize the number of his or her children.

But as we shall also see later in this chapter, humans are not limited to one reproductive-economic strategy. Different people, depending on the constraints they face and the opportunities available to them, will rationally choose to follow different approaches to reproductive success. Also, the same person may follow different strategies over the course of his or her lifetime, adjusting them to changing circumstances. Many different factors enter into the final calculation of whether an individual's long-run fitness is better served by investing in number of children, their quality, or in the bequest of non-human capital. Focusing on extended fitness provides an objective framework for the study of human behavior that is consistent with the basic tenets of both evolutionary and economic theory.

Gifts and Bequests

An interesting question concerns how parents allocate human and non-human capital among children of different inherent ability. It also serves as an indirect test of the power of extended fitness as a useful construct. There are two major sources of differences that might affect parents' decisions with regard to investments in human capital and bequests: siblings differ in their natural abilities and in their sex.

We have already seen that the optimal decision by parents should be to invest differently in children who differ in their ability to benefit from the investment. This pattern of investment will aggravate the income disparity among siblings caused by differing natural abilities. It is even more problematic how non-human capital, that is, gifts and bequests, should be distributed among children to maximize extended fitness. If there are returns to scale in investing in non-human capital, such that the rate of return is positively related to the amount of funds invested, we predict that inheritances would be concentrated in one child. This is what tends to occur when land is the primary form of wealth. In order to maintain the economic efficiencies of large holdings or the political power associated with them, large landowners have traditionally passed estates to their eldest son. Primogeniture guarantees that the "position" of the family—its power and prestige—will not be diluted over time. Concentrated wealth, with all the political power it brings, has long been important in determining the rate of return on property.

There is another reason for the concentration of inheritances, namely, a genetic reason to concentrate non-human capital in those children who appear most able. Such individuals will not only be most likely to produce the "best" offspring, but they will also be most likely to invest their inheritance in the most profitable manner.

All arguments for the concentration of parental gifts and bequests should be understood in the context of uncertain child mortality. Even when it is optimal to invest all resources in only one son, additional children are required, which is why the typical royal family always desired "an heir and a spare." Once substantial investments have been made in rearing and educating these insurance children, additional gifts to aid their reproductive efforts might be justified.

Other factors argue for a more equal distribution of gifts and bequests in the modern world than in pre-industrial, agricultural societies. One of the chief characteristics of a developed economy is a high return from human capital. It requires a fairly intensive investment in the human capital of most children before the rate of return on further investment is driven down to the market rate on non-human capital. If the marginal cost of having children increases with the number of children, then there is an advantage to parents in distributing the production of grandchildren evenly among their offspring. So long as the return from producing grandchildren of optimal quality is higher than the market rate of return on non-human capital, grandparents should gift the necessary funds to those of their children who do not have sufficient resources to invest the optimal amount of human capital in each of their children.

For example, assume that a parent has two children, Alice and Betty. Alice is the higher-quality child. More human capital was invested in her and she has a net wage high enough that she can afford three optimal-quality children. Since Betty has less ability, less human capital was invested in her and she can afford only one child. It is possible that neither Alice nor Betty can afford to have all the children that would maximize the resources of the next generation. Alice may be able to afford no more than three children even though a fourth would yield a return higher than that on non-human capital. The same can be true for Betty. She can afford only one child, although perhaps her optimal quantity is two. The grandparent should gift to each child enough to fund an additional child rather than give the entire bequest to one child.

This, of course, is an arbitrary example; it could well be that Alice can easily afford her optimum number of children. It could also be that Betty, the poorer child, shouldn't have any more than one offspring herself. The point we are making is that there need not be any necessary relationship between the quality of a child and the size of the transfer necessary for the child to produce the optimal number of grandchildren. A high-quality child who is poor through bad luck should receive more than a lower-quality child. This could be true even when the income of the unlucky child is higher than that of the siblings.

Since a parent cannot forecast the future, it is not unreasonable to make selective gifts during her lifetime that optimize the production of grandchildren. The parent can give preference to one child or the other based on the circumstances at the time, while leaving the remainder of her resources evenly divided among her children or grandchildren. For societies in which the return from human capital is not only high but has been increasing, a relatively equal division of bequests is not necessarily a sub-optimal solution. On the other hand, in cases where the return from human capital is unimportant, the argument leading to an unequal distribution may have greater weight.

Becker (1981) has proposed an even more egalitarian analysis of inter-generational transfers. In our theory, what is being maximized by parents is the net resources of their descendants; for Becker, it is the parents' utility, in which parents value their children's income. The income of each child enters the parents' utility function equally. Diminishing marginal utility to the parent of each child's income implies that an additional dollar of income for a rich child provides less utility than an additional dollar of income for a poorer child. Therefore, parents distribute their human and non-human capital in a way that reduces the income difference between their children:

> If parents invest in both the nonhuman and human capital of children, the marginal rate of return is the same for all children and equals the market rate on non-human capital..
> .. [I]ncomes are also the same for all children: neutral parents would fully compensate their less fortunate children (Becker, 1981, p. 123).

Nothing better illustrates the basic differences between our approach and that of Professor Becker than the issue of inheritance. Because his theory gives him no reason to refrain, Becker assumes that parents have equal affection for all their children and that the parent's utility is maximized when their bequests are distributed among the children so as to equalize their incomes. Our view, in contrast, sees parental bequests as an integral part of the parent's indirect reproductive strategy, aimed at maximizing his or her extended fitness. How a parent distributes bequests among his or her children will, in practice, depend on many considerations, some of which include differences in sex and quality of children, possible economies of scale in the return from non-human capital, and increasing costs in the production of grandchildren.

These considerations, combined with legal and social constraints faced by parents, will determine how they distribute their bequests. But we nonetheless predict that regardless of the tactics parents adopt in particular circumstances, their ultimate strategy is to distribute their bequests in the manner that will maximize their long-run reproductive interests.

Evolutionary anthropologists have begun studying the role of differential parental investment on genetic fitness. For example, James Boone examined parental investment among fifteenth- and sixteenth-century Portuguese nobility, and found that the strategy followed by four different status groups was consistent with the goal of maximizing total number of descendants. As to sex-biased parental investment, he concluded that,

> among the highest status families, where wealth is concentrated in male offspring, males out reproduce females, whereas among the lower nobility, where families are more likely to invest in dowries for daughters, females tend to out reproduce males (p. 201).

Parental investment is thus concentrated in the sex likely to produce the largest number of descendants in a given ecological situation.

The second pattern of differential parental investment analyzed by Boone concerns preferential investment in elder children of both sexes:

> Primogeniture is likely to develop as a reproductive strategy where wealth is a strong determinant of reproductive performance and where high mortality makes large family size a necessity in ensuring lineage posterity. (p. 210)

Primogeniture is also likely to develop where the source of wealth is dependable and does not vary with the personal characteristics of the heir. Boone contrasts the Portuguese case, in which the source of wealth was land rents, with that of the elites of the Italian city-states during the same period.

In Renaissance Italian city-states, the primary source of wealth was commercial enterprise, and the return on children's non-human capital depended on their expertise and on a great amount of luck: "Here, wealth was customarily divided up more or less equally among males, often in their early teens" (Boone, 1988, p. 210). Given the degree of uncertainty involved in commercial activity and the early age at which the children received their capital, an equal division makes sense to parents concerned—in the short term—with maximizing the family's fortune, as a part of their long-term, and often unacknowledged "concern" with fitness enhancement. Boone's work is consistent with our contention that parents will divide their estate among their children based on a reproductive strategy rather than on the basis of parental affection as suggested by Becker. Should we believe that Italians had a more equal love for their sons than did the Portuguese? Or is it more reasonable to suppose that different circumstances fostered different tactical responses?

Boone's approach differs from our own. As an evolutionary anthropologist, he is primarily concerned with how parental investment affects the fertility of children. But this is only a part of the story. Parents should primarily be concerned, not with maximizing the number of their children, but with maximizing their children and their grandchildren's wealth, and thus, their long-term extended fitness.

Demographics

What are the implications of extended fitness for population growth over time? According to our approach, population in any generation depends on the net resources available to the previous generation and the allocation of those resources among investments in number of children, as well as investments in capital, both human and non-human. Parents allocate their resources so as to maximize the net reproductive resources available to their children. The return on the marginal dollar invested in human capital must be equal to the return on non-human capital that equals the return from producing an additional child of optimal quality.

The net resources (after maintenance), available to the children's generation depend on the factors of production they inherit from their parents. If the production function that determines net income depends only on reproducible factors such as labor and capital, and if the relative cost of producing the various factors is constant, the growth rate of all factors of production will be equal. In the absence of technological change, the marginal return on capital and all other factors of production will be constant.[8]

If, however, there is a factor of production that is fixed and incapable of expansion such as land, then without technological advances, growth will come to an end. With a fixed supply of land, the expansion of labor and capital will lower the marginal product of the variable factors of production. Net per capita income will fall until the net resources available for investment are just sufficient to maintain the previous generation's level of physical capital, population, and human capital. This economy will be characterized by high land rents, low wages, and a low return on capital. Such stagnant demographic and economic performance is characteristic of much of human history, although usually it manifests itself as either very slow growth due to the accumulation of minor technological advances, or a gradual decline due to externalities or inefficiencies caused by predatory political structures.

The negative effect on growth caused by a fixed quantity of land and natural resources can be overcome only by improvements in productivity. In fact, technology can be considered a separate factor of production which, unlike the others, does not depreciate and which can be increased by investments in acquiring knowledge.[9] Where there are institutions and incentives to produce knowledge, prolonged technological advancement can occur and growth will continue even when an important factor of production such as land is fixed in quantity.

This is precisely the situation that the industrial world has experienced for the last two hundred years. Continuous technological advances have permitted a more or less continuous expansion in output despite no further expansion in the resource base. Over the last hundred years, this expanded output has coincided with a sharp reduction in the rate of population growth in the most industrialized countries. In Europe, the birth rate is currently below replacement level. For example, in the last decade, total fertility for Europe has declined to 1.45 children per woman, well below the replacement rate of 2.1. A challenge to our approach is to reconcile this low level of fertility with the fact of continuing economic growth.

At this point we must be content to suggest some possible forces that produced this so-called "demographic transition," paralleling a switch from r- to K-selection among other living things, and a pattern that is widely found when developing countries achieve a degree of industrialization and improved status of women. A below-replacement level of fertility is not limited to Europe but also extends to the other rich industrial nations. Currently the total fertility rate is only 1.5 for Japan. The fertility rate of the United States, 1.98, is also below replacement level; the continuing increase in total U.S. population is due to the additional effect of immigration (World Population Prospects, 1996).

The fertility decline in developed countries is not recent. The birth rates of all Western developed countries peaked before the early twentieth century. In fact, the decline began much earlier for France and the United States (Haines, 1994). The record for the United States is of particular interest. Table 5.2 presents the total fertility rate for White American women from 1800 to 1990. With the exception of the post-World War II baby boom, the record is one of almost continuous decline, beginning well before the late nineteenth-century decline in infant mortality. This decline in fertility occurred in a country with abundant land, rising income, and no well-established contraceptive technology.

Several reported studies are particularly consistent with the approach to fertility adopted in the present book:

An inquiry by Wahl ... finds that parents progressively traded off quantity (number of children) for quality (education, health care, etc. per child) as the nineteenth century progressed. As the price (cost) of quality declined (via public education, more effective public health and medicine), parents opted for greater human capital per child. (Haines, 1994, p.24)

This is the quantity/quality trade-off stressed by Becker and comprises one of the two important investment decisions required by our theory of extended genetic fitness.

Table 5.2
Fertility Rate for White American Women

Year	Rate
1800	7.04
1810	6.92
1820	6.73
1830	6.55
1840	6.14
1850	5.42
1860	5.21
1870	4.55
1880	4.24
1890	3.87
1900	3.56
1910	3.42
1920	3.17
1930	2.45
1940	2.22
1950	2.98
1960	3.53
1970	2.39
1980	1.75
1990	1.89

Source: Haines, 1994, Table 3.

Other studies reviewed by Haines, including those by Yasuba (1962) and Forster and Tucker (1972), found a close relationship between the availability of agricultural land and child/women ratios for the period prior to the U.S. Civil War (Haines, 1994, p. 21). This relationship is consistent with several theories of fertility, including the one we offer. So long as agricultural land is plentiful relative to the supply of labor, the wage or marginal product of "unskilled" labor will be high and the return from investing in quantity of labor will also be high compared to investing in quality of labor. This in turn will encourage parents to invest their reproductive resources in numbers of children.

Another demographer, Steckel, found some support for the land availability theory; he also found that the strongest predictors of fertility differentials for the period just prior to the Civil War were the presence of financial intermediaries (banks) and the ratio of non-agricultural to agricultural workers (Haines, 1994, p.23). This is consistent with our view that the greater the incentive to invest in non-human capital, the less will be invested in producing children, that is, fewer children of optimal quality will be produced. The remainder of the parents' reproductive resources will be invested in financial and physical capital as an indirect way of increasing their genetic fitness, by making more resources available to their descendants.

Anything that increases the cost of producing children relative to the cost of physical or human capital will result in a shift away from numbers of children toward these other investments. Since the fixed cost of producing a child is related to the value of the mother's time, any increase in wages will raise the relative cost of children. For mothers, this increase in cost is due to an increase in the value of their time. For fathers, it is due to an increase in the value of their mates' time. This is consistent not only with our presentation, but with the widespread observation by international organizations concerned with encouraging family planning in under-developed countries, that the most effective way to reduce family size is to increase the status of women. In addition, anything that increases the return from investing in human and non-human capital relative to the return from "unskilled" labor will also cause a shift away from numbers of children toward these other investments.

Any model of economic or demographic growth needs to also explain the secular rise in income and wages that a good part of humanity has experienced over the past one hundred or so years. Although technological advances can raise the marginal product of all factors of production, this does not guarantee that any increase will be sustained. If the supply of each variable factor of production increases sufficiently, there need not be any secular rise in their marginal products. All net income is invested in either children (quantity and quality), or in non-human capital. Technological advances increase income and therefore raise the supply of labor and capital. Unless technological change is faster than the subsequent growth in these factors, there will be no sustained rise in their rates of return.

Does our theory, then, fail the test of explaining the two central economic trends of the developed world, the rise in wages and the fall in fertility? Obviously we don't believe so, or we never would have put forth this theory. The key to our explanation is the fact that technological change doesn't have to be neutral, and usually it isn't. That is, it needn't increase the marginal product of all factors of production uniformly. Although skill and knowledge have always been important to human economic activity, it is only in the last several hundred years that there has existed a body of technical and scientific knowledge beyond the scope of even the most intelligent human mind. Increases in the stock of human knowledge tend to increase the rate of return from all factors of production, but they may have a disproportionate effect on the return from investment in human capital.

In the Middle Ages, literacy was of limited usefulness to the vast bulk of the population engaged in agriculture. Most useful knowledge was acquired by apprenticeship. There were very few books on practical subjects and these hand-copied manuscripts were very expensive. After Gutenberg's invention of moveable type, the cost of books fell and the number of titles devoted to technical and practical applications expanded dramatically. As the cost of books fell and the list of titles expanded, the return from investing in literacy rose. As the number of people who could read and write grew, so did the number of people who could contribute their particular knowledge to the general pool of recorded knowledge. Investments in human capital had a self-reinforcing effect on the return from such investments. Some students of social development (e.g., Eisenstein, 1979) consider the invention of printing to be one of the inventions that made possible the modern world with its characteristic of advanced technology.

Our model of extended fitness predicts that any development that raised the return from investments in human quality would cause parents to shift from an "r-strategy" of producing a large number of relatively low quality offspring to a "K-strategy" of producing fewer, each of higher quality. In essence, investment in quality becomes a more efficient means of producing labor inputs than investment in number of children. An improvement in the marginal product of human capital will increase the relative supply of human capital relative to the supply of both physical capital and number of children.

Following an increase in the marginal product of human capital, the future wage rate of a child will be increased and it will pay to invest more human capital in that child. Because of the increased optimal investment in quality, the cost of producing children will also increase. Even if the higher-quality child's net wage is double that of his parent, he need not be able to afford more children than his parent. That would depend on how much more it costs to produce children of the higher optimal quality.

The modern era, in short, has been characterized by an exceptional increase in the return from investing in human capital. This explains another potential paradox. Education, like child rearing, is a labor-intensive process, and it has not yet benefited very much from technological advances. On the face of it, therefore, there is no reason why an increase in wages should induce a shift away from numbers of children towards investment in their quality. Rather, a rise in wages should induce a shift toward physical capital. Obviously, this has not happened, presumably because the technologically induced increase in the marginal product of human capital has not only been greater than the increase in the marginal product of physical capital, but was large enough to offset the increased cost of producing human capital. The increase in cost of producing human capital raises the total cost of producing children of the optimal quality, further reducing fertility.

Even without any increase in the relative cost of producing human capital, the increase in the optimal investment in quality can reduce the desired number of children. For example, if human capital and raw labor are substitutes and if the marginal products of all factors of production—especially the return from human capital—were positively related to past levels of investment in human capital, it can be shown, using the common Cobb-Douglas Production Function, that the accumulation of technological advances due to past investments in human capital will eventually reduce the equilibrium ratio of population to physical capital and increase the equilibrium ratio of human to physical capital. This occurs because the rise in the productivity of human capital comes at the expense of the marginal productivity of raw labor (See Technical Appendix 5).

Technological change makes it more efficient to satisfy the growing demand for labor by investing relatively more in human capital and relatively less in number of workers. Human capital, in effect, substitutes for raw labor. Since each generation of workers has more human capital, wages will rise over time.

We suspect, however, that a portion of the amazing growth in per capita income that has occurred in the last two hundred years has been deceptive. Gross income has probably increased far more in absolute terms than has net income (the income available for reproduction), in part because much of consumption spending is directly or indirectly related to an individual's productive behavior (the optimal resources devoted to maintenance has increased dramatically).

Real per capita spending (i.e., adjusted for inflation) on clothes, commuting, health, shelter, and food, have all increased remarkably since the beginning of the industrial revolution. Whatever the effect on individual happiness, these expenditures have also increased the efficiency and prolonged the productive life of individuals. As increased knowledge of sanitation, hygiene, and advances in medicine extended human life, the return on human capital was substantially increased as its economic benefits were enjoyed over a longer working life. It is misleading simply to look at the rise in income and ignore the costs of producing it.

Another way income growth has been overstated has long been recognized by economists. The standard measures of income place no value on household production. The value added by a worker within the household is assumed to contribute nothing to national income. Whenever there is a shift from household production to market production, the resulting increase in recorded economic activity will be overstated. As wives have entered the workforce, families have replaced their household production by market services: restaurant meals, maid services, childcare expenditures, and so on. This leads to an increase in measured national income, at least some of which is misleading. We can all increase our measured income by doing each other's laundry, in which case measured income would rise but no one would be better off (because expenditures would rise comparably).

A great deal of the increase in earnings of the average family over the last thirty years has been due to increasing participation of women in the work force. Once we deduct the value of the reduction in household production, it is entirely possible that the income of the average family has stagnated or even declined over this period.

Thus viewed, it is not surprising that, during the period, fertility has stagnated if not fallen in the Western world. Couples may be having fewer children because, given their stagnant if not declining income and the increasing optimal investment in child quality, they can't afford more.[10]

Risky Business

Risk and uncertainty are the only constants of life. So far in our discussion of economics and evolution we have said precious little about this fact of life. Our discussions and analysis have generally assumed the absence of risk and uncertainty. Where we have introduced these twin concepts we have argued that people and other biological entities maximized the "expected" or average outcome of their actions, without explaining why this should be so. In chapter 6 we will be dealing with the implications for human and animal behavior of sexual reproduction. Sex is inherently risky. It, as explained in chapter 4, is one of the most uncertain and risky activities that can be engaged in. Our discussion of the optimal response to risk and uncertainty can be delayed no further.

The consequences of any act, or of the failure to act, are inherently uncertain. In the previous chapters, we have simply assumed that all organisms act according to the expected value of that action, where the expected value is the sum of all the possible outcomes of any action, with each outcome multiplied by the probability of it occurring. If an activity has two possible outcomes, success, S, and failure, F, and the probability of success is PS, and the probability of failure is PF, then the expected value, EV, of engaging in the activity is simply: $EV = PS \times S + PF \times F$.

Since there are only two outcomes possible, PF is equal to one minus PS. Let S equal $100 and F equal $20. If PS, the probability of success, equals 50 percent, the expected value of this activity is $60.

If an actor had to choose between two alternatives, he would choose the one with the highest expected value. For example, suppose Activity 1 has a payoff, if successful, of $100, and a payoff if it fails, of $20. Activity 2 pays $60 if successful, and $40 if unsuccessful. Each gamble has a 50 percent chance of succeeding. The expected value of Activity 1 is, as before, $60, whereas the expected value of Activity 2 is only $50. According to our logic, if these quantities were not dollars but units of fitness, natural selection would favor choosing the gamble with the highest expected value, Activity 1 in this case.

The logic of this argument is similar to that of why organisms must maximize their fitness. Any other strategy would be sub-optimal, causing the individual to lose in evolutionary competition with organisms that maximized the likely payoff from their actions. However, maximizing the expected value isn't always the best strategy. Before going into detail about this complex issue, we present the standard economic analysis of risk and uncertainty.

As presented by Friedman and Savage (1948, pp.270-304), the individual does not choose the activity that maximizes the expected value of his payoff, but rather that which maximizes his expected utility. Expected utility is simply the sum of the utility of all outcomes, each multiplied by the probability of its occurrence. In the two outcome case, the expected utility, EU, is equal to the probability of success, PS, times the utility of the payout if successful, U (S), plus the probability of failure, PF, times the utility of the payout of failure, U (F).

$$EU = PS \times U (S) + PF \times U (F)$$

In the earlier case, the individual was maximizing his utility by choosing the activity with the highest expected value. In this case, he chooses the activity with the highest expected utility. Since economists assume that utility is a positive but diminishing function of income, these two approaches can give very different answers. To illustrate this, let us assume the following levels of utility for different payouts.

Table 5.3

Payoff	Utility
20	60
30	80
40	90
60	96
80	100
100	102

The expected utility of Activity 1 is 81 units (.5 x 102 + .5 x 60); the expected utility of Activity 2 is 93 units (.5 x 96 + .5 x 90). According to this view of risk, the individual does not choose Activity 1, which has the high expected payoff, but rather Activity 2, which has the highest expected utility. The logic is that since every additional dollar of income has less utility than the previous dollar, individuals will be biased in favor of those activities that have a lower variance in outcomes. The individual will be willing to give up a little in expected value in order to guarantee himself a higher outcome if he fails. In other words, the $40 of extra payoff Activity 1 pays if successful isn't worth as much as the $20 additional income that Activity 2 pays if failure occurs. Activity 1 does not pay enough for the additional risk.

A person who maximizes his expected utility and has a diminishing marginal utility of income will be risk averse, while someone who maximizes the expected value of his income will be risk neutral. Economists have used this expected utility theory to explain why people buy various forms of insurance and why investments with a wider variance of outcomes have to pay higher rates of return. But this explanation of risky behavior has not been altogether successful. It doesn't explain why the same person who buys insurance also plays the lottery. The expected loss due to a fire is less than the premiums on a fire insurance policy, so a person who buys the policy must have diminishing marginal utility of income. Yet the expected payout of a lottery ticket is less than its cost, so only people with increasing marginal utility of income would buy it.

To explain this type of paradox, some economists have hypothesized about the utility or enjoyment received from gambling. Others have explained this contradiction by assuming that people with low incomes have increasing marginal utility while at higher income levels, the marginal utility begins to decline. This is used to explain why gambling is more prevalent among the poor, while the rich are more risk averse. But this doesn't explain why the relatively well off have been known to patronize Las Vegas and other similar adult theme parks. We understand the enjoyment from beating the house, but this can be accomplished as well by playing for low stakes.

We can define any organism's response toward risk by one of three reactions:

1.   *Risk Neutrality.* Regardless of the variance in the possible outcomes of an activity or gamble, a risk neutral individual will base his decision solely on its expected return. If forced to decide between two activities, he will choose the one that offers the greatest expected return regardless of its risk.

2.   *Risk Aversion.* In evaluating an activity, a risk averse individual will consider the variance in its possible outcomes to be a negative feature of that activity. If forced to choose between two activities which have the same expected return, a risk averse individual will always choose the activity with the lower variance in its possible outcomes.

3.   *Risk Preference.* An individual who has a preference for risk places a positive value on the variance in the outcomes of any activity. When choosing between two activities that offer the same expected return, he will always choose the activity with the higher variance in its possible outcomes.

The definitions of risk aversion and risk preference do not tell us anything about how much weight a decision maker would place on the riskiness of any potential activity. Economists would say it all depends on the shape of the individual's utility function and have little more to add. In contrast, the evolutionary biologist would claim that an organism's response to risk is shaped by the forces of natural selection and that the response to risk that maximizes fitness will be the one that ultimately prevails in any competition among organisms.

To discover what evolutionary theory can tell us about the optimal response toward risk, we invite back a troop of asexual globs. To start, let's divide our population into three groups of equal size. One group has a gene that leads it to be risk neutral, one group is genetically inclined to be risk averse, and the third group has a preference for risk. Let's also assume that each glob lives one year and has to take one gamble during its short life. It has to decide on a reproductive strategy: whether to devote its energy to having a large number of children or to feeding and protecting a smaller number.

Let us assume for argument's sake that there are three possible strategies. Table 5.4 presents the results of following each strategy under two equally probable outcomes, rain and drought.

Our risk neutral glob will obviously choose Strategy #2, because it offers the highest expected number of surviving offspring. Our risk-averse glob chooses Strategy #1. Even though it has a lower expected payoff, there is a smaller variance between success and failure. The risk-preferring glob chooses #3, even though it too has a lower expected return than #2. It likes the action, the high payoff from success.

If rain and drought are equally probable and randomly distributed among the globs, (each glob's gamble is independent of every other glob's gamble), the risk-neutral strategy will be the one that maximizes fitness. Roughly one half of all globs will succeed in

Table 5.4
Number of Surviving Offspring

Strategy	Rain	Drought	Expected value
#1	4	3	3.5
#2	6	2	4.0
#3	7	0	3.5

whatever strategy they adopt. Since the globs that adopt Strategy #2 will, on average, have more surviving children, they will eventually dominate the population. When gambles are independent of each other, the strategy with the highest expected value will be optimal and under these circumstances, those individuals who are risk neutral will be favored by natural selection. All that is needed is that risk-neutral globs are sufficiently abundant that the law of large numbers can work.

A more interesting case occurs when the successes of all gambles of a particular strategy are perfectly correlated with each other, that is, all globs who follow Strategy #1 succeed or fail together. Let's assume when it rains, it rains on everyone. If there is enough rain, then all globs, regardless of their strategy, succeed. If, however, there is a drought, all fail. The relative successes of the three strategies described above now depend, not on how they fare in one year, or in one generation, but on how they do over many years of both good and bad weather.

The number of descendants produced by any one strategy over, say, a four-year period, will be equal to the product of the return in each of those years. Since we know that in our example the probability of good weather is 50 percent, let us assume that there are two years of drought during this four-year period.

As table 5.5 shows, Strategy #1 yields as many expected descendants in four years as does Strategy #2, even though in any one year, the expected number of descendants from Strategy #1 is one-half child lower. And Strategy #3, which has exactly the same number of expected offspring in any one year as Strategy #1, leads to an expectation of extinction. The entire genetic line of risk-preferring globs will be wiped out in any drought year.

The strategy that eventually wins out will be the one that produces the maximum number of descendants in the long run. But how long is that long run and how can our globs evaluate each strat-

Table 5.5

Strategy	Total Descendants over Four Years
#1	144
#2	144
#3	0

egy? Is there a way of expressing the results of each approach that is independent of the number of years chosen? There is. It is the geometric mean of the results of each strategy. The geometric mean is simply the nth root of the product of n years' results. The geometric mean of Strategy #1 and #2 is 3.464 while the geometric mean of Strategy #3 is, of course, 0. For a strategy with only two possible outcomes of equal probability, the expected geometric mean is simply the square root of the product of the two outcomes. Once the geometric mean is estimated, we can estimate the population at any future period by simply taking the EGM (Expected Geometric Mean) to the nth power where n is large and is the number of generations between the starting and ending period.

It is not essential that each result from each gamble of a particular strategy be perfectly correlated with the other results of that strategy. When the results of reproductive gambles are correlated to any degree, that is, when there is systematic risk, natural selection will favor the gene that leads to picking the strategy with the greatest geometric mean. The lower the correlation between gambles of a strategy, the lower the variance of the outcomes of that strategy over time and the closer the geometric mean will be to the arithmetic mean. Biologists call this type of behavior bet-hedging and have found that many organisms, in fact, engage in this form of behavior (e.g., Philippi and Seger, 1989). In the finance literature "(t)he criterion can be viewed as maximizing the expected value of terminal wealth" (Elton and Gruber, p. 298).

In conclusion, risk-averse behavior maximizes fitness under certain circumstances. For risk-averse behavior to be optimal, the outcome of any strategy must depend on systemic factors that affect the fate of all individuals participating in that strategy in the same way.

The form of risk-averse behavior predicted by evolutionary theory is quite specific. By specifying that individuals will choose those strategies or series of gambles with the highest geometric means, evolutionary theory provides testable predictions about human behavior. All this applies when dealing with units of fitness. As long as the relationship between material resources and fitness is continuous and monotonic, there is no problem measuring outcomes in dollars and cents. But where there are discontinuities, individuals may appear to engage in irrational behavior.

Take for example a male with no close relatives and an expected level of net lifetime wealth (above what he requires for his maintenance) insufficient to attract a wife and raise a child. Let's suppose for the sake of argument that he has one half of the amount needed for procreation. You cannot buy half a child. If he does nothing but spend the surplus funds on his own amusement, the man faces genetic extinction. Let us provide him, accordingly, with the following gamble. Two coins will be tossed, if two heads turn up, his wages will be doubled and if any other combination occurs, he loses his bet (namely, his surplus funds). Should our imaginary friend accept this bet? The expected value of this wager is only fifty cents for every dollar bet, about the same for a New York State Lottery ticket. The bettor has one chance in four of doubling his money and three chances of losing it.

Put another way, our man has a one in four chance of affording a family and being able to reproduce if he makes the wager, compared to a zero chance if he does nothing. From the point of view of money, the gamble reduces the expected value of his surplus wealth by 50 percent, but from an evolutionary perspective, it raises his expected chance of reproducing from 0 to .25.

In an old joke, a man was asked why he continued to play in a weekly poker game, knowing that it was fixed. His answer: "Because it's the only game in town." Because children can only be purchased in discreet units, a little wealth does little genetic good for those who are very poor. Moreover, as explained in chapter 6, because human biology decrees that males are the competitive sex, low-status men are unlikely to be successful. Such considerations might help explain why the poor seem to show such a strong preference for risk. Perhaps traditional analyses have measured behavior on the wrong scale, based on dollars instead of genes.

Notes

1. Remember the utility function in modern economics is not about what makes people happy; it is not supposed to describe psychological states. It is solely an abstract representation of people's preferences and goals and the trade-offs that people will make among their preferences when they are in conflict.
2. $$\frac{Sr*}{C+Q*} = MP_Q$$
    where MP_Q is the marginal productivity of an additional unit of resources invested in quality on increasing the survival rate. $C + Q$ is the total price of producing an additional child. $Sr*$ is the optimal value of the survival rate. $Q*$ is the optimal investment in quality.
3. As usual, we can write this relationship as follows:
    $E = f(M)$, where E is total lifetime earnings and M is the amount spent on mainte-

nance. The goal of the individual is to maximize the amount of net earnings available for reproductive purposes. $R = E - M$ or $R = f(M) - M$, where R is net lifetime earnings. $dR/dM = df(M)/dR - 1 = 0$; $df(M)/dR = 1$.

4. For ease of discussion we assume that the problems of maximizing genetic fitness are separable, that is, can be solved independently of each other. In reality resources spent on maintenance also have an effect on genetic reproduction. For example, money spent on maintaining an individual's health not only increases lifetime earning potential but also may make the individual a more desirable mate. By ignoring the interrelationships between maintenance and genetic fitness, we simplify the analysis without changing the basic thrust of the argument.

5. For ease of analysis we also ignore investment in relatives other than children.

6. By now the reader should be familiar with the basic form of the argument. $W_G = g(Q)$. W_G, the gross wage of the child is a positive but diminishing function of Q, the amount invested in enhancing the human capital of the child. Since the child's net wage, W, is equal to his gross wage minus his optimal spending on maintenance, M^*, we can write: $W = W_G - M^* = h(Q)$ where, $h(Q) = g(Q) - M^*$. The sum of net resources available to an individual's children is equal to: $R_C = N \times h(Q)$. The parent must choose the combination of N and Q which maximizes the children's net resources, R_C, subject to the parent's budget constraint. $R_p = N \times P$, where R_p represents the net resources of the parent, N is the number of children and P is the total price of a child. P is equal to a constant cost per child, C, plus the amount, Q, invested in human capital: $P = C + Q$. The fixed cost, C, of a child is independent of the wage or wealth of the parent.

7. The solution to the more complicated problem involves each parent taking into account the effect of his or her decisions about the optimal number of children on the cost of his children having children. Because having more children reduces the cost of grandchildren, great grandchildren, etc., the more complete solution to the problem of maximizing the number of future descendants would involve parents having more children than would be necessary to maximize the next generation's net income.

8. This occurs when the production function has constant returns to scale, which occurs when there are no fixed factors of production or externalities.

9. In fact, knowledge can depreciate through social disruption, which destroys the institutions that pass on knowledge from one generation to the next.

10. Since children require more land in their production than does capital, the rise in land rents will also cause a shift away from numbers of children toward investment in human and non-human capital. The negative relationship between fertility and the cost of land is consistent with the universal observation that urban families produce far fewer children than rural ones. The higher cost of space, combined with limited opportunities for the employment of children, raise the net cost of producing children for city dwellers. The secular growth in urbanization has therefore had a negative impact on fertility.

6

Sexual Economics

In chapter 5, we suggested that human beings, along with all other living things, are "programmed" by evolution to maximize their contribution to the future gene pool. We also proposed that much economic activity—along with other behaviors—can be interpreted as serving this end. Non-human species accomplish this by having as many offspring of optimal quality as possible, which may include additional investments of time and effort, including material resources such as the bequeathal of territories, nests, and so forth.

Humans do essentially the same thing. For example, they can enhance their offspring's future reproductive success by gifting non-human capital to them. Therefore, to maximize their contribution to the future gene pool, humans must balance their investment of resources among number of children, their human capital, and the amount of non-human capital to be transferred to them. (Once again, bear in mind that much human behavior can be directed toward maximizing fitness without this being a conscious goal.)

We have presented a simple model of how parents might go about making optimal investments in these three "assets." Many assumptions were necessary to produce an easily comprehensible model. Although we are confident that these simplifications do not alter the basic dynamics, one assumption does crucially affect our model. In chapter 5, we assumed asexual reproduction, equivalent to assuming that both parents act in concert, that is, they have no conflicting interests and behave as if they were one individual with one utility function. This is true for lifetime exclusive monogamy, in which both partners mate for life, and in which each is the biological parent of the other's children.

This assumption is only an approximation. Polygyny is the preferred mating system in nearly 80 percent of human societies identified by anthropologists, monogamy, in less than 20 percent. However, this does not mean that the majority of men, for example, have been polygynously mated. Since the human sex ratio—like that of most sexually reproducing animals—is very close to unity, only a small proportion of highly successful men have been polygynists. Some remain bachelors, with the majority monogamously mated, simply because they can afford only one wife.

But at the same time, even in societies that are legally and culturally monogamous, there are numerous exceptions to the exclusive mating assumed in our model. Adultery, serial monogamy, and promiscuous sexual activity outside of marriage all complicate its basic logic—just as they complicate human life. Except when both are committed to lifetime monogamy, the reproductive strategies followed by men and women can be fundamentally different. To understand why this is so and how we must alter our model of human behavior to account for it, we next consider the biological differences between women and men, and how such differences affect their reproductive incentives.

Vive la Différence

In species that engage in sexual reproduction, individuals that produce the larger sex cells (eggs) are, by definition, female, while those that produce the smaller, more numerous sex cells (sperm) are males. Since each offspring is the result of a union of one sperm and one egg, the female invests more than the male in each offspring. Males, in turn, have the potential of fertilizing far more eggs than any one female can produce. The variance in male reproductive success is typically greater than that of females, because to some extent, male reproductive success is a zero-sum game: success for one occurs at the expense of another. By contrast, the reproductive success of one female is less likely to limit the reproductive success of another. Put in economic terms, eggs are the scarce resource in the production of offspring, and as a result, males are selected to compete among themselves for access to females (Barash and Lipton, 1997).

Because of these basic biological differences, the reproductive strategy of males and females will differ; this holds for mammals no less than most other animals, and for human beings no less than for other mammals. Not only do female mammals continue to nourish the egg after fertilization, but they devote scarce resources to nursing those offspring for a considerable time after birth (in fact, the caloric investment during lactation greatly exceeds that of pregnancy). Given the requirement of nursing their children, women—without the assistance of wet nurses, animal's milk or formula—are essentially limited to one child every two or three years. A realistic maximum for a woman's lifetime is about a dozen children.

The biological limit for men is very much higher. Ismail, for example, a seventeenth-century king of Morocco, is reputed to have fathered 1,056 children (Barash, 1979). Ismail hit the genetic jackpot; his genes were disproportionately represented in the next generation. Obviously, to have achieved this prodigious reproductive feat, Ismail must have enjoyed the favors of hundreds of women, women who were no longer available to mate with less fortunate men. It is probably not coincidental, as well, that he was known as Ismail the Bloodthirsty: just as with all harem-forming species, success in polygynous society is often associated with physical prowess and cunning, as well as a propensity for threat and violence. For every male who strikes it genetically "rich," there are numerous bachelors who never get to reproduce at all. This is not true for women. Given the cheapness of sperm, it is truly the rare and unfortunate woman who can't find a man willing to provide the wherewithal for fertilization. Since women contribute so much biologically to each child compared to the negligible contribution of men, it would appear as if evolution has arranged for the exploitation of women by men. To some extent this is true: sperm (consisting of virtually no caloric contribution), compete among themselves because the winners get to profit from resource-laden eggs. But as any economist could understand, male exploitation of women is not an equilibrium situation.

Both men and women have finite resources available for reproduction. A man can advance his reproductive interest by successfully impregnating as many women as will accept his attentions if— and this is a big if—the mother can raise a child of reasonable quality with little or no assistance from him (recall the situation of the pied flycatchers described in chapter 4). Among mammals, females bear virtually all the cost of child rearing. But in such a situation, the demand for females by males vastly exceeds the demand for males by females.

Since the demand for one sex by the other is equivalent to an offer of supply, there exists an excess demand for females. When demand exceeds supply, something has to give; the price of the scarce resource is bound to rise. In the case of human mating systems, females get to choose from a surplus of suitors, who, as we have seen, must compete with each other for access to feminine charms. A male has several ways of inducing a female to mate with him rather than with another. For example, he can force females, by violence or the threat of violence, or by effectively eliminating the competition. In such cases, females have essentially no choice, as when bull elk compete among themselves and the winner "gets" the females.

Alternatively, when males are unable to control female sexuality, the focus essentially switches from male initiative (i.e., male-male competition) to female choice. Since females provide—in most cases, by definition as well as biological fact—the bulk of parental invest-ment, they are often able to drive a hard bargain: providing sexual access to their eggs (and, among mammals, the promise of subse-quent pregnancy and lactation) only to select males. For convenience, and, incidentally, a play on words that is especially appropriate for economists, we can say that females choose those males who are best able to provide the three "goods"; namely, good genes, good behavior, and good resources (Barash, 1982).

When male competition is especially intense—as in classic harem-forming species such as elk or elephant seals—a few dominant males father nearly all a breeding group's offspring. Dominant males dur-ing breeding season expend immense energy beating back competi-tors and inseminating harem members. In such cases, male compe-tition guarantees that females will receive the highest quality genes from their mates.

When female choice is paramount, females typically show an ac-tive preference for good genes. In some cases, genetic quality is not objectively measurable; good genes for one female may be less good for another. This is especially noticeable in cases of potential in-breeding, such that sexual reproduction among close relatives re-sults in an increased frequency of genetic defects, and thus, lowered fitness for the offspring produced as well as for the parents in ques-tion. Not surprisingly, animals show a range of adaptations for avoid-ing inbreeding, including dispersal before sexual maturation is reached, inhibition of ovulation in the presence of male genetic rela-tives, and inhibitions against sexual behavior involving individuals with whom one has had extensive early experience. It is noteworthy that this latter adaptation is characteristic of human beings. Israeli kibbutz residents, for example, reared in communal groups from infancy, and which therefore mimic a situation of genetic sibships, are especially unlikely to treat each other as potential sexual partners when they mature (Shepher, 1971).

Female preference for males with good genes appears to be a major driving force behind elaborate male ornamentation among many animal species, as well as time- and energy-consuming courtship display (the famously ornate tail feathers of the peacock are a classic case). Females may also be selected to choose impressively ornamented males because by so doing, they increase the chances that their male offspring, in turn, will be sexually attractive to females. This so-called "sexy son hypothesis" (Weatherhead and Robertson, 1979) has received impressive empirical support among animals. In such cases, female choice is driven by the evolutionary advantage accrued by the *grandchildren* of the females doing the choosing—more precisely, only one-half their grandchildren: those produced by their sons—rather than by the direct reproductive success of these females.[1]

Good behavior is relatively difficult to assess, simply because males could essentially "promise" to behave well—that is, in a way that enhances the fitness of the chooser—then renege in practice. However, there is evidence that animal courtship often involves guarantees of forthcoming good behavior, especially in cases of monogamy, in which the success of the choosing individual depends heavily on a behavioral contribution to be made by the individual being chosen. Indeed, in such cases, courtship serves as an opportunity for mutual assessment.

Among many predatory birds, for example, courtship involves elaborate aerial maneuvers, during which each prospective partner gets to demonstrate his capacity as a hunter, and thus, the probability that it will be able to bring home the bacon. Generally speaking, there is a positive correlation between duration of courtship and degree of monogamous commitment among animals: a long "engagement" period provides a greater opportunity for the "betrothed" couple to evaluate each other's behavior—including, notably, whether either one is maintaining another mate elsewhere.

Even non-monogamous species evaluate each other's behavior prior to mating. Among coral reef-dwelling Hawaiian damselfish, for example, females are especially prone to spawn with males who demonstrate—as part of courtship—that they are capable of behaving aggressively toward the potential egg-predators that abound in their environment (Barash, 1981).

Finally, concern over good resources is widespread among animals, especially choosy females. The quality of one's resources is generally harder to misrepresent than that of one's genes or one's promised behavior. Especially when a species is polygynous, males often compete to maintain territories, which are then evaluated by females, who preferentially mate with males whose territories offer such resource-based advantages as good feeding opportunities, safe and convenient nest sites, and so on. An influential "polygyny threshold model" has shown how the differential resource bases maintained by different males gives rise to a predicted distribution of females (Orians, 1969).

In this model, developed originally to explain why some redwinged blackbirds remain monogamous while others may have harems of five or six females, females distribute themselves in accord with the resources offered by males: some females forego the monogamous assistance offered by otherwise unmated males in order to become the fifth or sixth mate of a polygynist, if the latter's resource offerings are sufficient to compensate for the loss of his direct parental assistance. The result, interestingly, is that females tend to have comparable reproductive success, whether they are monogamously mated to a relatively "poor" male, or one of numerous cowives of a comparatively "wealthy" male.

The situation among human beings parallels that of other animals. (When one of us lectured on the role of good genes, good behavior, and good resources in an undergraduate animal behavior course, a student immediately piped up, "Oh, I get it. You mean looks, personality, and money!") Let's look at this more closely.

Human beings are perfectly good mammals. They have hair, are warm-blooded, and nurse their young. They are also unusual—although not unique—in that males will often make a substantial postcopulatory contribution to the success of their offspring. There is overwhelming evidence that human beings are biologically polygynous: males are generally larger than females, females become sexually mature earlier than males, and males are more prone to aggression and violence, not to mention the anthropological evidence showing a preponderance of polygyny in pre-contact societies. On the other hand, *Homo sapiens* is only mildly polygynous.

Monogamy is almost certainly the most common reproductive arrangement among human beings worldwide, even when polygyny is permitted (and preferred by men able to achieve it). This, in turn, is at least consistent with the fact that human infants are so vulnerable and needy at birth, as well as having a very long period of growth and dependency, that they benefit greatly from the assistance of two committed parents.

And so, intra-sexual competition among human beings is not strictly male-male. Female-female competition also takes place, although it appears to be generally subtler and less violent than its male-male counterpart. In addition, sexual selection—whereby members of one sex choose potential mates from among those of the other sex—is not limited to female choice, as in many other animals. Just as human females prefer males with certain traits, human males are also remarkably fussy, as mammals go (consistent with the fact that human males provide more parental investment than any other known mammals).

These preferences tend to be remarkably consistent with evolutionary proddings related ultimately to the probability of reproductive success. Men, for example, consistently prefer women who are young, who possess waist to hip ratios that indicate suitable levels of estrogens and the promise of efficient childbirth (as well as not being already pregnant!), whereas women prefer men who are relatively tall and otherwise healthy, and both sexes are attracted to unblemished skin, lustrous hair and physical symmetry—which also correlates with a lack of disease, of parasitism, and of developmental anomalies.

When considering potential mates for a monogamous marriage, each individual must be concerned with the genetic quality of a prospective partner, his or her behavioral inclinations, and the resources that either will bring to the union. Resources are comparatively easy to measure and can readily be expressed in monetary terms, although this does not mean that people cannot attempt to fake them, such as by renting a Mercedes, or costume jewelry. Behavior, too, can be faked, which as we have seen, likely puts a premium on prolonged courtships and lengthy betrothals. Genetic qualities are relatively difficult to reduce to one index. Health, beauty, strength, height, intelligence, and so forth, can all play an important role in fitness. Some of these traits have an obvious impact on an individual's ability to acquire resources, while others, such as symmetry of features, are just now being unraveled (Thornhill, Gangestad, and Comer, 1995).

Breast development among women provides an interesting conundrum, insofar as they are sexually appealing to men and seem to promise ability to lactate. Yet, since non-lactating breast tissue is composed almost entirely of fat, it seems that a simple fitness-enhancing explanation is too facile. The intriguing possibility exists that pronounced non-lactating breasts (a human specialty), are an example of female deception. If so, then male fondness for a characteristic waist/hip ratio might be a counter-adaptation, by which men keep women honest as to their overall level of body fat (Barash and Lipton, 1997).

As to more traditional economic factors, note that it is not necessarily in the best genetic interests of a woman to mate with a man of high genetic quality, if he provides little or no material support. It is often to her advantage to choose a lower-quality male who is willing to devote most if not all his reproductive resources to her children. Given the long gestation period of the human baby and its much longer period of dependency, most women find it difficult to raise children without assistance. Therefore, it is adaptive for them to demand resources from males as the price of bearing their children. (Such demands, incidentally, go a long way toward equalizing the evolutionary balance sheet, such that males, reproductively speaking, are in a sense no more exploitative of females than females are of males. When a young woman demands and receives money and lavish gifts from her male lover, it is not immediately clear who is exploiting whom!)

Men will generally agree to provide resources to women, for two reasons. First, given the excess demand for women, it is simply the price a man must pay for access to a woman of childbearing capacity. Second, men also have a genetic interest in enhancing the quality of their children. At the same time, however, their polygynous propensities insure that men have an interest in shifting the cost of child rearing onto the woman so as to conserve resources that could then be spent having children with other mates.

The Dating Game

"There will always be a battle between the sexes," according to George Burns, "because men and women want different things. Men want women and women want men" (Burns, 1996). If only it were this simple!

The logic of human sexual reproduction dictates that men and women have distinct and at times, irreconcilable interests. It is not that men, as a group, are united to oppress women, or vice versa. Rather, the optimum reproductive strategies of men and women often clash, generating what has been termed "strategic interference" (Buss, 1999). This occurs whenever the optimal strategies of one person conflict with those of another. For example, optimal strategies of men are generally to achieve the maximum number of copulations; optimal strategies of women are generally to withhold copulation until there is further commitment of behavior and resources. To be sure, such strategic disagreements are ultimately reconcilable, but not without conflict.

At the risk of oversimplifying, there are two, not necessarily mutually exclusive, reproductive strategies available to a man. First, he can be a dutiful husband and father, siring the optimal number of children by his wife or wives and investing the optimal amount of human capital in each of them. The remainder of his resources, if any, is then invested in non-human capital to be bequeathed to his children to aid them in their reproductive efforts. This is the strategy laid out in chapter 5. Alternatively, he can use his resources to engage in a life of promiscuous sex, hoping to impregnate as many women as possible. This strategy will succeed best if others can be convinced or, in the case of adultery, fooled into providing resources to invest in his children.

For the first strategy to succeed, a man must have a high degree of confidence in the paternity of his children; otherwise, it makes no genetic sense to invest in them. For this reason, he has a vested interest in the "virtue" of any potential or actual wife. But some men also follow the promiscuous strategy in which they actively attempt to seduce all suitable females. As women once complained, "men wish to marry virgins, but spend their lives trying to make sure that none are available."

Men consistently have lower standards than women when it comes to the requirements for casual sex, as measured, for example, by estimates of the minimally acceptable intelligence required in a casual sex partner (Kenrick et al., 1990), or how long they would have to know someone before sexual relations would be an acceptable option (Buss and Schmitt, 1993).

We emphasize that this is precisely the pattern to be expected if mating preferences were ultimately driven by unconscious considerations of fitness maximization. The "battle of the sexes" is not a generalized struggle between males and females, and certainly not one in which either sex is somehow united in desire to oppress or defeat the other. Rather, individual males and females are each influenced by their own evolutionary-appropriate agendas, which simply result in strategies that tend to conflict. What is good (that is, maximally fitness enhancing) for men is not necessarily equally good for women, and vice versa.

Women, no less than men, have their own distinct genetic interest to worry about. Given the long dependency of a human child, the worst reproductive bargain a woman can make is to allow some low-quality male to impregnate her and then provide no material support. Far better is to attract a male of high genetic quality who is rich in material resources and is willing to devote them exclusively to supporting her and her children.

When we discussed the marriage market, we assumed that individuals had accurate information about the relative characteristics of prospective mates. But, this need not be true. In fact, individuals may not even have accurate knowledge about their own qualities, especially how they rank relative to their competitors. Given this lack of information, it is not surprising that the courting process should be characterized by so much disappointment and deception. Each prospective partner is attempting to evaluate the strengths and weaknesses of the other, while at the same time trying to put him or herself in the best light.

According to the interests of each sex, the male, in seeking mates, should emphasize his material riches, or at least his prospects for such, as well as his devotion and commitment, essentially promising that he will not abandon his wife. He also should appear healthy, strong, intelligent, brave, and able and willing to defend her and her children.

The female, on the other hand, especially wishes to appear attractive: that is, healthy and capable of child bearing. She may also need to appear intelligent, coy, and modest. Any woman who appears too eager for sex will have no problem getting a "date," but may find it more difficult to get a man committed to supporting her children, since for him the danger of cuckoldry is too great. Although the advent of reliable birth control has changed these dynamics somewhat, men still tend to have a whore/Madonna classification of women, preferring one-night stands with the former, and marriage with the latter.

Numerous studies of "singles ads," from cultures as diverse as the United States, India, and Germany, have confirmed these expectations. Thus, women preferred such words as "loving," "reliable," "monogamous," "career oriented," and "emotionally stable," whereas men responded most positively to "good figure," "attractive," "trim," "sexy," "good-looking," and "young." It may also be noteworthy that longer advertisements held special appeal for women, who, being the choosier sex, can be expected to hold out for more information. In contrast, briefer ads are more attractive to men, consistent with their inclination to hone in on a simpler dimension: sexual availability and attractiveness. Finally, men on average receive fewer responses per advertisement than do women (1.50 to 4.53), which is precisely what we would expect in a world in which women have something that men want (Thiessen, Young, and Burroughs, 1993).

In a series of cross-cultural studies involving thirty-seven different cultures, men and women were queried as to their preference in a mate. Although both sexes indicated that "kindness" (a component of good behavior) was the number one priority, men and women differed consistently from each other and also in accord with evolutionary theory (Buss, 1989). Thus, men tended to value physical characteristics in a prospective spouse, with resources being less important, whereas women tended to assess resources above physical traits.

The possibility exists that female concern about male wealth and earning potential (i.e., resources) does not reflect an evolved behavioral tendency so much as the simple economic fact that in virtually all societies, men control most of the wealth. If so, then women who are themselves wealthy should not be especially concerned about that of their partners, since they would be less dependent on them. But a study focusing on wealthier women found that such women preferred men who are wealthier and higher status yet (Wiederman and Allgeier, 1992)! In addition, there is no correlation cross-culturally between degree of male-female economic disparity and female preference for wealthy husbands (Buss, 1989). (The above findings, consistent with the sociobiology of hypergamy—in which women are especially inclined to "marry up"—brings to mind the folk song whose refrain asks, "If I were a carpenter, and you were a lady, would you marry me anyway? Would you have my baby?" The answer, in most cases, would be a resounding "No!")

This fits with the concept of strategic male-female interference, described earlier. For example, it makes genetic sense for men to push their dates for sex, since such behavior tends to be a win/win strategy for them. If successful, sexually aggressive men will get the proximate satisfaction of a sexual encounter plus, possibly, the ultimate benefits of producing a child without being necessarily obliged to provide support, and if not successful may have discovered a woman suitable for marriage. (Again, don't be deceived by the fact that in such situations, most men would disclaim any desire to father a child. Such a disclaimer may well be "true" in nearly all cases, but this doesn't mean that their biology is not following a different agenda.)

Depending on a man's social position and the probability that he might be forced to marry the woman or provide child support, he may be very anxious to avoid conception and may even take the lead in employing birth control. In fact, to the extent that the male loses by initiating a pregnancy, a female might win by getting pregnant. A high-quality young male from a respectable family might, in certain societies, find the scandal revolving around an out-of-wedlock child devastating to his future prospects and to his family's social standing. Therefore, sexual reticence is not always the best strategy available to all women. It is not for nothing that pre-marital sex was at one time termed the "Tender Trap."

Whether taking this risk is in the woman's best interest depends on weighing the gains from snaring a husband better than she could otherwise expect versus the real possibility that she may have misjudged his and his family's reaction and be bought off or left with nothing but the child. When a woman decides to trap a man into marriage, she still has to be selective: the prospective "victim" must be of high enough quality to be worth the risk, but not too good as to be unattainable. In fact, one explanation for the rise in illegitimate births is the demise of the shotgun wedding, which, especially for lower classes, usually followed pregnancy. Legalized abortion, by giving women other options, has reduced the need or willingness of men "to do the right thing by her"—or alternatively, it has opened up a major new way of defining the "right thing," namely, pay for the abortion.

In his book *The Selfish Gene*, Richard Dawkins provides a useful analysis of male and female sexual strategies and how they interact. Employing the concept of Evolutionarily Stable Strategies pioneered by evolutionary theorist John Maynard Smith (1988), Dawkins attempts to discover if there are ESSs for male and female courtship.

Remember from chapter 4 that a strategy is an ESS if, once adopted by most members of a population, it cannot be bettered by an alternative strategy. Dawkins is concerned with basic male/female behavior and not just with that of men and women. However, we believe that the basic model and his conclusion shed light on human sexual behavior.

Dawkins identifies two male strategies that he calls faithful and philanderer. The faithful male is willing to expend substantial resources courting a female and will, when she gives birth, stay with her to help rear her young. The philanderer quickly loses interest in a female if she will not mate immediately, and even if she does, will not stay to help her; instead, the philanderer goes off looking for other females with whom to copulate. Females also have two strategies, coy and fast. Coy females will not mate with a male unless he is willing to spend substantial resources courting them. Fast females will copulate with anyone, immediately.

Dawkins assumes the genetic payoff from offspring to be 15 units for both mother and father. The total cost of rearing a child is 20 units, and the cost of courtship is 3 units for both sexes. In a totally monogamous population of faithful males and coy females, each partner gains 15 units of genetic benefit from mating, and pays half the cost of rearing the children, 10 units each, as well as his or her courtship costs of 3 units. Therefore, each sex has a 2-unit profit from the mating.

Introduce a fast female into this population. She does better than the coy female, since she does not pay the cost of courtship and even though she is fast, her mate is faithful. Her payoff is 5 units. Her genes, and therefore the fast strategy will come to dominate the female population.

But, as the fast females increase in abundance, they open the door to philandering males. When the female population consisted totally of coy females, the philandering male strategy was a flop. Such a male could find no one to mate with him. Now that the population is dominated by fast females, however, his genes will prosper, enjoying a payoff of 15 genetic units and bearing no cost. At the same time, the fast female who mates with him will have to raise the kids all by herself and will lose 5 units (15 - 20 = -5). Philanderers therefore prosper and spread through the male population at the expense of their faithful competitors, while fast women will suffer and decline relative to their coy counterparts. Eventually, coy females expand in numbers, reducing the opportunities for philanderers. In this example, equilibrium is reached when 5/6 of the females are coy and 5/8 of the males are faithful. (It is not necessary that there are literally two different "kinds" of males and females; rather, individuals could vary their behavior such that 5/6 of the time, females are coy and 5/8 of the time, males are faithful.)

Human behavior is far more complicated than this, but the above model raises two very interesting points. First, it is possible for two different reproductive strategies to co-exist in the same sex, and without necessarily assuming genetic or other differences between fast and coy women, or between faithful and philandering men. If there are such differences that explain why certain individuals specialize in a particular strategy, they could be "conditional," that is, keyed to various conditions in a man or woman's environment (e.g., "if a wealthy female, be coy," etc.).

The other interesting conclusion is that the equilibrium distribution of strategies need not be stable. Small changes in conditions can lead to large changes in behavior. The repeated swings that appear to have taken place in sexual morality over the last 500 years in Western societies may not be a response to fundamental changes in the nature of society (and certainly not in human nature), but rather, natural oscillations produced by the working out of the four sexual strategies described by Dawkins. For a time, these swings are self-reinforcing. After a certain point, however, they become self-limiting. After one set of strategies has gone to its extreme, the pendulum begins to swing back the other way. Biologists refer to such situations as a "mixed ESS," in which two or more discontinuous strategies can be maintained in a population indefinitely.

Economists are very familiar with the theory of unstable equilibrium; it can occur in markets in which the current period's supply depends on last period's price and there is no inventory or forward markets to provide stabilizing speculation. In such markets, if the demand curve is steeper than the supply curve, any departure from the equilibrium price or supply will be self-reinforcing. The result is termed the cobweb theorem (Samuelson, 1985, p. 405).

Figure 6.1 presents the demand and supply of corn. The supply depends on the price in the previous year. Farmers are assumed to have no foresight and to simply assume that this year's price will be equal to last year's price.

Figure 6.1
Demand and Supply of Corn

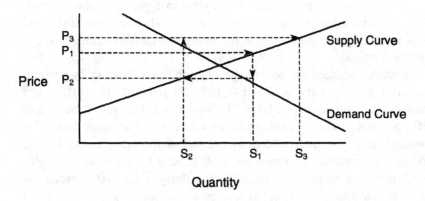

Figure 6.2
Supplies of Sexual Strategies

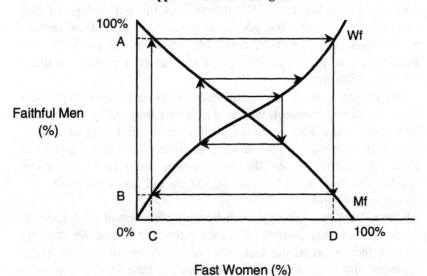

Price, P1, is above equilibrium. It leads to an increase in supply, S1, which leads next year to a fall in price to P2, which the following year leads to the reduced supply S2, and so forth. As long as the demand curve is steeper than the supply curve, the swings in production and price will grow larger each subsequent period.

We can present Dawkins's model using the same type of dynamic analysis. Instead of the supply and demand for corn, we have the supplies of the various sexual strategies. In figure 6.2, the percentage of women following the fast strategy, Wf, is on the horizontal axis and the percentage of men following the faithful strategy, Mf, is on the vertical.

In each instance, the percentage of each sex following its particular strategy can vary between 0 and 100 percent. The difference between the percentage of men following the faithful strategy and 100 percent is the percentage of philanderers. The same holds for women. Every woman who does not follow the fast strategy is coy. When 100 percent of women are fast, it pays for all men to be philanderers and none to be faithful. Similarly, when 100 percent of men are faithful, it pays for all women to be fast, to avoid the cost of courtship. In figure 6.2, Wf is the curve that describes how women in one generation determine their optimal strategy, given the percentage of men in the previous generation following their two strategies. In particular, curve Wf determines the percentage of fast women in this generation, given the percentage of faithful men in the previous one. Similarly, curve Mf describes the percentage of faithful men in this generation, given the percentage of fast women one generation ago.

Any deviation from the equilibrium ratios, determined by where these two curves intersect, will lead to a self-reinforcing move away from equilibrium. This is shown by the small spiral with the arrowheads indicating the direction of causation. Over time, given the slopes of the two curves, these ratios will cycle each generation, with faithful men going between A and B, and fast women alternating between C and D.

It is at least possible that such instability in sexual strategies explains the recurring periods of sexual laxity and Puritanism that appears to have marked the last 500 years of Western history. Much empirical and theoretical work needs to be done in this area. The study of the dynamic interaction of male and female sexual strategies is a prime candidate for the joint application of economic and evolutionary theory.

Liars and Lovers

Real life is far more complicated than the simple models constructed by biologists and economists, more complicated, even, than our attempts to merge the two. For example, the ability to deceive a potential sexual partner about one's true intention can bring huge genetic benefits. Take Dawkins's philanderer. He doesn't lie. If a woman won't immediately copulate with him, he leaves her in search of another, more willing. He could instead adopt a more devious strategy; thus he could spend the time, effort and expense necessary to court her (i.e., pretend to be faithful) only to abandon her after conception. With this strategy, he wouldn't get the 15 units of genetic pay-off that he receives from mating with a fast woman, but he would receive a very respectable 12-unit profit (15-3). Coy women who fall for this deception would be even worse off than their fast colleagues since they would not only have to raise the child by themselves, they would also endure the added expense of a lengthy courtship.

But once again, women are not helpless; given time, natural selection would devise counter-strategies to detect or punish cads and bounders. In effect, an arms race would ensue between liars and truth detectors, with evolution continually improving the moves and counter-moves employed by each sex. Some students of evolution believe that this sexual arms race—notably, the need to develop stratagems necessary to acquire and retain mates—has been the primary stimulant for the explosive growth in human brain size and intelligence.

In such a process, one side never vanquishes the other; rather, there is a continuing, shifting battle between the sexes. Evolutionary theorist Leigh van Valen (1977) first pointed out the similarity between such unending competitions and the Red Queen in Lewis Carroll's *Through the Looking Glass*, who famously urged Alice to run, simply in order to remain in place—because everything else was moving so quickly! (To get anywhere, the Red Queen helpfully suggested, it was necessary to run twice as fast.)

Evolution, operating on the human psyche, seems to have developed a technique for getting males to tell the truth about their qualities and characteristics. Any male can claim to be an eccentric millionaire who just chooses to wear dirty jeans, drive a run-down Yugo, and live in single-room occupancy hotel. But not many women would fall for that line. To convince a desirable woman that you are a man with the "goods," it is generally necessary to prove it. Expensive suits, luxury automobiles, swanky apartments, and Rolex watches have certain utilitarian features not shared by cheaper alternatives, but they are primarily a way of advertising one's wealth. A Rolex watch does tell accurate time and a Mercedes is a well-engineered car and a large apartment on Park Avenue with a doorman does provide comfort, safety, and convenience, but their real value lies in the fact that only the rich can afford them.

Biologists have recognized this phenomenon among other animals. The peacock has a large decorative tail that has no survival value and is, in fact, a severe impediment. But peahens find these displays very sexy and the larger the tail, the greater the turn-on. Why should peahens choose males whose sons are going to be similarly afflicted? One possibility is that only a strong, healthy male can afford to grow and carry around such a burden and live long enough to breed (Zahavi and Zahavi, 1996). The peacock's tail would thus be his Mercedes, a proof that he carries genes that will produce high-quality sons and daughters.

Of course a beautiful tail or a flashy car is no guarantee that a male will hang around after he copulates. To insure that he does, females need to make males spend their resources on them. Any large expenditure of resources would make a male less likely to leave after copulation to seek another female, assuming that his resources are finite and if he has reason to expect that the next female would demand the same effort. Better yet—from the female's perspective—this expenditure should be of direct value to her, should the male take a powder. A single, "perfect rose" may have sentimental value (and possibly suggest something about the prospect of male "good behavior"), but a diamond engagement ring has real value that serves as a bond attesting far more to his serious intentions.

The danger to the reproductive future of a woman and her family from her being impregnated and subsequently abandoned by a male is so great that in almost all cultures, sexual relations are regulated by law and custom. Thus, although copulation itself is among the most private of human activities, it is at the same time widely regarded as a matter of concern to the entire community. Marriage is and has always been recognized as a form of contract. Contracts exist when the values exchanged by each party to a transaction occur at different times. This is certainly true for copulation. The man gains a great portion of his potential genetic reward at the moment of conception. In exchange, he is supposed to provide, over time, appropriate behavior and material assistance in raising the child. Marriage as an institution exists to enforce this contract.

Even when contracts are not legally enforceable, they can still be effective since a public breach of contract will have an adverse affect on the guilty party's reputation. This partially explains why marriage is always an important social event, celebrated and—even more important—publicly acknowledged by friends and relatives of both the bride and groom. By making marriage a public event, the bride and her family guarantee that the entire community knows of the sexual contract. Therefore, any subsequent abandonment of the wife will have severe negative implications for the man's reputation and his relationships with other members of the community, particularly other potential mates.

This might help explain why in Europe and North America it is so often the custom for the bride's family to pay for the wedding. As divorce has become more prevalent, the value of any dowry should diminish, yet it appears that at least for middle- and upper middle-class Americans, the expense of weddings has not diminished in recent decades. Perhaps the increased frequency of divorce has inclined many a bride's family to buy a kind of insurance policy against subsequent male abandonment.

There is another reason. Dowry payments can be adaptive in monogamous societies in which men invest heavily in their children. In such cases it can easily "pay" for the parents of a daughter to help her "purchase" a worthy man. This should be especially true in monogamous cultures that are highly stratified socio-economically, because in such cases, there is a substantial difference between the perceived value of wealthy *versus* impoverished men. Dowry payments, interestingly, are fifty times more prevalent in socio-economically stratified monogamous cultures than in cultures that are non-stratified, or polygynous (Gaulin and Boster, 1990). Once again, people are intuitively good evolutionary economists.

Truth in Advertising

Evolutionary theorist Alan Grafen (among others) has wrestled with the question of truthfulness in male advertising; specifically, can males deceive females into thinking they are of higher quality than they really are? Is that Rolex real, or is it a knock-off? Do you own that Mercedes, or did you borrow it from your uncle? Grafen (1990) developed a mathematical model of sexual advertising based on four basic assumptions:

1.   Males vary in real quality.

2.   Females can't perceive male quality directly but have to rely on male advertising.

3.   Males know their own quality.

4.   Females can evolve rules of their own, such as "Believe males," or "Ignore all advertising," or "Assume the opposite of what a man says."

Grafen was able to demonstrate the existence of an evolutionarily stable system with the following properties:

a.   It is optimal for males to choose a level of advertising that displays their true quality.

b.   Females are right to trust male advertising.

c.   The best advertising is costly. This is the reason that a particular form of advertising is chosen. It imposes real burdens that can't be faked and which reduce the fitness of lower-quality males.

d.   Lower-quality males face a greater risk from a high level of advertising than do higher-quality males.

These results are important, carrying implications beyond sexual advertising. They are consistent with one of the theories economists have developed to explain why large firms selling nearly identical products often spend so much on non-informative advertising. The sole point of such advertising is to prove that the firm is successful and profitable enough to afford it, telling the world, in effect, that the firm has too much at stake to risk its reputation by producing sub-standard products.

Grafen's results also suggest why the rich and powerful engage in so much conspicuous consumption, expenditures that seem to do little to directly enhance their fitness. They are advertising their wealth in a way that cannot be copied by those with fewer resources, calling to mind the famous potlatch ceremonies of Pacific Northwest Native Americans, in which valuable resources were conspicuously and competitively destroyed, with the "winners" being those whose losses cannot be matched by others.

The theory of sexual advertising that we have been discussing leads to a testable hypothesis. We would expect that in small, stable, homogeneous societies where individuals and families have detailed knowledge about their neighbors, there would be less benefit from costly displays to both the advertiser and the consumer than among more anonymous societies in which information about potential mates is difficult to come by. In fact, the success of such groups as the Amish and the Hasidim may be augmented by the fact that their rules prohibit the types of wasteful, ostentatious displays common in the larger society. The resources saved can be invested in children or in other forms of productive capital. The closed and intimate nature of these groups insures that members can acquire accurate information about other members at relatively low cost.

Arranged marriages, which are also common in traditional societies, are another way of reducing the cost of sexual advertising. A professional marriage broker can specialize in acquiring accurate information for his or her clients, which is no different from the use of real estate brokers to reduce the search cost of buying or selling a house.

In Grafen's model, males do the advertising. But there are plenty of wealthy women who engage in conspicuous consumption. Presumably, they are signaling either their wealth or their husband's. If the latter, then their intention is probably not sexual. (Why would they announce to potential female competitors the superior qualities of their spouses?) Perhaps they do it to please their husbands, serving as walking billboards announcing their husband's success. This is unlikely; most women do not have to be pressured into wearing diamond rings or expensive dresses. We think it more probable that conspicuous female consumption is intended to demonstrate to their peers how much their husbands love and value them, as well as perhaps signaling that they are so well-off that they are likely to be well-protected and zealously guarded. It is also likely that women are advertising the wealth of their nuclear family on behalf of their children, in order to attract higher-quality spouses for them.

Studies of "mate retention strategies" have also found interesting correlations between the husband's income and the frequency with which wives engage in "enhanced marital vigilance, appearance enhancement, possessive ornamentation and submission, and self-abasement" (Buss, 1999). By contrast, mate retention strategies on the part of men are more closely correlated with their wives' youthfulness, perceived attractiveness and risk of infidelity, all of which is consistent with the male-female differences already described.

In chapter 5, we listed four types of expenditures, namely, maintenance (resources required by an individual to maximize lifetime income), those contributing to both the quantity and the quality of offspring (and other kin), and finally, investment in non-human capital. To this list, we must now add a fifth type of expenditure: spending to enhance status, to advertise an individual's genes, behavior and resources in competition for mates for one's self as well as one's offspring.

In general, spending on status can be considered an intermediary good, something that facilitates the production of long-run fitness. As we shall see in chapter 7, devoting resources to enhancing status can also be beneficial in enhancing one's earning potential and/or that of one's descendants. Since the effects of spending on status persist over time, it has the attributes of a capital good. People will invest in it until its rate of return is equal to the return on other available investments. Therefore, the theory of extended fitness maximization leads to two more categories of testable propositions.

First, people will devote their energy and resources to five types of activities:

1. Activities that enhance or maintain their productive power.

2. Producing children.

3. Investing in the quality of their children.

4. Acquiring physical or non-human capital.

5. Altering how others view them so as to facilitate the previous four goals.

Second, people will spend resources on each of these activities until the rate of return on the last dollar spent is equal for all of them. Otherwise, it would be possible to enhance long-run genetic fitness by shifting resources from those activities yielding a lower rate of return to those yielding a higher rate. This view is in direct contrast to that of Kaplan who argues that much of modern behavior is non-adaptive. "In fact, as wealth has increased over the course of the last century, none of the increase has been allocated to increased fertility, and all has been allocated to increased consumption and investment in embodied capital" (Kaplan, 1996, 125). The difference between his approach and ours is the difference between looking at short-run rather than long-run genetic fitness.

"Till Death Do You Part"

Despite their different sexual and reproductive interests, men and women must cooperate in at least the conceiving and most often in the rearing of children. To better understand human sexual strategies, let us abstract from the many qualities that distinguish competitors in the sexual marketplace, and assume that each man and woman can be characterized by two parameters, one signifying the individual's net wealth that is, resources available for reproduction, and the other signifying genetic quality. (Although good behavior is also crucially important, its incorporation will have to await a more sophisticated model.)

Consider the case of lifetime exclusive monogamy, in which each man and woman is permitted no more than one mate. Individuals will then sort themselves in a way similar in some respects to Becker's marriage market model described in chapter 3. In Becker's model, each participant enters a possible marriage with a given amount of resources. Due to the advantages of specialization, the total product of the joint household is greater than the sum each participant could produce by remaining single. The marriage market determines the division of household product between each husband and wife. An equilibrium sorting occurs when no man or woman would be better off together than they are with their current spouses; this equilibrium guarantees that the total additional output produced by the sum of all marriages is maximized. Each partner's utility depends solely on his or her share of the household's product.

However, in our model of extended fitness, as in any genetic fitness model, the utility of each spouse depends solely on the number of copies of his or her genes that will exist in some future generation. In the case of exclusive monogamy, each copy of the husband's genes can only be projected to the next generation when accompanied by his wife's genes, and vice versa. Thus, the genetic fate of each partner is intrinsically bound to the other. A couple then maximizes the number of its future descendants by investing its available resources in a manner that maximizes the net wealth of its shared offspring. In exclusive, monogamous marriages, anything that increases the utility of one partner increases that of the other: such a couple can be treated as having a single shared utility function. But this is true only *after* they are married. When choosing a mate, each individual tries to acquire one with the highest genetic quality, the best promised behavior, and the most resources. A spouse's high-quality genes will raise the anticipated quality of their shared children, just as fitness-enhancing behavior by either will enhance the payoff to both, as will the provisioning of reproductively relevant resources. (We must note at this point that even self-consciously hardheaded economists might argue for another consideration: love. Our response: love, in such situations, is the word used to designate the intense human emotional response to individuals who maximally meet these requirements.)

For the sake of argument, we now assume that a child's genetic qualities only affect the relationship between a child's future wage and the total cost of producing that child. In chapter 5, we showed that the total return from producing a child is equal to its future wage divided by the price of the child, where this price is equal to the fixed cost of producing one child plus the cost of the optimal investment in human capital. We showed that when every child is identical, the return on each child would, in equilibrium, be equal to the return on non-human capital. It is also true that when children differ in genetic endowment, they could easily have different returns. Even with an optimal investment in human capital, some will yield a rate of return higher than that available on physical capital, while others—who also have the optimal amount of human capital—will experience a below-market rate of return. We can therefore measure the genetic quality of any individual by "g," the ratio of his or her wage to the cost of producing that individual. In our monogamous marriage market model, every man and woman is judging and being judged by potential mates on the basis of two measures: g, his or her rate of return, and R, the quantity of resources he or she has available for reproduction.

In table 6.1, male number one, M1, has earned a rate of return of 10 percent on his cost of production and has 40 units of resources to invest in offspring. Female number one, F1, also has earned a ten

Table 6.1
Rates of Return and Resources of Three Hypothetical Males and Females and Expected Rates of Return and Resources of Offspring of Various Pairs

		Females (Rate of Return, Resources)		
		F_1 (10, 40)	F_2 (10, 60)	F_3 (20, 80)
Males (Rate of Return, Resources)	M_1 (10, 40)	*(10, 88)*	*(10, 110)*	*(15, 138)*
	M_2 (20, 60)	*(15, 115)*	*(15, 138)*	*(20, 168)*
	M_3 (40, 100)	*(25, 175)*	*(25, 200)*	*(30, 234)*

percent rate of return and has 40 units of resources. If they marry, they will have a total of 80 units to invest in offspring. For the sake of simplicity, we assume that any offspring produced by M1 and F1 will have a rate of return equal to the average of its parents. The children of M1 and F1 will have an expected rate of return on their cost of production of 10 percent and 88 units of resources (80 plus 8 due to the 10 percent return on their parental investment in them), to invest in their own children.

The matrix of table 6.1 gives the expected rate of return and the resources available to the offspring of all potential marriages. As you would expect, the quantity of resources available to each individual is correlated with his or her rate of return. Even if all men and women had received similar investments in human capital from their parents, those with the highest genetic quality would earn a higher rate of return on this investment and would earn a higher income. In addition, higher-quality individuals will likely have had higher-quality parents who will have bequeathed them more non-human capital as well.

M1 would maximize his genetic fitness by marrying F3, but she can do better. F3 will do best by marrying M3 and F3 is also the best match available to M3. Once these two individuals are married, the best M1 can do is F2, but she can do better by marrying M2, and is also his best match. M1 is stuck with F1 and F1 can do no better than he. There is pure assortive mating, one of the most robust aspects of human mate selection; the richest, most handsome and highest quality men marry the richest, most beautiful and highest quality women, and vice versa.

This result is different from Becker's model, in which individuals who produce the highest valued joint product will marry. In Becker's model, those couples that produce the highest value added over what they could produce if they remained single, will marry. In ours, the only product individuals are concerned about is extended fitness. In this idealized monogamous world, no product can be produced by remaining single. Also, since the only product that enters the utility function is descendants, and all descendants are the joint product of both spouses, there is no way to divide up the output of the marriage between the two partners.

In Becker's model, there will be assortive mating only when male human capital and female human capital are complementary, that is, when they enhance each other's productivity. In Becker's world, one should not see rich lawyers marrying each other. Two individuals who totally specialize in market-oriented human capital will not add anything to each other's productivity. Our theory does not depend on pure economic gains from trade to justify marriage. This is not to deny gains from specialization in household production, but rather, we assert that such gains are a secondary feature of the marriage market. The primary activity is the formation of an alliance to advance the genetic interest of both parties.

Because of bequests and the variation caused by sexual reproduction, it is not always true that individuals with the highest level of resources will also have the highest level of genetic quality. It is not uncommon for rich, highly competent parents to produce ne'er-do-well heirs. (Consider, in addition, well-known genetic defects such as hemophilia, associated with certain lines of European royalty, apparently because of excessive inbreeding.) When there exists such a disparity in available "goods," the decisions faced by participants in the marriage market become more complicated.

Suppose we add an additional male, M4, to our market. This incompetent heir has a rate of return of zero and resources of 135. His offspring with F3 would have a rate of return of ten and resources of 236.5. Should F3 choose him over M3 since the mating of F3 and M4 produces children with slightly higher resources? This would obviously be a mistake. For a slight gain in resources (about 1 percent), F3 would be substantially lowering the expected quality and future rate of return of her children (from 30 to 10 percent). The grandchildren resulting from a M3 marriage would be expected to have a higher rate of return than those from a M4 marriage. Their higher earning power could easily make up the small difference in resources produced by these two potential marriages. By mating with M3, F3 gets to use M3's high-quality genes to advance her own genetic interest. This linkage will last for many future generations, but will be reduced in importance as each member of future generations carries fewer and fewer genes contributed by F3 and M3.

Besides the direct gain of producing more competent children, higher-quality children make it easier to attract higher-quality mates for them. So, F3 has to decide between quality of genes and quantity of resources. She has to value the future benefits that higher-quality genes will bring to her descendants. Although this calculation is difficult and freighted with uncertainty, it is done all the time when dealing with non-human species. There is, for example, a well-defined market for stud services. Racehorse breeders and dairy farmers have no difficulty assessing the economic value of high-quality sperm, and will pay handsomely for it.

Remember that non-human capital is an alternative to investing in children. If the expected return from children of optimal quality is below the return from non-human capital, parents should choose to have relatively few children, investing their surplus reproductive resources in the higher yielding investments. (In the absence of close kin of exceptionally high quality, parents would not choose zero children). This is a partial explanation of why some of the very rich have relatively few children. By preserving their wealth, they can hope that their children will marry up in genetic quality. It is not uncommon to see an old moneyed family welcome a talented but poor son-in-law. Similarly, it is the hope of many bright but penniless young men to marry the "boss's daughter."

In societies where wealth is based on agricultural rents rather than on commercial success, considerations of genetic quality will be less relevant for the wealthy. When wealth depends primarily on inheritance, marriages will be arranged with less emphasis on the personal qualities of the partners than on what property they bring to the marriage.

Anthropological findings in this respect are especially suggestive. Thus, in polygynous societies there is a positive correlation between a woman's reproductive success and her husband's wealth (Borgerhoff Mulder, 1987; Mace, 1996). Moreover, although Americans and Europeans are particularly familiar with dowry payments, bridewealth payments (in which the man and his family pay the bride's family) are far more common, occurring in 66 percent of the 1267 societies listed in the Ethnographic Atlas (Murdock, 1967). Dowry payments, by contrast, are found in just 3 percent. This is what evolutionary theory predicts, since as we have seen, females are generally the limiting resource for the reproductive success of males. Furthermore, bridewealth payments are especially common in polygynous societies (found among more than 90 percent of them). When a small number of men monopolize many of the marriageable women, the remaining ones become especially scarce and thus, particularly valuable. To "get" them, men must pay, and they do.

Note also that in polygynous societies, wealthy parents can get an especially high reproductive payoff by directing their wealth disproportionately to their sons, which they also do (Borgerhoff Mulder,

1988). Not surprisingly, there is a strong cross-cultural correlation between polygyny and inheritance rules that favor sons (Hartung, 1982; Cowlishaw and Mace, 1996). At the same time—and as expected—there are very few societies that bias inheritance toward daughters, because in most cases, the fitness of daughters cannot be enhanced as readily as can that of sons.

At least one revealing exception has been uncovered, however (Cronk, 1994). The Mukogodo people of Kenya are in transition from a hunter-gatherer to a herding lifestyle; accordingly, most are poor, and socio-economically subordinate to adjacent tribes. As a result, a Mukogodo son is unlikely to obtain the necessary brideprice to obtain a wife, whereas a daughter has the prospect of "marrying up," thereby repaying the greater parental investment. Mukogodo sons have an average family size of three; that of daughters is nearly four. With regard to fitness, therefore, daughters appear to be better investments than are sons, and sure enough, Mukogodo parents typically invest more heavily in their daughters than in their sons, as measured by the provisioning of food, education, and medical care.

Mommie's Baby, Daddy's Maybe

If, in the marriage market model we presented above, the difference between the resources of M4 and M3 was very large, F3 would face an interesting possibility. Her situation would be greatly improved if somehow she could manage to acquire the wealth of M4 and the sperm of M3. The best way to accomplish this is obvious; marry M4 to gain access to his money, have an affair with M3 to get his sperm; convince M4 that she is a faithful wife while hoping M3 is the father of her children. (Barach and Lipton, 2002).

F3 is not the only woman with an incentive to cheat. In our original example, shown in table 6.1, F1 could do no better than M1. Not only was her husband poor, but he was also of low genetic quality. No man of greater quality or wealth would be willing to marry her. But she also has an alternative to improve her situation. She marries M1 to get his meager resources—as well as his behavioral assistance—for her children, and convinces M3 to donate a little sperm for her cause (which also becomes his). Her outcome is less favorable than that of F3, but even though she has less money, she has access to the same quality sperm. Both these schemes depend on getting a high-quality male to cooperate, and on fooling the husband. Given the high genetic payoff to M3 of siring children who will inherit M4's money, F3 should not have to try hard to convince him to play along. With regard to F1, even though she is of low genetic quality and her husband is poor, the cost of sperm is so low that F1 should not find it hard to find a high-quality male with whom to have an affair.

Fooling the husband may prove more difficult. Both M1 and M4 realize their wives' temptation to cheat on them. They will likely exert great vigilance, therefore, in protecting the virtue of their wives. F1 and F3 have to balance the risk of getting caught and subsequent abandonment against the gain from increasing the genetic quality of their children.

M3 has less to worry about.[2] Since his wife can't find a higher-quality father for her children, she has no incentive to cheat on him. It is she who has to worry. Her husband is getting a lot of female attention. But as long as her husband is contributing nothing but sperm to the others, her vital reproductive interests are not threatened. She has little to fear from either low-quality F1 or even from F3, who is not likely to give up her rich husband. She would only have to fear a rich, high-quality female who can offer her husband a better total deal. This is one reason for the double standard.[3] Cheating by wives poses a high long-term evolutionary threat to their husbands, whereas cheating by husbands need not pose much of a threat to their wives.

However, this is not quite accurate. A high-quality wife does have something to lose from her husband's extramarital relationships. A high-quality, wealthy man may find it optimal to divert resources to aid in the rearing of his illegitimate offspring. It is therefore significant, and confirmatory of our fitness-minded perspective, that men find the prospect of their mate being *sexually* involved with someone else to be especially upsetting whereas women are particularly agitated by the prospect of their mate being *emotionally* involved with another person (Buss et al., 1992). Once again, men are primarily threatened by genetic cuckoldry on the part of their wives, who in turn are especially vulnerable to diversion of the husband's resources. Fitness threats for the former are therefore primarily heralded by sexual involvement, and for the latter, by emotional involvement.

From the perspective of wives, strong laws or social stigma against divorce and adultery reduce the threat posed by their husband's extracurricular activities. Although he is less able to leave her or recognize his illegitimate children, in genetic terms, men such as M3 are still in the catbird seat; they get to attract a high-quality mate and raise a high-quality family, but still—in a system practicing the "double standard"—have the opportunity to sow their wild oats and, with a little bit of luck get some other man to support his illegitimate children.

Recent findings suggest that adultery—and the production of children as a consequence—is more common than previously believed, and that the anatomy and physiology of human sperm production may reflect male-male competition taking place within the vaginal tract (Baker and Bellis, 1995). In addition, the use of DNA fingerprinting in field studies of animal behavior has revealed that even among many supposedly monogamous species—notably passerine birds, long thought the epitome of monogamous fidelity—upwards of 20 percent of the offspring are produced by "extra-pair copulations" (Birkhead and Moller, 1992; Barash and Lipton, 2002).

In such cases, male motivation is easily understood: increased numbers of possible offspring. Female motivation is more complex, generally involving such considerations as increased probability of fertilization, increased genetic quality of offspring, enhanced access to the resources of the "extra-pair" male, additional assistance by the "extra-pair" male in provisioning offspring as well as in defending them against predators, and—perhaps especially in some primates—insurance against infanticide on the part of males who might have fathered the offspring in question. In any event, no single consideration appears to be paramount; different factors are more prominent in particular species (Westneat, Sherman, and Morton, 1990).

Among animals, both males and females run risks by seeking extra-pair copulations, notably the prospect of abandonment by the cuckolded mate, as well as the risk of enduring a violent response. Among human beings, this risk appears especially great. Sexual jealousy is a prime ingredient in the great majority of spouse killings (Wilson and Daly, 1992), and in marital conflicts that result in lesser forms of violence. This phenomenon can be self-reinforcing. Low-quality males are likely to realize, as described above, that the loyalty of their wives is tenuous and that paternity of her children may be questionable. This could leave them less willing to devote all their reproductive resources to the maintenance of those children. In chapter 4, we related the work of Hamilton that shows an individual maximizes its inclusive fitness by expending resources of behalf of relatives (including children) based on the degree to which those relatives share the individual's genes. A man should therefore value a child in direct proportion to his confidence that he is the child's father.

Among species that experience internal fertilization, such as human beings, one of the great asymmetries of the biological world concerns confidence of genetic relatedness: females have it, males don't. Significantly, such confidence correlates strongly with care of offspring. In those species for which fertilization occurs outside the female's body—notably fishes and amphibians—males and females are about equally likely to partake in childcare. When fertilization is internal—notably in birds, mammals and reptiles—childcare is female-biased. And when females are specially adapted to nourish the young (notably mammals), childcare is overwhelmingly a female task.

Indeed, it can be argued that part of the reason why male mammals are generally so non-paternal is that females, not males, have functional breasts. But there is no convincing physiological or anatomical reason why males couldn't lactate; evolution has produced more remarkable adaptations than this, and moreover, male lactation would seem not only fair, but efficient, given that a mammalian mother has already undergone the stress of pregnancy and birth. But only females do so, almost certainly because among mammals it is they—and not the males—who enjoy sufficient confidence in their genetic relatedness that they are selected to make the huge additional investment that lactation entails.

Significantly, those unusual species of mammals that demonstrate paternal behavior tend to be monogamous (beavers, foxes, gibbons, marmosets), such that the males in question have a relatively high confidence of being the father.

Human beings can and do behave paternally, and yet, it is a cross-cultural universal that fathers do less fathering than mothers do mothering. The importance of parental certainty in this respect is highlighted by the following research, which is so robust in its confirmation as to have surprised even many evolutionary biologists. Consider this: since fathers are necessarily less confident of their parenthood than are mothers, this asymmetry should be exaggerated when an additional generation intervenes. Thus, the least confident grandparents should be paternal grandfathers, who are connected to their grandchildren by two father-father (FaFa) links, each of them necessarily somewhat uncertain. By contrast, maternal grandmothers (MoMo), with their two mother-mother links, should be the grandparents with the greatest genetic confidence, whereas maternal grand-fathers (MoFa) and paternal grandmothers (FaMo), each with one high-confidence maternal link and one low-confidence paternal link should be in between.

Surveys evaluating this prediction among American college students with all four living grandparents found precisely this relationship, as measured by feelings of emotional closeness, amount of time spent with the subjects, and gifts received from the respective grandparents (DeKay, 1995). Comparable findings were subsequently found from a sample of students in Germany (Euler and Weitzel, 1996). In the same vein, maternal aunts (mother's sisters) were predicted to invest more than paternal aunts (father's sisters), just as maternal uncles (mother's brothers) should invest more than paternal uncles (father's brothers). This too has been confirmed (Gaulin et al., 1997), providing yet more evidence that human beings tend to invest in children proportional to their confidence of genetic connectedness.

It is also interesting in this respect that nearly one-third of human societies practice a kind of "mother's brother" form of child responsibility, in which the primary "father figure" is not a child's father but rather, its mother's brother. This has been cited as evidence against an evolutionary view of family structure, since the mother's brother is at most related to a child by a factor of 1/4, whereas the father is related by 1/2 (Sahlins, 1976). Further investigation, however, revealed that such systems are in fact among the exceptions that confirm, if not prove, the rule of genetic relevance: "mother's brother" societies are typically characterized by sexual mores such that the mother's husband is likely to have a low level of paternal confidence. By contrast, the mother is guaranteed to be related (by 1/2) to her offspring, and her brother is likewise guaranteed to be related (by at least 1/4) to her; as a result, a mother's brother has a guaranteed relatedness to his nieces and nephews of at least 1/8 (i.e., 1/2 x 1/4). In such cases, men are behaving adaptively by favoring a 1/8 return over one that might be as low as zero (Hartung, 1985).

In modern Western societies as well, people invest parentally in proportion as they are genetically related. For example, a trio of anthropologists investigated the impact of paternity uncertainty on the tendency of men in Albuquerque, New Mexico to invest in their children's college education (Anderson, Kaplan, and Lancaster, 1997). All three of their hypotheses were confirmed: (1) more money was allocated to the men's children than to their stepchildren; (2) when paternity was uncertain, investment was less than when it was more certain; and (3) more was invested in children whose mother was a current mate than a former mate. (The latter finding suggests the use of paternal investment as a mate retention strategy.)

By reducing support for children of doubtful paternity, even in modern Western societies, the husband reduces the stake the wife has in the marriage and therefore in remaining faithful. Even when a wife is faithful and gives the husband no grounds for suspicion, the prevalence of adultery within the couple's social group could well diminish the husband's confidence in paternity, inclining him to withhold full support from his family, and thereby increasing the likelihood that his wife will engage in the very conduct the husband fears. In effect, the fear of adultery can become a self-fulfilling prophecy.

A male's concern over the paternity of "his" children is probably also related to child abuse. By weakening the male's commitment to the well being of "his" children, fear of cuckoldry is likely to increase the chances that the normal frictions of daily life will spill over into violence. While we are unaware of any study that links child abuse and adultery, there is abundant evidence that being raised by adults other than one's natural parents can be harmful to one's health (Daly and Wilson, 1996). In fact, being reared with nonbiological parents is by far the most serious risk factor ever identified for child abuse and neglect.

It is commonly stated that small children are the real victims of divorce. This typically refers to the sense of abandonment and other psychological problems these children experience. But, mental anguish may be the least of these children's worries. Since divorced individuals usually remarry eventually, their children must cope with one of the most dreaded figures of mythology, the stepparent. Fear of stepparents is more than just the stuff of fairy tales or the irrational emotional reaction of children resenting the displacement of a loved parent.

Daly and Wilson (1988) found that in 1976 in the United States, a child living with one or more stepparents was one hundred times more likely to die as a result of abuse than was a child living with biological parents. This finding is not particular to America. For example, in 1980, a Canadian child two years old or younger was seventy times more likely to be killed by one of its parents if it lived with a stepparent and a biological parent than if it lived with both biological parents. Although only a tiny fraction of children living with stepparents are killed, incidents of non-fatal child abuse are far more common when a stepparent is present in the household. Daly and Wilson (1988) also report that non-fatal child abuse is approximately forty times greater in a household with a stepparent compared to one with two biological parents.

These results should not be surprising or shocking to anyone familiar with evolutionary theory. Among animals, infanticide is well documented, and is typically performed by non-parental adults, most commonly after a male drives away the existing harem-master and takes over control of a group of females (e.g., Hrdy, 1979). Stepparents generally place little or no reproductive value on their stepchildren. Evolution would not favor the survival of genes that led individuals to squander their resources on non-relatives (unless, for example, they are rewarded for their tolerance and generosity by receiving reproductive benefits from their new spouse, as by enhancing the newly established pair bond).

In this discussion, incidentally, a distinction must be made between step parenting and adoption (see chapter 7). But do not miss the forest for the trees: we are not concerned with casting aspersions on stepparents, the great majority of which do remarkably well, under trying circumstances. Rather, we are emphasizing the degree to which parental investment is gene-directed.

Given that women are guaranteed to share genes with their offspring whereas men can only take their wives word for it—and given, further, that women have an interest in receiving an ongoing supply of parental investment from their mates—we can also predict that women and their families should seek to reassure their husbands as to paternity. A study of spontaneous observations on the part of family members immediately after childbirth found that adult family members are significantly more likely to comment on paternal than maternal resemblance to the child, as in "Oh look, he has his father's chin," or "She has her father's dimples." Not only that, but such comments are significantly more likely to come from the mother's family—who have a particular interest in convincing a potentially dubious male in-law (Daly and Wilson, 1982).

The Economics of Adultery?

Every adulterer requires a partner. It is in the wife's genetic interest to select the highest quality partner possible. If she had her druthers, and was safe from detection, she should select the most intelligent, healthy, ambitious, and successful male. If she is of lower socio-economic class, she may be able to entice her boss, or she might have to settle for someone in the neighborhood who shows more promise than her husband. She may even hope that this male will be willing to support her and her children, should her husband desert her. In such cases, infidelity becomes, in effect, both a cause of and an insurance policy against desertion.

Women are not alone in their vulnerability to adultery. Men, although otherwise happily married, will be tempted to engage in transitory reproductive activities with both single and married women. In fact, every married man must make the following calculation. How much of his limited resources should he invest in his wife's—and hopefully, his—children, and how much should he invest in extra-marital affairs? Although sperm are cheap, having an affair or maintaining a mistress often isn't. However, if someone else can be found who will support any resulting children, an extra-marital affair can still be a reproductive bargain.

A more respectable way to gain the genetic advantage of nonmarital sex is for a man to delay marriage. This accomplishes two things; it gives him the opportunity to "sow his wild oats" and the time to accumulate more resources so as to attract a more desirable wife. Some high-quality men, even those with relatively ample resources, will be so desirable as casual sexual partners that they may never marry. Such men are called playboys.

Men and women who engage in a strategy of nonmarital sex run various risks. Most obvious is disease. The human reproductive tract, being dark and moist, is a hospitable breeding ground for a range of bacteria and viruses. In addition, there is nothing like adultery to undermine trust in a marriage. Even though a husband's sexual dalliance does not put the parentage of his own children in doubt, adultery can undermine a wife's willingness to devote all her resources to their common venture. Most wives can be expected to resent their husbands' diversion of resources, regardless of the amount, as well as being rightfully concerned about diseases that an unfaithful husband may inadvertently transmit to her. Most importantly, she is likely to worry about possible alienation of affection, if, in his extra-marital wanderings, her husband finds a woman he considers superior to his wife. This fear could even induce her to hedge her bets by having an affair of her own.

Even if he doesn't leave her, there is always the danger that an out-of-wedlock child fathered by him may have an emotional, if not legal claim to some of his resources. After all, from a genetic point of view, it may be as good for him to invest in an illegitimate child, as in his legitimate children. He would be disinclined to support his illegitimate children only if such support would jeopardize other sources of support, such as from welfare, the mother's parents, or her husband. Also, he might withhold support if recognition of such children would cause him to bear other costs, such as the wrath of his wife or social disgrace. Another reason why men would be inclined to invest less in "their" illegitimate children is the uncertainty of paternity. The women likely to engage in such affairs are unlikely to limit themselves to one partner.

A common objection to any reproductive analysis of adultery is that it misses the point. Men and women, the argument goes, do not engage in extra-marital sex in order to maximize their genetic fitness, but for the purpose of sexual variety. After all, sleeping with the same man or woman, year after year, can get predictable and boring. Monogamy equals monotony, and the purpose of extra-marital sex is recreation, not reproduction. In answer, we point out first that adultery does result in the conception of some children, not only today but probably even more so in the past, when the bulk of our behavioral predispositions were established, and when birth control was substantially less effective, as well as less available. (Barash and Lipton, 2002).

Moreover, the above objection misses a deeper point, recognized by evolutionary biologists as the distinction between proximate and ultimate causation. The proximate causes of a given act include those factors immediately responsible for it; its ultimate cause is the adaptive significance, the evolutionary rationale for the behavior in question. For example, people and other living things eat because they are "hungry," which is mediated by a variety of factors (gastric motility, lowered blood sugar, time-conditioned responses, etc.) and not because they understand the biochemistry of digestion or even the connection between caloric intake and survival. Similarly, insofar as people seek out sexual partners, it is often for the various direct, proximate pleasures this may provide (gratification, danger, orgasmic release, and, especially in the case of men, sexual excitement associated with novelty itself), not "because" of ultimate reproductive pay-offs. But as with eating, there is every reason for confidence that such proximate mechanisms are means toward the ultimate end of fitness maximization.

Till Divorce Do Us Part

Adultery is not the only threat to monogamous "bliss." When divorce is a viable option, the sexual strategies of men and women are substantially altered. The extent to which men and women's optimal reproductive behavior changes is likely to depend on the nature of the legal and social constraints that control divorce. In the current American situation of basically no-fault divorce and little or no social stigma attached to divorce, men and women enter marriage with a different set of expectations and different reproductive options than did their grandparents.

In a traditional marriage, both parties gain because the male trades material resources (along with very little biologically mandated parental investment) for the comparatively scarce material resources (along with large biologically mandated parental investment) of the female. Because the relative cost of reproduction is so much greater for the woman, she benefits from a long-run commitment of support to raise her children and to prevent exploitation by the man.[4]

Men are more or less willing to enter into marriage for three principal reasons. First, it is the price demanded by the market for reproductive services, that is, for sexual access to a woman of sufficient quality and virtue. Second, it is the best way to guarantee that an optimum amount of human capital will be invested in each of his children. And third, there are gains from division of labor within the household.

We can distinguish between two types of divorce, those that occur during the wife's prime reproductive years and those occurring after her prime childbearing years are over. Divorce during the early years of marriage, particularly before the arrival of children, can be considered simply a failure of the marriage market. People can't conceivably obtain detailed and accurate information about a large number of potential mates. They usually make their decisions with incomplete information and after a relatively limited search. We suggest that early divorce occurs when one or both parties discover the prospect of making a better match. Given that the couple has probably not yet accumulated much property and especially if there is no child to support, there is little cost to divorce for the spouse that has found a better opportunity. The situation for the other spouse is less sanguine. At best, he or she will have to undertake the cost of a new search, and there is no guarantee of finding a mate of comparable quality. (At the same time, it may be better for all concerned if the departing spouse's disposition to "cut and run" is revealed earlier in a marriage rather than later.)

Any heightened uncertainty about the permanence of marriage should reduce the incentive of both husband and wife to make large investments, and this in turn could further endanger their marriage. Women in particular should be hesitant to undertake a pregnancy early in an uncertain marriage (although some people attempt to have a child "to save the marriage"). Because a young divorcee with a child generally finds it more difficult to attract a replacement mate, it would be in her interest to wait and see if the marriage has staying power. Ease of divorce also encourages both spouses to continue looking.

Newly married people can continue to remain in the marriage market, forever looking for a better "deal." Studies have shown the divorce rate to be much higher when young marrieds live in proximity to each other than when they live in a more heterogeneous environment.

Remaining in the marriage market aggravates the natural paranoia of each spouse concerning the other's sexual fidelity. This is particularly true for the male who fears the genetic consequence to him of being cuckolded. To some extent, therefore, easy divorce increases behavior that tends to produce divorce, another self-fulfilling prophecy. And, as divorce becomes more frequent, there is more incentive for young couples to remain in the marriage market, if only for self-defense: Better to have a replacement handy, just in case your spouse decides to bail out of the marriage.

Early divorce probably carries a greater load of negative consequences for the reproductive success of the wife. Since her reproductive years are more limited than her husband's, and since fertility in women declines with age, anything that interrupts her reproductive activity can substantially reduce her chance of having the number of children she desires. For women in particular, fertility delayed is fertility denied. But, in general, the cost and gains from divorce are basically similar for both sexes.

As soon as children enter a marriage, the dynamics change. If before marriage a man must win the heart of the woman, after children, a woman must keep the loyalty of her mate. During pregnancy and for a considerable time after childbirth, a woman needs substantial support. Thus, a woman might fear that her husband will seek other sexual partners during her pregnancy, when sexual contact with her has no direct reproductive value. The insecurity women feel during the latter months of pregnancy and the continuing need for reassurances about their husband's love is far from irrational. Who knows whether the husband may dally during this period, and if so, what the consequences might be? He may decide to "stick" her with the baby hoping that someone, such as her family or society as a whole will provide support.

Once a baby enters a marriage, the balance of power shifts substantially. Before, the wife's ability to provide or refuse sex gives her substantial power. After all, there is an excess demand for women. After a child arrives, the leverage of the husband increases. Unless there is an adequate substitute for the level of support provided by the husband, the wife has a lot more to lose from a breakup of the marriage than does the husband. It is easier for the man to replace the wife and child than it is for a woman with a young child to find a man who is willing to support someone else's child. (Among many non-technological societies, a child without a father is substantially at risk, and is often killed as a precondition of the mother remarrying.) Even where child support laws are adequately enforced, they rarely compensate the woman adequately for the time she must spend raising the child and for her lost division of labor within the marriage.

For Better or Worse

In our model of the marriage market presented above, we assumed that people have full and accurate information about the genetic quality and lifetime income of themselves and their potential partners. Since in the real world, most first marriages occur near the beginning of a person's reproductive and working life, individuals must base their judgements on partial information. In time, more accurate estimates of income ("good resources") and inclination ("good behavior) will become apparent. Since men specialize in market activity, there will be, in general, a greater variance between their actual and expected lifetime incomes than there is for women. And any substantial deviation between actual and expected should lead the partners to re-evaluate the reproductive strategies, including choice of mate.

When new information becomes available early in a marriage, the results are fairly predictable. A husband who is much more successful than expected will tend to re-evaluate his marriage. All of a sudden, the wonderful girl he was lucky to marry doesn't seem as smart or pretty. She has failed to "grow" as much as he has. The husband finds, perhaps for the first time in his life, that beautiful women are attracted to him. His success seems to have made him taller, more intelligent, and handsomer, at least in the eyes of other women. In the recent past, it was not uncommon for a young wife to accept menial jobs and deny her own professional advancement while helping her husband through law school or medical school, only to have him leave her—comparatively unprepared for an economically successful life—as his own prospects improved.

On the other hand, should the husband prove a failure, the shoe is on the other foot. Now all his faults, which she once overlooked, loom large. She suddenly finds her male acquaintances far more interesting than before. If she already has children, she may not be able to find another man willing to take on these responsibilities, and might then have to settle for what she already has, perhaps with an occasional dalliance on the side.

Of course, not all spouses respond in this fashion. Many remain loyal to their partner, taking their marriage vows seriously. But any severe and unexpected change in economic circumstances doubtless places a strain on a marriage, as it will on any commercial contract.

Early in a marriage, such strains are roughly symmetrical, as we have described. But with the arrival of children, things change. Indeed, the response to changing economic circumstances is generally asymmetrical, with the husband getting the better of the situation. Once a wife is past her prime reproductive years, her options are essentially closed. Since she is unlikely to bear more children, and is typically seen as less attractive as well (such diminished attractiveness is a proximate signal of reduced reproductive potential), she is unlikely to find a more successful man to replace a husband who has suffered an economic reverse. The clearest reproductive strategy open to her is to maximize resources for her existing children, or otherwise aid them in their reproductive efforts.

The evolution of menopause is probably relevant here. Thus, women are unusual, if not unique, in experiencing a shutdown in their reproductive potential while still facing several decades of life.

A promising explanation has come to be known as the "grandmother hypothesis," whereby menopause might well be adaptive in view of the increasing risk of morbidity and mortality associated with a pregnancy late in life, combined with the fact that among human beings, middle- aged and older women are likely to have something of value to convey to their offspring, namely, assistance in rearing *their* children, who are the grandchildren of the post-menopausal women. Insofar as it is valid—and studies of South American hunter-gatherers suggest that it is (Hill and Hurtado, 1991)—the grandmother hypothesis for the evolution of menopause is entirely consistent with the underlying theme of this book: that human beings are profoundly motivated to act in support of their fitness.

The foregoing also suggests a potentially important and hitherto unrecognized source of domestic stress among middle-aged couples. Assume that post-menopausal women have in fact been selected to maximize their fitness by helping care for their grandchildren (genetic return = 1/4), since it is no longer effective for them to produce additional children (genetic return =1/2). Although their middle-aged husbands will also profit genetically by such investment in their grandchildren, these men stand to do better yet by producing additional children, with each of whom they would share 1/2 their genes. The stage is thus set for middle-aged men to leave their post-menopausal wives, for younger women whose fertility is still high. After all, even though older men produce sperm in diminished numbers and with reduced viability, they remain capable of fathering children into old age.

Evolutionary economics suggests that this scenario is all the more likely, since it is not uncommon for men to acquire status and wealth as they age. Such men can offer a young woman abundant resources plus even the promise of good behavior, while his genetic contribution is not substantially diminished. It is interesting that whereas youth is considered essential to female sex appeal in every human society, "mature" men are more likely to maintain their attractiveness. This is why middle-aged, physically unappealing men such as Henry Kissinger have been considered "sexy," whereas, as former Congresswoman Patricia Schroeder once ruefully noted, middle-aged congresswomen don't seem to have nearly the same sex appeal as their male colleagues!

Thus, the age preferences of both men and women for prospective mates reflects consistent sex differences in their respective reproductive strategies: whereas young men are comfortable with women who are about their age, older men tend to prefer women who are significantly younger than themselves (that is, those women considered desirable, by both young and old men, are those who are still fertile). By contrast, women are much less likely to be "turned off" by older men than men are by older women (Kenrick and Keefe, 1992).

Serial monogamy, in which a man goes from wife to wife, is little different from polygyny. In both cases, high status males command a great deal of resources and monopolize the prime reproductive years of more than one woman. By giving some men disproportionate access to a number of fertile women, serial monogamy, like polygyny, results in a shortage of mates for less successful males, increasing the competition among men for women

Here Come the Brides

Every human society has some system of institutionalizing sexual unions between men and women. Of these, the rarest by far is polyandry, in which one woman marries several men. Polyandry's rarity makes sense in terms of evolutionary economics, since it requires men to acquiesce in, what is for them, a distinctly sub-optimal and inefficient means of assuring their own fitness. After all, since the maximum reproductive success of any woman is strictly limited, and only one husband can be the father of her children at any given time, most of the co-husbands are in a genetically disadvantageous situation.

In this regard, it is noteworthy that there is a strong predisposition toward fraternal polyandry; in those highly unusual situations in which polyandry arises, the co-husbands are very likely to be brothers. Under such an arrangement, even though a man may not become a father, he is at least guaranteed to be an uncle (and thereby gain an inclusive fitness benefit via the child or children he assists). Similar patterns have been found among many animals, such as lions, in which brothers are especially likely to share the same pride (Bertram, 1978).

As to polygyny, its evolutionary economics are in principle the same as presented in our standard model. To illustrate this point, let us assume for the moment that all men and women are equal in genetic quality and in the amount of human capital invested in them. The only difference among men is the amount of non-human capital inherited from their parents. For now, also assume that women do not inherit non-human capital. The optimal investment in the human capital of each child still occurs when the return in increased future wages from the last dollar invested in the human capital of a child is equal to the return from non-human capital.

Since women face a biological limit to the number of children they can produce, the cost of having an additional child rises as a woman has more children. To maximize her fitness, a woman will continue to produce children of the optimal quality until the cost of producing a child exceeds the discounted value of the child's future wages.

Men, by contrast, face no effective biological constraint on the number of children they can father. By adding wives, they can continue to produce children that yield a higher rate of return than that available on non-human capital. The number of wives a man can have is limited only by his resources and his ability to monitor their fidelity. Since, taken as a whole, the children of a woman are a better investment than non-human capital, a man should add wives as long as resources permit, or until the additional cost of monitoring additional wives erases the gain from more children.

Figure 6.3 presents a visual representation of this situation. Wife number #1 will produce N1 children, and the last child she produces has a cost not greater than the discounted value of that child's future return on investment; the average cost of her children is below the cost of her last child. Given the cost of adjudicating disputes among

Figure 6.3
Optimal Number of Children

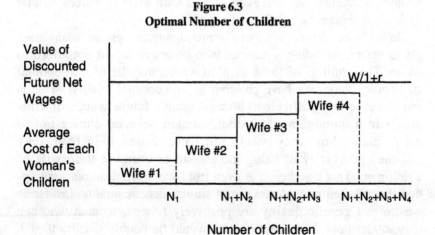

wives and the cost of guaranteeing their fidelity, the average cost of a wife's children increases with each wife (although there may be economies of scale insofar as wives can be induced to care for each other's offspring). In our example, the husband would, like all good Muslims, have no more than four wives. Even if he had sufficient resources, he should not have more than this, because at that point he would increase the resources available to his children—especially his sons—by investing in non-human capital. (In practice, very wealthy, observant Muslim men by-passed the limitation of four wives by having numerous concubines.)

Since each wife is assumed identical, each will have the same number of children, and each child will receive the same investment in human capital. Every husband has to provide each of his wives sufficient resources such that, combined with her contribution, she can afford the total cost of her children. A notable feature of polygynous mating systems is that—contrary to the popular view, in which they oppress women—a case can be made that they actually promote women's equality. No longer is the prosperity of the wife and her children dependent on the prosperity of the husband she can attract. No longer is the wealth of a very rich man permitted only to benefit one woman. With polygyny, the competition of the marriage market insures that all women of similar quality receive the same resources from their husband. (In biological parlance, polygyny results in a so-called "ideal free distribution," a situation of evolutionary stability in which the pay-off to each woman is equal. Recall the polygyny threshold model discussed earlier, as a result of which females distribute themselves in accord with male resources so that each, on average, is equally successful.)

On the other hand, in a strictly monogamous system, many men get to marry, including a number who otherwise could not afford to do so. The families of these men, however, may be of non-optimal size and/or they may have children of non-optimal quality. (This is true because it is difficult to borrow against future wages of children.) In a monogamous system, women have no choice but to marry men whom they would not have chosen if instead, they had the opportunity of being the second or even the third wife of a rich man. This conclusion is even truer when we drop our assumption that all men and women are of similar genetic quality. Insofar as wealth and genetic quality are positively related, women who can only attract poor, low-quality males would be doubly disadvantaged.

Under monogamy, assortive mating can be expected: rich men of high genetic quality tending to marry women who are similarly endowed.

Monogamy is thus egalitarian with respect to men, but has the opposite effect for women. High-quality, rich men would prefer polygyny, as would resource-poor or low-quality women. Monogamy benefits rich or high-quality women who get to monopolize a man with similar attributes, and poor or low-quality men who otherwise could not afford to marry. By limiting the number of wives that rich men can "consume," monogamy in effect reduces the prices of wives to a level that all but the most disadvantaged males can afford.

At least one economist has already noticed this:

> Today, when my wife and I argue about who should do the dishes, we start from positions of roughly equal strength. If polygamy were legal, my wife could hint that she's thought about leaving me to marry Alan and Cindy down the block—and I might end up with dishpan hands. (Landsburg, 1993, p. 170)

The major beneficiaries of monogamy appear to be men rather than women, for two reasons: it reduces the bargaining power of women, while also reducing the potentially violent consequences (to men) of high levels of male-male competition, something that is especially characteristic of polygyny.

Polygyny results in a larger number of superfluous men than does monogamy. What happens to men who cannot afford to buy a wife in a polygynous society or to attract and maintain a wife in a monogamous one? What do they do with the few reproductive resources they can accumulate? After all, you can't buy half a wife or produce half a child.

Such disadvantaged men have several alternatives. First, they can provide their surplus resources to a brother or sister or other close relative to aid them in their reproductive effort (i.e., they could seek to enhance their inclusive fitness via the "indirect" or "kin selected" component). In terms of genes, their relative's children will only be worth a fraction of what their own would be worth, but if this is their only alternative, something is better than nothing. But there are other alternatives. The individual male who has only a fraction of the resources required to produce a child may gamble with his resources, hoping to win enough to reproduce. Consider two brothers, neither of whom has enough resources to produce a child. They could pool their resources to allow one brother to father a child.[5] The lucky brother will be able to reproduce 1/2 of his genes while the losing brother gets to reproduce, on average, 1/4 of his genes. If the brothers flip a coin to decide who gets to mate, the expected genetic return from the gamble is .375, equal to the probability of winning times the genetic payoff from winning plus the probability of losing times the genetic payoff from losing. If our individual did not have a brother to gamble with and had to play with a stranger, the expected genetic return is only .25. Unlike the case of the brother winning, there is no genetic return from the child of a stranger. The expected return from a gamble with a stranger is exactly the same as from gifting the resources to a sister or brother who have only half the resources necessary to produce an additional child.

The general conclusion that can be drawn from this example is that males whose genetic quality or economic prospects put them below the reproductive threshold will be more inclined to take risks to better their situation than will their better endowed colleagues. Such risk taking can take many forms, from gambling to engaging in more hazardous occupations including crime. Criminal activity, whether it involves so called victimless crimes such as drugs or illegal gambling, or crimes against persons and property, is predominantly engaged in by poor young males who have a lot to gain and nothing to lose. From a genetic point of view, the enforced celibacy of prison is no worse than the celibacy enforced by economic circumstances.

Evolutionary economics of this sort are revealed among the Gusii people of Kenya. During the late 1930s, brides were expensive, costing a man from eight to twelve cows, one to three bulls, and eight to twelve goats. As a result, many younger men couldn't afford a wife, and both livestock-theft and rape soared. As one anthropologist summarized it:

> When a Gusii man lacks the economic means for a legitimate bridewealth marriage and does not have the personal attractiveness or seductive skill needed to persuade a girl to elope with him, he may resort to desperate measures. (R. A. LeVine, 1977)

Later, when marriage prices went down, so did the Gusii crime rate. Several decades after that, in the 1960s and 1970s, when the brideprice climbed again, the frequency of theft and of rape did the same.

Although most crime is only indirectly involved with sex, rape is, by definition, sexual. Some argue that rape is less about sex than about power, that rape is an expression of male dominance. This leaves the question: why do men wish to dominate women, what do they have to gain? The answer provided by evolutionary theorists is as stark as it is simple. In order to reproduce their genes, men require sexual access to women. As with anything people need and cannot produce themselves, they can acquire it by trade or by force. Power is not an end in itself, but it is a means to an end. It is true that rape is about power, but power is ultimately about sex and reproduction—and so is rape.

If rape were purely a matter of male violence against women—as some scholars have suggested—then the age distribution of rape victims should match that of murder victims. It doesn't. Rape victims are significantly more likely to be younger, and thus, more fertile. In fact, rape victims are most likely to be of reproductive age (Thornhill and Thornhill, 1983).

Rape is the risky reproductive strategy of losers, of men without any better reproductive alternatives. It is the fundamental denial of a woman's right to choose. It prevents her from pursuing her own reproductive strategy. It takes from her the "bargaining chip" she needs to induce men to help support her children. It not only damages the reproductive interest of the woman, but also of other family members who have a stake in her reproductive success. This is one reason rape is usually considered such a serious crime and is so severely punished.

There is still one more strategy available to men who are too poor to afford a wife and family. They can agree to share a woman. While, as we mentioned earlier, formal polyandry is very rare and is statistically likely to involve brothers, the informal sharing of women is very common and exists in all cultures, namely, prostitution. Prostitution is usually considered merely the provision of sexual services in exchange for money. Its reproductive aspects are typically ignored.

Before the advent of modern birth control, prostitutes faced an ongoing risk that one of their transactions could lead to a pregnancy. Once again, as with adultery, it can be argued that men do not visit prostitutes in order to reproduce; their motivations are likely complex and manifold, including desire to overcome loneliness, to feel important, or simple lust. Our point is that all these proximate mechanisms induce men to seek sexual satisfaction, and often, to be willing to pay for it, because underlying these satisfactions is a potential fitness pay-off. (Consistent with evolutionary thinking about the cost of sperm vs. eggs, note that virtually all prostitutes are women, just as the consumers of pornography are nearly all men.)

Cinderella's Slipper

There is another common feature of the marriage market that warrants mention, namely, hypergamy. Women tend to marry up, choosing men whose families are richer and of higher social status than their own. This is even true where there is strong assortive mating. As a result, a woman and her family tend to gain more from the marriage than does the husband and his family. Through her children, her genes gain access to her husband's resources. How is this to be explained?

Given the reproductive advantages available to rich men even in monogamous cultures, there is strong reproductive advantage to concentrating family wealth in a few male heirs. Accordingly, a wife is unlikely to inherit the bulk of her family's wealth, and its exact size is not terribly important in determining her desirability as a wife. More important would be her health and overall genetic quality. She also must be able to fulfill the proper social role demanded by her class.

Part of the difference in resource contribution is offset, in Western culture, by the payment of a dowry by the wife's family. The dowry is an institution that is almost exclusively a feature of monogamous societies; a bride-price—described earlier—in which men pay for women, is far more common worldwide. Dowry payments appear to serve as a flexible mechanism that equilibrates both the relative contributions of both families, as well as the limited abundance of rich husbands to the more plentiful supply of available wives.

When all men in a society are essentially equal in access to resources, monogamy naturally results. As predicted by the polygyny threshold model, if male "goods" are equivalent, there is no pay-off to a female in becoming the "n-th" wife of a man when she could monopolize the resources of another. Such economically imposed monogamy can explain why societies that rely on the plow for agricultural cultivation tend to be monogamous, while pastoralist societies, for example, are more often polygynous. In plow cultures, it takes the strenuous effort of one man to grow enough food to support one family. There is little surplus available to support another wife. Among pastoralist cultures, by contrast, one man can accumulate substantial wealth as measured by the size of his herds.

And in modern Western societies? We are monogamous by legal, social, and religious restrictions, but mildly polygynous by nature. This does not mean that enforced monogamy does not have a real effect on the distribution of reproductive opportunities. However, such rules are rarely as restrictive as they sometimes seem. Almost by definition, any system that severely limits the reproductive potential of its most powerful members cannot persist. At the same time as the wealthy and highly successful can often afford to ignore traditional rules, there may well be a similar tendency among the "dregs" of society to flaunt social and legal prescriptions, if only because they stand to lose little if caught; this probably leaves the middle class stuck with what has aptly been called "middle-class morality"!

It seems evident that monogamy has historically been flexible enough to accommodate the polygynous interests of those with the power to challenge the system. Fifteenth and sixteenth century Portuguese society was, by law and morals, a strictly monogamous society, but over 20 percent of the offspring of the highest status males were illegitimate (Boone, 1988). This is certainly an underestimate, since it only considers those illegitimate children recognized by their fathers. When the man's partner was a married woman, paternity would be uncertain and also not willingly revealed.

Throughout history, rich and powerful men have found ways to enjoy the favors of more than one woman, even when the culture they lived in was nominally monogamous. In such monogamous societies as ancient Rome, female household slaves were sexually available to their owners. In Pompeii, there is a famous house that was once occupied by two bachelor brothers. In this house, there was a small room near the female slave quarters that was decorated with pornographic sculptures and paintings. In this room, the brothers "serviced" their servants.

Even in such strictly monogamous societies as medieval Europe, polygyny existed but was kept disguised (Betzig, 1986). This is not to deny the existence of powerful women such as Cleopatra, Catherine de Medici, Catherine the Great, Queen Victoria. But the facts of sexual reproduction limit the number of offspring that even the most influential woman can produce; in fact, it approximates that of any other woman. Only rich men are capable of hitting the genetic jackpot. In economic terms, they can leverage their wealth to produce many children.

What about modern times? During the period coincident with the emergence of bourgeois capitalism, there seems to the casual reader of history to have been a marked reduction in the appetite of rich men for additional mates. When we think of the great barons of the industrial revolution—Rockefeller, Ford, Carnegie, Morgan, et al.— sexual promiscuity is not the first trait that comes to mind. Quite the opposite: these people were almost paragons of ascetic self-discipline. More recently, Bill Gates can afford to buy an island and establish a breeding harem of thousands of women. But he just doesn't seem the type.

There are several explanations for this, not the least being the role of conscious decision-making, which we address in chapter 7. But this does not exclude a substantial role for evolutionary economics. As we argued in chapter 5, non-human capital or wealth can, from the genetic point of view, be considered a reasonable substitute for numbers of children. Individuals with the ability to earn a high rate of return on their investments in non-human capital might well maximize their number of descendants in some distant future generation by electing a kind of K-selection strategy, devoting the bulk of their resources to non-human capital and producing only enough children to secure their genetic line. Therefore, extended fitness offers a consistent explanation for what appears to be non-adaptive behavior. In cultures where property rights are secure—for example, modern bourgeois societies—the gifting of non-human capital to descendants can provide rich men with a reasonable, if not superior, alternative to polygyny.

The evidence is in fact overwhelming that people bequeath wealth to their relatives. (It is so "obvious" as to be taken for granted; as we pointed out earlier, such "obviousness" is often the hallmark of evolutionary machinations, which underpin human behavior so thoroughly as to seem to require no explanation.) In *The House of The Seven Gables (20)*, Nathaniel Hawthorne acknowledged the tendency of people to pass their property in the same direction as their genes.

> But there is no one thing which men so rarely do, whatever the provocation or inducement, as to bequeath patrimonial property away from their own blood. They may love other individuals far better than their relatives,—they may even cherish dislike, or positive hatred toward the latter; but yet, in view of death, the strong prejudice of propinquity revives, and impels the testator to send down his estate in the line marked out by custom so immemorial that it looks like nature.

A century and a half later, a study of 1,000 probated wills in Vancouver, Canada, strongly confirmed that the custom of leaving property to one's "blood relatives" does not so much "look like nature" as it *follows* nature (Smith, Kish and Crawford, 1987). Inheritance patterns reveal that relatives are consistently favored over non-relatives or impersonal organizations, and closely related kin are favored over those more distantly related. To be sure, when making out their wills, people sometimes "disinherit" close relatives in favor of more distant ones, or even non-relatives. But this is rare, and because of its rarity—as well as, presumably, the fact that it violates basic "common sense"—it often receives quite a bit of attention when it occurs. Not surprisingly, when a wealthy old person leaves the bulk of his or her estate to an unrelated butler, or a favorite pet, this often leads to the will being contested, and by whom? No surprise here: by relatives, especially any existing offspring. Moreover, the favoring of non-relatives over close kin is so rare that when it occurs, it is typically presented as *prima facie* evidence of mental incompetence!

Notes

1.   The role of sons in propagating the genes of high quality women may provide a clue to solving the puzzle as to the existence of the male sex (see chapter 4). Given the physical reproductive limits of females, "sons" give high quality females an indirect mechanism to leverage their genes.

2.   In our example, if F_3 married M_4, M_3 would marry F_2 and M_2, F_1. M_1 would have to remain single.

3.   Another reason is that throughout most of human history it is men who have made the rules, and they benefit from the double standard.

4.   By expolitation we mean that if a woman knew that she would be abandoned by her husband, she would never have agreed to mate with him. She might instead have sought to be fertilized by a higher-quality male. She only agreed to marry her husband because she was trading off quality for material support.

5.   This assumes that there is a woman available who will mate with a man who has resources which are only sufficient to help her produce and raise one child.

7

Rules, Roles and Reputations

Morality and economics are more closely related than many people think. Similarly for economics and social rules. After all, every economy operates in a context of laws and rules that reflect the moral values of its society. Property rights, without which a market economy could not exist, are themselves dependent upon and a reflection of a moral system. Any discipline that claims to call itself a social science must offer some scientific explanation of how moral values arise and what causes them to change over time.

Good and Evil

From the perspective of rational self-interest, we would expect individuals to classify events and other people in terms of how they affect their own well being. But morality is more than simply individual classifications of how events affect each person. When people make moral statements, they appeal to abstract general principles. They characterize events and people in moral terms even when these are remote and have no bearing on themselves. Why do they do this and what determines these principles of morality and justice?

One attempt by an economist at a scientific explanation of the origin of moral rules was by F. A. Hayek, who stressed the limits of human reason, arguing that the customs and institutions of human society were not the result of design but arose spontaneously through interactions of individuals, each guided by his or her self-interest. We have already seen how this concept was used by Adam Smith to explain the functioning of a complex economic system.

Hayek (1973) proposed a simple theory of cultural evolution whereby those societies that managed to develop the appropriate set of rules, customs, and laws that allowed their members to cooperate best with each other in economic production and in meeting threats

191

posed by other societies were the ones that thrived and spread their rules by example or conquest. These concepts of morality and justice are not biologically inherited, but are passed down from one generation to another by acculturation and learning. This is a theory of cultural evolution operating via group selection.

Hayek's theory has nothing to say about the behavior of the individual members of a society. It cannot explain how different groups in the same society have different values, how and why these values change over time and why people adhere to moral values and internalize them in the absence of fear of punishment. Most important, he has no explanation for how or why these abstract rules we call moral laws arose in the first place. If all the benefits of moral behavior accrue to the society as a whole, what motivation does each individual have to be moral? These rules could not have been imposed by the leader of each group, for that would violate Hayek's concept of the spontaneous order.

Hayek does, however, have a theory for the origin of individual primitive moral sentiments. Unfortunately, these are not conducive to the functioning of a complicated impersonal society. According to Hayek, certain natural moral sentiments evolved, by the process of group selection, in that long period of our history in which we lived in small, closely related groups or bands. These sentiments, based on mutual dependence and intimate personal knowledge of all members of the group, were beneficial to the survival of our hunter and gatherer ancestors. For Hayek, these sentiments are part of humanity's biological nature. They are the feelings of solidarity, sympathy, and empathy found within families. They also include jealousy, envy, and resentment, emotions which are appropriate to small equalitarian bands of hunters who must cooperate and share their resources. At the same time, such emotions are inimical to the functioning of more impersonal, complex societies, which depend on division of labor for their prosperity and require abstract rules of property and commerce that encourage the inequality that our primitive emotions find so hard to accept.

Given that our biological moral sentiments are so inconsistent with the type of rules required for the formation of complex societies, we must ask how such advanced societies were ever established. Hayek does not explain this. Moreover, he leaves untouched the question of how, once established, they survived, given the biological foundation of the more primitive moral sentiments. We can easily imag-

ine a society in which people eat two meals a day, or four, instead of
three, or in which people take a mid-day nap. But we cannot imagine a society in which people do not eat at all, or in which they sleep
twenty-four hours a day.

Our point is that whereas human nature is flexible, it cannot be
flaunted altogether. By the same token, it seems impossible that any
society could persist for any length of time if its moral rules were
fundamentally inconsistent with human nature. But even though
Hayek's effort at explaining the origin of morality is incomplete, it is
at least an attempt to place discussion of morality and other rules of
behavior on an objective and scientific basis.

The Kindness of Strangers

In recent decades, evolutionary biologists have made a serious
attempt to explain the evolution of moral systems by linking it with
an explanation of altruistic behavior. In some ways these problems
are similar and they do overlap. Any rule-determined behavior will
at times require an individual either to engage in some activity from
which he derives no direct benefit or to refrain from activities from
which he would benefit. Since pure altruism is essentially an act of
self-sacrifice, it would appear that explanations of morality and altruism would have much in common. But this connection has one
unfortunate consequence. It reinforces the association of moral or
ethical behavior with selflessness, in which any behavior that benefits the actor is immoral or at best, ethically neutral. According to
this, the only behavior that is truly moral is something from which
the actor derives no benefit.

Economists and evolutionary biologists are unlikely to take such
a point of view seriously. After all, as we mentioned in chapter 2,
economics rests (legitimately and comfortably) on the assumption of
individuals acting in their own self-interest and the theory of evolution shows that the forces of natural selection insure that individuals
will act to maximize their genetic interest. If morality is defined to
consist of only bona fide altruistic behavior, neither economists nor
biologists can have anything useful to say on this subject, and we
would be forced to leave all such discussions of morality to philosophers and theologians where it has resided for several millennia.[1]

In any event, evolutionary theorists have sought to explain the
evolution of moral systems in a manner consistent with the laws of
natural selection. Such explanations may not speak cogently about

what people ought to do, but they are eloquent about how people actually behave, how they evaluate the actions of others, and why.

Reciprocity and Genetic Hostage-Taking

As pointed out in chapter 4, modern evolutionary theory has a cogent interpretation of the role of genetic relatedness in orchestrating social interactions: the closer the relative, the more benevolent the interaction, because near kin enjoy a higher probability that genes influencing such benevolence (usually called "altruism") are present in the recipient as well as in the donor. A nephew may be "worth" only one half as much as an offspring, but maximizing one's inclusive fitness still requires taking the nephew into account in any genetic cost-benefit calculation. This may be why it is easier to do "business" with blood relatives; there are natural limits to the degree to which they will take advantage of you.[2] In societies lacking a well-defined legal system or in which the cost of information is high, most business establishments are family based. In pre-modern societies, a businessman would rarely place a non-relative in a position of great trust.

But what about cooperation among non-relatives? Stimulated once again by a theoretical insight from Robert L. Trivers (1971), evolutionary biologists understand that seeming altruism can be selected for even between non-relatives, indeed, even between members of different species. The basic requirements are as follows: the initial cost to the altruist must be low, the benefit to the recipient must be relatively high, there must be a sufficient probability that the situation will be reversed in the future, and when that happens, the initial recipient must be willing to return the favor and by his reciprocation, repay an adequate benefit to the original donor.

Trivers recognized that the major block to the evolution of reciprocity is the initial recipient's temptation to receive benefit and then fail to repay it. After all, unlike a simple economic exchange, such as trade or cash payment for an item, reciprocating systems involve a time lag between the benefit originally received, and when it is subsequently repaid. During this interval, the donor has lost fitness, and the receiver has gained; accordingly, there could be an evolutionary payoff if the latter simply walks away, refusing to play any more. This situation is modeled—albeit imperfectly—by the well-known mathematical "game" known as Prisoner's Dilemma, which obtains when the payoffs are arrayed in a particular way, with individuals having a limited number of options (typically, "cooperate" or "defect"). Thus, a Prisoner's Dilemma arises when the highest return is derived from defection when the other cooperates (the so-called Temptation to defect), the next highest when both cooperate (the Reward for mutual cooperation), followed by the return when both defect (the Punishment of mutual defection) and finally, the lowest payoff: from cooperating when the other defects (whereupon the cooperator receives the Sucker's payoff). In short, when $T > R > P > S$, then by the strict logic of the maximizing payoff, both players are driven to defect.

This is because each player, not knowing the other's move, is trying to maximize his return. He reasons as follows: "If the other player cooperates, then my best move is to defect (so I get T, which is higher than what I would otherwise get, namely, R). Alternatively, if the other player defects, then once again my best move is to defect (so I get P, which is higher than what I would otherwise get, namely, S)." Since both players analyze the game identically, both defect.

This result mitigates strongly against reciprocity. However, aside from its oversimplifications, the Prisoner's Dilemma also presumes a one-time game. For individuals living in a stable social group, and who can potentially profit from a series of reciprocations, the added benefit of a single defection may be less than the cost of having to forego subsequent reciprocal benefits. Trivers pointed out, therefore, that to some extent, would-be cheaters can be kept in line by "moralistic aggression," whereby a failure to reciprocate evokes condemnation, fitness-reducing ostracism, or even violence.

In addition, political scientist Robert Axelrod (1984) has demonstrated that in the case of iterated games, there exists a simple and efficient way for people (and other living things) to avoid the trap of the Prisoner's Dilemma. Known as tit-for-tat, it establishes a possible framework for human cooperation even among non-relatives. The requirements are that individuals cooperate on their first move, then subsequently repeat whatever the other player has done. In this way, they avoid being "suckered" by a non-cooperating defector, while also keeping the door open for a mutually rewarding, reciprocating relationship.

It should be clear that to some extent, reciprocity is not really altruism at all. Thus, participants in a successful reciprocating system do not suffer in terms of their personal fitness (although they run the risk of such suffering, if the other player defects). Rather, insofar as the system works, they profit selfishly, via pay-offs directed back toward them by the other player. Hence, reciprocity is appropriate to any individuals seeking to maximize their fitness.

But it isn't simple. Tit-for-tat represents a winning strategy only if both players know that the current game is not their last. It still pays to cheat if your partner will not have a future opportunity to punish you. At first blush, this objection doesn't seem fatal. After all, reciprocity could readily prosper if people cooperated all their lives and only cheated on their deathbeds. But unfortunately, this is not what the logic of game theory implies.

Suppose two would-be reciprocators know from the start that they will have ten opportunities to cooperate; each knows that the tenth "game" will be the last, so the optimal strategy is to cheat on this game. Since they both anticipate this, there is no way for either to punish the other for also cheating on the ninth. Given this, the optimal strategy is for both to cheat on the ninth game as well. But since it is optimal to cheat on the ninth game, there is no way to punish someone for cheating on the eighth. Reasoning backward from this, neither party should cooperate in the seventh, sixth, fifth, or any earlier game. It can be argued, however, that this problem is not as serious as it appears, since people do not know for certain how many games they will play in their lifetimes. They can never be confident which will the their last, so under the benevolent awning of this future uncertainty, reciprocity could nonetheless flourish, even in a primordially selfish world. But this may be a little too facile.

Realistically, each person is likely to make an estimate of how long he and any potential partner are going to live. We might be reluctant to enter into any deal with an eighty-five year-old, for example, out of fear that this would be his last and he would therefore find it optimal to cheat. So an eighty-five year-old will find very few partners. Knowing this, we should also fear doing business with an eighty-four year-old. Since the eighty-four-year old knows that no one wants to do business with someone a year older, he might view this as his last deal and therefore be more inclined to cheat. Extending this logic, we could eventually say the same thing about a partner of any age.

Is there any way to save reciprocal altruism as the building block of not only human cooperation but of morality? We believe there is. If the series of games or encounters is potentially never-ending, there is no reason to begin cheating. The problem, then, is to reconcile this requirement with the fact that individuals have finite lives.

Here is a solution consistent with evolutionary theory, and with the approach espoused in this book. Each individual should adopt the following rule: If you partner cheats, punish him and his relatives (notably his children, if there are any). Even better, insure that your relatives also punish his relatives. Remember that this is not a question of fairness or justice but of creating the proper incentives to insure cooperation. Imagine two elderly individuals who are considering a joint enterprise. Each is aware that this may be the last "game" for each of them. The temptation for each to cheat is therefore great. However, if each knows that his partner and his partner's family will punish him and his family for bad conduct, he will behave as if he expects to live forever. (According to evolutionary theory, he can: via the potential immortality of his genes.)

It does not serve an individual's interest if by cheating on his last game, he earns a big pay-off but his children are barred from cooperating with his disgruntled partner's family (not to mention possibly being attacked by them). Admittedly a child shares a genetic overlap of only one half with a parent, but this does not eliminate the force of this rule, since children and other close relatives are the only avenue to future genetic success. In chapter 5, we showed that if a parent is rich enough to leave bequests, he would be willing to trade one dollar in his lifetime for $(1 + r)$ dollars of additional resources for his children, where r is the return on non-human capital. If this return is 5 percent per year, the parent will discount the consequence of future non-cooperation for his children by this rate before deciding whether it pays to cheat. This situation is no different from what a young person faces. He will also discount the costs he would bear from cheating and compare it to the possible current gains. Individual lives may be finite but gene lines can go on forever. By linking the punishment for non-cooperation to the gene line, the problem of the "last game" is solved.

The foregoing also suggests certain precautionary strategies. To protect oneself from being cheated, avoid partners who don't have or will never have identifiable close relatives. Also, be wary of partners who are poor and therefore have discount rates much higher than the market return on capital.

Do people actually behave this way? Are the sins of the father truly visited on the sons? In traditional societies it is not uncommon for family feuds to last generations. Russian anthropologist Sergei

Arutiunov described the situation of many Georgians, Abkhasians, Armenians, and Azeris:

> Among the Caucasus highlanders, a man must know the names and some details of the lives and the locations of the tombstones of seven ancestors of his main line. People fight not only for arable land; they fight for the land where the tombstones of their ancestors are located. Revenge is not only for events today, but also for the atrocities from wars eight generations ago. (1993, p. 6)

Although varying in intensity, such considerations are characteristic of many people, throughout the world. Familial honor is something that human beings die for. On a more benevolent level, a rule that holds children responsible for the conduct of their parent helps explain why so many enterprises in traditional societies are family affairs. It is not simply, as argued earlier, that one can only trust family members, but that no one will trust *you* unless there are family members in the business, who can be held hostage to your good behavior.

This solution to the problem of human cooperation also applies to informal relationships in which the mutual obligations of each partner are never made explicit. An individual will do a favor for a "friend" without any expectation of immediate reward. Sufficient is his confidence that when he requires assistance, his "friend" will reciprocate. He has this confidence because the "friend" knows that failure to reciprocate may terminate the friendship and all the future gains that can be expected from it, and also because such interactions have likely happened in the past. "One good turn deserves another," or, as people often reassure themselves, "That's what friends are for."

A Good Reputation is More Valuable than Money

In Axelrod's simulation of the Prisoner's Dilemma, each party could remember how its partners behaved in the past, but could not learn from the experience of others. But in real life, people can and do alter their strategic approach to others based on how those people behave in third party dealings. Basing our behavior toward others on their reputation, rather than just on how they have treated us and our family, creates a powerful incentive for mutual cooperation. This modified tit-for-tat strategy means that the cheater not only faces retaliation from his victim, but must also take into consideration the possibility of retaliation from all who learn of his "bad" behavior. (The readiness of people to brand cheating as reprehensible suggests that *Homo sapiens* have been deeply primed to assess cheating and to discriminate against cheaters; here, incidentally, is another intriguing candidate for a selective pressure leading to the rapid evolution of human intelligence, since reciprocity was probably important to our evolutionary success, and it may well require a substantial IQ to avoid cheaters—or to cheat successfully!)

When engaged in any dealings with another person, we are, in effect, also performing for an audience, which judges how well we cooperate with our partners, how well we keep our word, our fairness, honesty, reliability, and so forth. Based on this information, people adjust their behavior toward others. Since everyone can't directly observe the behavior of everyone else, information about cheaters is shared among the members of a community.

Gossip is an ubiquitous feature of human society, and it, like reciprocity, has antecedents among animals as well (Dunbar, 1997). Information about the honesty of potential partners is a much-desired good. It can prevent us from making costly mistakes. Because it is a valued commodity, this information is bartered or exchanged among individuals. Providing accurate information about others is usually the act of a friend, giving rise to the expectation that at some point it, too, will be reciprocated. Reputation is the crystallization of this process of information exchange. As evidence about the behavior of individuals accumulates, the community comes to a consensus about that person; essentially, his or her "character" is established. Someone of bad character is a person who has adopted strategies that make him a dangerous or unreliable partner in any interaction. Someone of good character is someone you can count on, someone you can "do business with."

Reputation, because it is a general consensus about one's reliability and not a private judgment, requires a vocabulary to allow information to be speedily and efficiently transmitted from one person to another. Instead of having to remember all the details of someone's life that give rise to that person's reputation, it is easier to devise abstract concepts that summarize the public information about him. If someone tells us John is a liar or a cheat, we do not need all the details of his life to draw the necessary conclusions. Statements concerning the behavior of people that involve such moral concepts are not made matter-of-factly, as if conveying information about the closing prices on the New York Stock Exchange. They usually involve expressions of shock or at least disapproval from the speaker, who expects the listener to react similarly.

Moral judgments involve more than the exchange of information; they call forth righteous indignation from both parties. Moral indignation is understandable since the exchange of information about others is itself an interaction or dealing. Thus, failure to express the appropriate response when confronted by a tale of someone's perfidy might cause one's own character to be questioned. Since the very act of conveying information reveals something about the character of the parties to the exchange, natural selection would favor those individuals who express the appropriate indignation, regardless of whether they really feel it.

Conveying information about another's character is itself capable of strategic manipulation. It can be provided for the honest purpose of helping a friend avoid a mistake, in the hope that he won't forget the favor, or in the hope that it might harm a rival. To achieve the latter goal it is not essential that the information be accurate. It is sufficient that it be plausible. The cost of avoiding someone may be trivial compared to the damage done by dealing with the wrong sort of person. For this reason, it is perfectly rational for people to be willing to believe the worst about someone else. The costs of believing a lie and of ignoring the truth are not necessarily symmetrical.

Given the importance of a good reputation in encouraging people to cooperate with an individual and in protecting him from the harmful actions of his rivals, developing and maintaining a good reputation should be an important goal in and of itself. A rational person should be willing to invest considerable time, effort and resources in such a valuable asset. He should be willing to take occasional, small, avoidable losses in his dealings if doing so will preserve or enhance his reputation. By the same token, if the stakes are high, then the lawyers are called. After all, no one really expects the honest practitioner of reciprocal "altruism" to be an altruist!

Tit-for-tat is a more forgiving strategy than one resulting from an emphasis on a potential partner's reputation. In tit-for-tat, once a cheat cooperates, new partners will cooperate with him. But where the response to a new partner depends on his reputation, one act of cooperation may not be sufficient to overcome the perception that the person cheats.

The willingness of people to forego short-term gains to enhance their reputation for the sake of larger, long-term gains is, in principle, no different than any investment decision, including those in children and other relatives that we have emphasized in the preceding pages. In all such cases, the discounted value of the future reward must exceed the current cost of the action. Therefore economic theory is perfectly suited to analyze status-seeking behavior, especially when informed by evolutionary insights. People will invest in their reputation up to the point that the return from such investment is equal to the return on alternative investments such as those in physical capital, or in the quality and number of children.

Indirect Reciprocity

The attempt by individuals to enhance their reputation (status) is a key ingredient in zoologist Richard Alexander's *Biology of Moral Systems* (1987). This important book seeks to show how moral systems could evolve as a result of individuals acting to enhance their fitness. The key to Alexander's approach is his concept of "indirect reciprocity." In unadorned or direct reciprocity, as we have seen above, individuals provide something of value to a nonrelative only if they expect to receive something of greater value in return. In indirect reciprocity, such person-specific cost-benefit analysis is expanded to include the effect that any action will have on reputation. Therefore, as we have just discussed, one might be willing to take a loss on a specific transaction if the gains to reputation were large enough.

Appreciating the importance of indirect reciprocity to reproductive success has led Alexander to propose an ingenious explanation of the evolution of human consciousness and related aspects of the mind such as self-awareness, self-reflection, foresight, planning, purpose, conscience, and free will: these faculties evolved in an arms race between individuals competing for status, resources, and ultimately reproductive success.

> More specifically, the collection of these attributes is a means of seeing ourselves and our life situations as others see us and our life situations, so as to outguess, outmaneuver, and outdo those others... [and/or cause them] to interact with us in fashions that will benefit us and seem to benefit them. Consciousness, then, is a game of life in which the participants are trying to comprehend what is in one another's minds before, and more effectively than, it can be done in reverse. This is the reason for the great significance of time, foresight, and planning in human activities, and for the bringing of time-related and time-sequenced activities into consciousness (p. 113).

Alexander assumes that sometimes people make mistakes and serve the interests of others rather than themselves. This, in turn, opens the door for the evolution of deceit, namely, deceiving others into serving our interest rather than their own. Such deception is very common in plant and animal behavior, whether it be carnivorous plants that lure insects to their death or harmless butterflies that mimic the coloration of their poisonous cousins. Obviously the forces of natural selection will also favor the evolution of defenses to such exploitation. The race between deception and detection gives rise to social, mental, and emotional complexity, especially when it goes on within the same species.

The evolutionary game of move and counter-move is capable of immensely subtle variations. If efforts to manipulate people to serve another's ends are sometimes successful, then it might pay the intended victims to realize what is going on, to deceive the deceiver, and perhaps to pretend to serve his interests while secretly advancing a selfish agenda. Of course, deception occurs even between people who have no misconception about the motives of the other; thus, fraud and cheating are ever-present dangers.

At this point Alexander puts forward a startling hypothesis, one that should shake our very conception of who we are:

> Provided with a means of relegating our deceptions to the subconscious ... false sincerity becomes easier and detection more difficult. There are reasons for believing that one does not need to know his own personal interests consciously in order to serve them, as much as he needs to know the interest of others to thwart them. ... Consciousness is a way of making our social behavior so unpredictable as to allow us to outmaneuver others; and that we press into the subconscious ... those things that remain useful to us but would be detrimental to us if others knew about them (p. 115).

Rather than consciously lie about these matters, with the risk that we could make a costly slip, we submerge them. It has long been known that "Liars must have good memories." Alexander carries this further, noting that the best liars are those that believe their own lies.

Similarly, it is probably advantageous if individuals are not perceived as evaluating their costs and benefits from following society's rules, but instead, are acting out of an uncalculating sense of duty or generalized beneficence. But what if the rules we were taught or accepted are not beneficial to us? What if they require us to do things that are against our interest? What if cheating on them would be optimal? Are conflicts between the id, ego, and super-ego the results of such "reality checks"?

Evolution would favor an early warning system that told us when we are about to go too far. Conscience, then, is that still, small voice that tells when we are about to incur intolerable risks. "It tells us not to avoid cheating but how we can cheat socially without being caught" (Alexander, 1987, p. 253).

Thou Shall Not

Indirect reciprocity can help explain the development of moral concepts or categories, such as honest, reliable, cheat, liar, and so forth. However, human societies do not rely exclusively on such a moral grammar but develop it into a fully articulated set of rules whose transgressions are punished. The basic moral grammars of different societies are probably very similar (Wilson, 1993), having evolved to solve the same fundamental problems of human cooperation. The rules that societies actually enforce can vary considerably across cultures depending on their particular histories and constraints.

Rules define how people may appropriately pursue their own self-interest. They set the limits to an individual's behavior and determine when a person has done unacceptable damage to the interest of others. Just as moral concepts may well have evolved out of the logic of direct and indirect reciprocity, the more detailed rules also probably grew out of these concepts and the requirements of complex interpersonal interactions.

It is at least possible, for example, that the concept of property rights developed (perhaps even evolved in the biological sense), when human beings became engaged in settled agriculture, which required defense of the resources expended in ground preparation, obtaining seed, planting, and harvesting. If so, these new rules were probably not the product of a conscious decision process, with farmers sitting down and deciding what social strictures were necessary for the formation of an efficient agricultural system. More likely, each farmer realized by trial and error (or by imaginative insight) that to reap the benefits of his investment, he had to exclude others from "his" land and its products.

Since defending one's land against all comers is expensive, agriculturalists would have benefited from entering into agreements with their neighbors to respect each other's property. As these bilateral agreements spread through the community, a system of property rights would have been established. From this it is only a short step for individuals to realize that anyone who challenged the right of any landowner was a threat to all. It would then be rational to assist a neighbor in defending his claim, since that neighbor could be expected to reciprocate if need be.

In this admittedly speculative case, the rules in question are readily seen to be beneficial to the participants. But interestingly, it is not necessary that all rules be logically appealing in this respect. Many are arbitrary; for example, it doesn't matter if we drive on the left side or right side of the road. All that counts is that everyone in a given population picks one side and all abide by it. In this sense, social rules are contractual in nature. They can also be analyzed in terms of what biologists call Evolutionarily Stable Strategies (Maynard Smith, 1988), even though in many human cases—such as driving on one side of the road, or everyone stopping on red lights—the phenomena are maintained by cultural pressures.

We propose that a detailed cross-cultural evaluation of social rules will show that they too are strongly predisposed to protect the fitness-maximizing behavior of those making such rules. Insofar as this is so, then human culture and biology are likely to be mutually reinforcing rather than contradictory, even as individual human beings are likely to follow their own—often conflicting and competing—paths toward evolutionary success.

Rules

As we have seen, indirect reciprocity can encourage the evolution of complex systems of rules that facilitate human cooperation. Included are the basic dictums of morality, the "Thou Shalt Nots," the customs that permeate the basic structure of every society and which its members take for granted, as well as the formal rules of law that are enforced by state power.

The content of these rules determines the culture of any society. As cultural anthropologists have long pointed out, cultures vary markedly from each other. They can also change over time. Identifying the determinants of culture and cultural change form one of the basic challenges of any social science.

Every human has been born into a culture rich in rules. As individuals, we have no choice about the rules of the societies into which we are born. Those we encounter as children are as much beyond our control as is our genotype, our sex, or the wealth of our parents. But as we mature and begin to enter into meaningful inter-personal exchanges, actions are not only constrained and affected by rules, but can, in turn, alter them.

In seeking to advance their own genetic interest, people are continually attempting to use existing rules to their own advantage. Of-

ten, it is optimal for the individual, that the behavior of others be rig-
orously rule-bound, while the individual is left free to advance his or
her own interest. Even when rules are not violated outright, individuals frequently interpret them in ways that are most favorable to
themselves. Since all rules are, by their nature, abstractions that cannot anticipate all possible situations, there is always room for strategic maneuvering. But then again, everybody else is trying to do the
same thing.

When a rule is stable, then either it is so basic—like those against
theft and murder—that no social cooperation could exist without it,
or the circumstances facing the society and the relative power of
different individuals or factions within the society are also stable.
However, if the balance of individual interests that maintain the stability of a rule is altered, then the rule will evolve until a new balance is found. Under most circumstances, such rule changes are not
the conscious decision of any individual or group, but rather the
cumulative result of everyone seeking his or her self-interest. This is
a good example of the emergence of spontaneous order.

Not all rule changes, however, are the unintended consequence
of human behavior. Some are the direct result of deliberate and
purposeful action. Individuals—or more likely coalitions of like-
minded individuals—often campaign to alter the rules to their advantage. The evolution of rules governing public smoking provides a good example of how a conscious attempt at rule changing
can work. During the 1950s, smoking was ubiquitous. People
smoked in restaurants, movie theaters, sporting arenas, airplanes,
trains, stores, banks, offices, colleges, and hospitals, and there were
few private homes where the owner would object. The conspicuous exceptions were elementary and secondary schools, churches,
and courtrooms.

As the evidence of smoking's ill effects accumulated, many groups,
including the American Medical Association, began to lobby for
changes in smoking laws. Initially they sought only restrictions on
advertising and labeling, not on the behavior of smokers. Given the
number of smokers, such an attempt would likely have been futile.
Instead, opponents promoted government sponsored anti-smoking
campaigns and lobbied for non-smoking sections in restaurants, airplanes, and trains. As the percentage of the population that smoked
declined and potential opposition weakened, the anti-smoking coalition became more aggressive, ultimately banning or severely re-

stricting the right to smoke in all public places. Buttressed by the damaging effect of second-hand smoke on non-smokers, anti-smoking activists have gradually made what was once viewed as an accepted social practice into an increasingly antisocial behavior.

Contrast this attempt to change the rules governing smoking with the change in rules governing sexual behavior. Here, we must be very careful to distinguish between what people say and what they actually do. It is almost certain, for example, that premarital sex was more common in the fifties than was admitted and not as common as claimed in the late sixties and seventies. Nonetheless, it seems clear that the sexual revolution was real. Between 1962 and 1972, choosing two arbitrary dates, there was a fundamental change in sexual behavior that is amply reflected in the statistics on illegitimacy (Murray, 1984, p. 126) and divorce (Becker, 1981, p. 229).

These changes in behavior were coincident with changes in the formal and informal rules society uses to control this behavior. Colleges that once strictly prohibited visitation by members of the opposite sex in dorm rooms not only abandoned all attempts at control, but soon adopted co-ed dorms. Parents found themselves permitting their daughters to sleep with their boyfriends under their own roofs. The change in these rules was a reaction to the change in behavior of millions of young adults. This revolution occurred not in the streets, but in the bedrooms of America.

The reasons for this change are unclear and probably manifold, including the increased availability of antibiotics for the treatment of sexually transmitted diseases as well as the advent of birth control pills and other convenient methods of contraception. In addition, the women's movement had gained intellectual momentum, urging not only greater economic and social freedom, but also enhanced sexual equality. Another possible explanation of this shift involves the demographic consequence of the maturing of the "Baby Boomers." Thus, by the early 1960s the first representatives of the baby boom generation were reaching sexual maturity. Recall that for sound evolutionary reasons women prefer men with status and resources, and of course, it is easier for a woman to evaluate the long-term prospects of a "man" of twenty-two than of a "boy" of eighteen.

On average, women in America marry men several years older than themselves. Because of this, the girls of the baby boom may have faced a serious problem: since from 1946 through the 1950s, each birth cohort was larger than that of the previous year, for well over a decade there were more women available then there were men of the appropriate age. This, in turn, would have altered the normal excess demand for women.

When supply and demand shift, something has to give. Women could have settled for younger men who were relatively plentiful or they could have competed for the more "desirable" older men. They may well have done both: instead of insisting on a long courtship to test the man's commitment, some women may have adopted a fast strategy (Dawkins' term), in the hope that one or more casual dates might be transformed into a permanent relationship. As some women changed their strategy, additional pressure was placed on those who continued to pursue the coy strategy. Of course, males were not passive observers of these events. As the proportion of fast women increased, the optimal male response would have been to shift toward philandering, which in turn, would have reduced the pay-off of the fast strategy, eventually equilibrating with the partial return to more "traditional" morality that we see today. (Other considerations, the AIDS epidemic not the least of these, have also doubtless been important).

No one planned these changes in rules governing sexual behavior. The rule-changes were responses to changes in the incentives of millions of men and women. It is not that rules governing sexual behavior are unimportant. Certainly, during those periods in which various rules were stable, they had an encouraging or inhibiting effect on behavior. But rules can be fully effective only when they codify behavior that is consistent with the balance of incentives in a society, that is, with what the Soviets used to call the correlation of forces. When rules do this, they play an important role in pushing all behavior toward this consensus or balance.

Out of Eden

Since European explorers first encountered Neolithic societies, there has persisted the myth of the "Noble Savage," that all problems and discontents can be attributed to the corrupting influences of civilization. In their original, primitive state, humans ostensibly lived in an egalitarian utopia free from the greed, jealousy, and competition that characterizes civilized society. Although this view was more a reflection of wishful thinking than an accurate portrayal of life in non-technological societies, it had a powerful influence on the development of the social sciences. From Rousseau to Marx, to the twentieth century social sciences, this idealization of primitive culture served as a benchmark for the criticism of western bourgeois society.

A central tenet of this view holds that before the invention of property rights, people lived in egalitarian societies where all property was held in common, free from the conflicts arising from competition over resources and free from the constraints of hierarchy and status. What do economic and evolutionary theory conjoined have to say about this picture of primitive human societies? To start with, common ownership of property is not a sufficient condition for the avoidance of either inter or intra-group conflict. Just because each group or tribe holds its property in common does not mean that the group as a whole will not attempt to expand its holdings at the expense of another group.

Neither is common ownership a guarantee against intra-group competition and conflict. Each individual or family might (indeed, probably will) attempt to acquire more resources than is consistent with the demands of others. Even if hierarchical control over resources exists, competition among factions to monopolize the allocation of resources might be quite intense. And hierarchical control itself is likely to be contested by those whose interests are less well served.

Traditional economic theory has a lot to say about competition for resources. There will be an absence of competition for a resource only if it is so abundant that its marginal utility in consumption or its marginal product in the creation of other goods is zero. Recall from chapter 2 that this has nothing to do with the average usefulness of the resource, but only with the value provided by the last unit consumed. Air is free even though it is essential, because it is so plentiful that its marginal utility is zero.

If the environment is so rich that all the food a group can eat can readily be picked from surrounding trees, the price of unpicked fruit will be zero. Because the marginal value of fruit is zero, the price or marginal value of fruit trees will also be zero. Under these conditions there will be no incentive for anyone to attempt to control any fruit tree for his own use. But, given the super-abundance of resources, evolutionary theory would predict a high birthrate. In the absence of offsetting factors, the local population should grow until eventually the demand for fruit at a zero price will exceed its supply.

When the price of fruit trees becomes significant, the incentive for establishing property rights over them will exceed the cost of doing so. The zero price of resources is only sustainable if there is some external check on population growth, independent of the availability of food.

Disease, predation, or severe climatic or other environmental conditions could provide such a check. So, notably, could the presence of other human beings. A primitive group can permanently exist in a rich resource environment if the death rate is high enough to offset the maximum possible birth rate. Under these conditions, the resource limiting the growth of the population is women. In such an environment, evolutionary theory predicts a high level of competition for women. When little effort must be expended acquiring food, a male could sire and support a large number of children, which, given the equal sex ratio of men and women, would induce him to devote much effort to competing for mates. In short, even a theoretical paradise has its likely drawbacks.

Accordingly, it is not surprising that the early reports of tropical Shangrilas, populated by non-aggressive, sexually permissive, delightfully androgynous "innocents" by anthropologists such as Margaret Mead, have been revealed to be combinations of naivety and/or misinformation (Freeman, 1983). Such societies are in fact characterized by intense sexual competition, adultery, and jealousy. Depending on the nature of the external threats facing the group, competition for mates can reach cataclysmic proportions. This is exactly what happened on Pitcairn Island.

In their flight from the British Navy, the mutineers from *HMS Bounty* took their Tahitian lovers and some native men and fled to a remote island. This small population had access to adequate resources and faced no external threat, except for possible discovery by the British Navy (against which they knew themselves to be helpless). Accordingly, there was not much to be gained from trade or cooperation in defense. Each man viewed every other as simply a sexual competitor, and after an eighteen-year period, only one of the adult males was left alive! One had died of natural causes, one committed suicide, and the rest had been murdered (Brown and Hotra, 1988). This is sexual competition run wild.

Although an extreme example, Pitcairn Island provides an important lesson. Absent any need to cooperate with other men to defend against predators of both the four and two-legged variety, and when significant male effort is not required to support his children, there is likely to be ruthless competition among men to monopolize the available women. So much for primitive paradise! Situations such as Pitcairn Island are very rare. Most primitive groups, even those that face no significant resource constraint, have sufficient enemies to encourage at least some male-male cooperation. Primitive warfare commonly takes the form of raiding parties whose goal is to acquire the women of neighboring groups (Keegan, 1993). This should come as no surprise to students of the classics. According to Homer's *Iliad*, the Trojan War was started by the kidnapping of Helen. Virgil recounts that the founding of Rome involved the rape of the Sabine women, in which the early Romans, needing wives, kidnapped the women of a neighboring tribe.

One of the great inducements for solidarity among the men of a group is the need to protect their women from other men. To be able to cooperate with each other in defense, a group of men must reduce their own internal conflicts over women, recognizing and enforcing one another's claims to exclusive access to women. Insofar as such mutual acknowledgment of claims is the essence of property rights (Wilson and Daly, 1992), then marriage, not land, may be the first property right, one that is intimately connected with evolution and fitness.

Even when men formally recognize each other's claims, competition persists. Intra-group competition for wives in non-technological societies can be quite intense. Thus, evolutionary anthropologist Napoleon A. Chagnon (1979) has found that within such a society, the Yanomamo of Venezuela, women are men's major preoccupation and that competition for wives forms the basis for most political maneuverings. Although access to resources may be equal, reproductive success among men certainly is not. A few politically important men, who have the support of a large number of relatives, are able to have many wives and father a very disproportionate number of offspring. There is also a distressingly strong correlation between male homicidal violence and reproductive success (Chagnon, 1988).

Among the Yanomamo, resources are abundant and not subject to property rights, although effort must still be expended in harvesting food. A man, by his own efforts, can support multiple wives and their children, but eventually, limits on his time place constraints on his reproductive achievements. The very successful man is able to harness the effort of others to help him, convincing younger men—who need his influence in arranging marriages—to provide material assistance to him and his children.

Where the availability of resources is a constraint, one effective way a man can achieve extraordinary reproductive success is to leverage his efforts off the labor of other men. This does not necessarily mean that the others are worse off as a result, since mutually beneficial trade can advance the reproductive interests of all. But this does not mean that all parties benefit equally. Economic exchange allows the most talented to leverage their skills by employing the willing cooperation of others to achieve success beyond that attainable by one individual working alone. This type of leverage is common in modern market economies. Michael Jordan, Bill Gates, and Luciano Pavarotti could not have achieved their wealth without the support of countless individuals, each of whom has been pursuing his or her own self-interest.

In short, individuals rarely act alone. They advance their self-interest via coalitions. These may be small and involve only members of the immediate family, or they may be as large as modern corporations, political parties, or even nations, all of which supposedly attempt to advance the interest of their members. Sometimes they do so to the detriment of others. To repeat an earlier point, in every society or group of any size, we expect to find coalitions or factions of individuals competing with each other to alter the rules of the society to their own benefit. Such is the essence of politics.

Coalitions, and the Logic of Predation and Restraint

Social stratification is a common feature of human groups. Everywhere there are haves and have-nots. Certain individuals and families get to enjoy a disproportionate access to the economic resources available to a society. What are the sources of this advantage? The economists' natural reply is that some people are simply more productive than others, better artisans, hunters and fishers, more productive farmers. Although such differences in ability account for much of the inequality in modern market economies, it is less important in non-technological societies, where inequality is predominately based on unequal ownership of economic resources, on the unequal distribution of the goods produced by resources held in common, or by enforcing claims on the output of others.

Such an asymmetric distribution of resources is directly translatable into unequal reproductive success. An analysis of pre-market/pre-state societies has shown that "people with power will try to exploit it to their productive and reproductive advantage," noting that in such societies, men of rank traditionally enjoyed control over economic resources, and often transformed such control into increased numbers of children (Betzig, 1985, p. 51).

High-ranking clans worldwide have a definite reproductive advantage over lower ranking clans, and it is in the joint interest of the high-ranking clans to support each other's prerogatives. "Upper classes are in part political alliances, or even conspiracies, to maintain shared advantage" (Barkow, 1992, p. 633). We point out that, although this advantage may be political, social, military or economic, the fundamental, behind-the-scenes driving forces are likely to be reproductive.

One question that naturally comes to mind is how elites are able to establish and maintain themselves, given that their disproportionate consumption of a society's resources must engender opposition in the rest of the population. How do the coalitions and conspiracies manage to convince the rest of society to acquiesce to their ascendancy?

The primary answer to these questions, we believe, is force or the threat of force. In any group of individuals there is a subset that can physically dominate the remaining members. Anthropologists report, in fact, that the social, and political (as well as reproductive) leaders of many non-technological peoples are literally called "Big Men." Given the differences in human size and strength, the dominant subset does not have to be a majority of the group. With weapons and skill in utilizing them, the dominant faction may, in fact, be relatively few in numbers. In small-scale societies, coalitions are largely organized along kinship lines (e.g., Chagnon and Bugos, 1979), with the common genetic interests of relatives serving as a unifying element. A recurring danger for any coalition is the development of sub-faction fighting over the distribution of the spoils, but even in such cases, conflicts are less frequent when the average coefficient of genetic relationship is high.

There are several ways a dominant coalition can exploit its power. It can take for itself all or part of the losing group's property. It can tax them, enslave them, or kill them and take their women. The optimum policy for a ruling coalition will depend on many factors, such as the productivity of labor, the need for assistance in repelling external threat, the stability of the coalition, and most important, the amount of force required to achieve a given end. This latter consideration is of special importance, since the benefits for each member of a ruling coalition vary inversely with the relative size of the coalition. An elite of 5 percent of the population can exploit nineteen individuals for every member of the elite. If a ruling coalition is 20 percent, then the ratio will only be four to one. The potential ruling coalition faces a dilemma. The larger the coalition, the more secure and powerful it will be and the more it will be able to extract from each non-member. However, the larger the coalition, the smaller will be the population left to exploit and the greater the number who will have to share in the spoils.

There is yet another complication, revolving around the question of genetic relatedness within each coalition. An animal example may offer some insight. Among lions, larger coalitions among males are generally successful in ousting smaller coalitions; this would seem to suggest that lions should join larger coalitions whenever possible. But the larger the coalition, the lower the chance that a subordinate lion will achieve any matings even if his coalition is successful. In a sense, then, subordinate lions that join a large coalition are being more altruistic than those joining a small one, since larger coalitions confer a greater benefit *on the leader* while imposing a greater cost on each subordinate. Interestingly, large lion coalitions tend to be made up of closer relatives than small coalitions. The evolutionary logic appears to be as follows: For a male lion to join a small pride, the prospect of an occasional copulation is sufficient. But to join a large one—in which such possibilities are slim—there must be the alternative possibility of gaining a kin-selected benefit via the success of relatives (Packer, Schell, and Pusey, 1990).

For both humans and animals, there are two basic ways to acquire wealth: produce it or take it from others. Among human beings at least, both "predator" and "prey" are generally aware of this fact. The prey's incentive and ability to produce is negatively affected by predation. If the producer has no confidence in his ability to retain the results of his effort, he will not produce. A farmer will not waste seed corn and labor if he knows that his entire harvest will be taken from him. Unrestrained predation destroys the supply of prey. Even though, over the long run, this is a self-defeating strategy, each predator realizes that if he shows restraint, he is simply leaving valuable resources to be taken by other predators.

An individual fisherman has no incentive to refrain from over-fishing, even though he realizes he is destroying his future liveli-hood: If he doesn't take the next fish, another boat will. The prob-lem with fishing is that there is no easy way to exclude competitors. If someone were able to establish control over a fishing bank, the catch could be limited to maximize its long-run potential. Other-wise, we have the well-known "tragedy of the commons," in which private greed leads to destruction of public resources (Hardin, 1961). Paradoxically, solutions to this potential tragedy lead in two politically conflicting directions: either toward privatization of the resource in question, or greater governmental and even international restrictions.

Human predators can attempt to maximize their long-run take from a population of producers by limiting their predation while also pro-tecting it from other predators. This is directly analogous to what shepherds and herders ideally do: They protect their flock and limit their own exploitation of these resources so as to maximize the value they can extract from them over the long run.

A state of managed exploitation is also better for the prey. Ex-ploited humans often know that the alternative is far worse. They may begrudge the tribute or taxes they have to pay their "protec-tors," but they may also prefer to be fleeced for their wool than be slaughtered for their flesh. The amount the protector can extract de-pends on the size and wealth of his subject population. It may even be in his interest to encourage growth in the population of prey by restraining his exploitation even further, thereby leaving resources that can be used in reproduction and investment. In formal economic terms, the exploiter wishes to maximize the sum of the discounted value of all future tribute.

Such rational "resource management" depends on one crucial factor, which justifies our discussion in the present context. The "pro-tector" must have some confidence that he, his children, or other relatives will be in control and thus able to profit in the future from any restraint in the present. Absent this expectation, it would be irra-tional for him to hold back today in the hope of a greater reward in the future. This is not an all or nothing situation, since he can never be sure that he will not be displaced in the future by some stronger predator. The less confidence he has in his tenure, the greater his incentive to take immediate advantage of his prey's resources.

Analogously, employees of any modern corporation rightly fear and loathe a take-over by a "corporate raider" whose only goal is short-term profit. When businesses are managed for the long-term, notably in the case of certain renowned family-owned enterprises, workers tend to be treated better, just as the business itself is more likely to survive.

Dilemma of Democracy

Although most people associate democracy and freedom, equality, and liberty, as essentially related concepts, they are in fundamental conflict. The central principle of democracy is political equality: one citizen, one vote. Unless wealth is uniformly distributed within a society, there will always exist a possible majority voting coalition in favor of income redistribution. And unless opportunities (biological, social, economic) are uniformly distributed, there will always exist a tendency for wealth to be inequitable.

Consider a society evenly divided into two groups. The first group invests all its net resources (after maintenance) into producing children of only modest quality. They enjoy a small comparative advantage in producing numbers of children rather than quality. The second group has a comparative advantage in producing human and physical capital. In addition, the two groups never inter-marry and their relative comparative advantages are passed on from one generation to the next. Even if the two groups started out equal in numbers and equal in wealth, they will diverge as these different reproductive strategies are pursued. The population of group one will grow more rapidly than that of group two, while the per capita wealth of group two will grow faster than that of group one.

Let us suppose that in the initial period, the two groups, being equal in all apparent ways, decided to form a democracy, which initially established a government limited to preserving the peace and defending the country. Harmony reigns and the only political struggle is over who is elected sheriff. After a period of time, however, the egalitarian utopia will have changed dramatically, having become divided into two classes, a large majority of poor versus a small, rich minority. Political battles are no longer fought over minor pork-barrel issues but now involve the basic distribution of wealth within the society. Political dialogue is filled with how the rich have exploited the poor, how unfair it is that children should go hungry while the rich shower themselves with luxuries, matched by patronizing rhetoric about the need for people to take responsibility for their lives, and to plan ahead if they wish to get ahead.

Both these groups have been attempting to maximize the resources available to future generations for reproduction. But they have followed different reproductive strategies. In each generation, the net resources (after maintenance) available to each group will be approximately equal. The lower per-capita resources of group one are offset by their greater numbers. Genes of the original members of both groups command an equal potential for representation at any time in the future. Even though from a genetic point of view, both groups are equally well off, the social situation is now asymmetric. Group one has the potential for greater political power, and it is in its interests to use its new majority to redistribute wealth from group two to itself. If it can form a ruling coalition, it can change the "rules of the game" to its benefit. At the same time, group two has greater economic power, and with it, the potential to manipulate the political arena in its likely efforts to maintain the current rules, by which its members benefit in terms of educational, medical, and recreational benefits, and so forth.

It is uncertain whether group one will succeed in generating any redistribution. Group two, realizing its vulnerability as well as its economic power, may be able to frustrate the workings of democracy and use its wealth to "buy" elections either overtly or covertly, or if all else fails, it may attempt to overthrow the existing political structure and install an oligarchy. It might be able to "buy" the loyalty of enough military support to offset group one's superiority of numbers. (All of which brings to mind the adage that politics consists of obtaining money from the wealthy and votes from the poor, by promising to protect each from the other.)

Even if it succeeds in preventing its exploitation by the other group, the members of group two may be worse off than before, since they will have to expend resources to defend their property. The only way they can break even or improve their situation is to form a ruling coalition and exploit group one. Once group two has to expend resources to defend itself against group one, it might as well go all the way and "buy" enough force to take control.[4]

If the initial members of group two had realized that someday their descendants' wealth could be in jeopardy of being fully or partially expropriated, they would have had less incentive to follow their capital intensive reproductive strategy in the first place and would have been more inclined to adopt a strategy closer to that of group one. The less secure property rights appear in the future, the more strongly individuals are driven to adopt a low quality, number intensive reproductive strategy.

One fertile source of data to test this prediction might come from the new market economies of Eastern Europe. The reduction in birthrate in Eastern Europe has been explained as a result of falling incomes or increased economic uncertainty. We have an alternative explanation, the key evidence for which is that fertility has declined even in those central and Eastern European societies such as eastern Germany, the Czech Republic, and Hungary that have made a fairly successful transition to a market economy.

Communism severely skewed the private returns from the three reproductive strategies available to individuals. Given the overall level of productivity in these economies, the return from private investments in human capital was diminished by the equalitarian wage policies, and the return from private investments in non-human capital was virtually non-existent. In view of this situation, it would be rational for parents to invest the largest proportion of their net resources, meager as they might be, in the production of children. With the emergence of market economies and private property, it is possible that the return from investments in human capital and from investment in non-human capital far exceeded the return from having children. In such an environment it would be rational, from a genetic perspective, for individuals to shift resources from numbers of children to these other investments. This argument also suggests that the emergence of secure property rights and free markets might do wonders for population control in other countries, such as China.

Notes

1. On the other hand, it is at least possible that this is precisely where such discussions belong, even assuming that an evolutionary perspective on the origins of morality is valid. Thus, insofar as people are "naturally" inclined toward selfishness, perhaps morality is precisely a matter of transcending these natural inclinations.
2. Many would disagree with this statement. The way close relatives treat each other depends on the facts of the situation. If the genetic benefit is high enough, brothers are more than happy to kill each other. But under most normal situations, they will be allies against the world.
3. Maxim of Publilius Syrus, 1st century B.C.
4. Group two might do this anyway even without the threat from group one, but the existence of the threat reduces the opportunity cost of doing so.

8

Philosopher's Dream

"There are more things in heaven and earth..." according to Hamlet, "than are dreamt of in your philosophy." He could have been talking to us, to sociobiologists, or, more generally, to anyone with the hubris to put forward a purportedly all-encompassing theory of human behavior. We are painfully aware that our particular gesture toward a consistent, coherent, social science based on the integration of economic and evolutionary theory is, at best, a useful simplification of a more complicated reality.

There are indeed more things in human behavior than are explained by evolutionary biology and economics, even were the two more creatively combined than we have accomplished in these pages. There are glaring exceptions, behavior that does not appear to enhance fitness. Such "exceptional" behavior occurs in many forms, and lends itself to different explanations. For example, many, perhaps most, of our inclinations evolved during the 99.9 percent of human evolutionary history that we spent in small hunter-gatherer groups roaming the Pleistocene savannahs of Africa. Moreover, cultural evolution has progressed very rapidly since then (accelerating at an extraordinary pace in recent decades), whereas human biological evolution continues to crawl along at a snail's pace (Barash, 1986). As a result, human tendencies are often better suited to a long-gone ecological situation than to the conditions of modern technological life.

This view is compatible with the approach taken by Gary Becker (1976) in his theory of the household production function. As we related in chapter 3, he terms these proximate goals "commodities" and the (Pleistocene-determined) trade-offs between them form the structure of Becker's utility function. Human behavior is, according to this approach, limited in flexibility because humans do not rationally consider how these trade-offs affect the ultimate evolutionary goal of fitness maximization. For the sake of computational efficiency, important relationships were "hard wired" in our brains, sometimes inclining us toward behavior that is evolutionarily misguided in the modern world.

A good example can be found in our taste preferences. Most people are attracted to food that is high in sugars and in fats, despite the fact that both are bad for us. The reason seems straightforward: during our vast Pleistocene species-infancy, sugars signaled ripe fruit (healthful for a primate such as ourselves) and fat is rich in calories (and also sparse in wild game). "Thanks" to modern technology, we have the confectionery industry as well as feed-lot produced, "well-marbled" beef. To make matters worse, modern lifestyles doubtless mandate less exercise than was the case 200,000 or even 50,000 years ago. The result is an epidemic of obesity, heart disease, and possibly cancer.

In such cases, human behavior is clearly sub-optimal. Nonetheless, one can readily trace the basis for such preferences, and it seems very likely that this basis is firmly embedded in fitness-maximizing inclinations, even if they occasionally go astray.

There exists, however, an even more potent reason for human behavior to flaunt evolutionary optimality. *Homo sapiens* is capable, through conscious decision-making, of over-riding most genetically inspired inclinations, including even such powerful urges as the male penchant for sexual variety, or even for sexual gratification altogether. Toward the end of his life, for example, the deeply religious Isaac Newton stated that his greatest achievement had been—lifetime celibacy! And as for the accumulation of capital as a semi-satisfying proxy for fitness, Mother Teresa and her followers took voluntary vows of poverty as well as of chastity.

In short, people retain sufficient free will and plain old orneriness to do all sorts of things for which no theory of rational action (genetic, economic, psychologic, sociologic, etc.) could ever fully account. They can even starve themselves to death, on purpose. Our consciousness gives us the opportunity to say NO to just about any hankerings—including that for extended fitness and its correlates—that whisper within us.

But this, too, misses the point: The crucial observation is not that we are *capable* of denying our own evolutionary proddings and thus, of making hash of *any* explanatory theory, but that most people, most of the time, do not do so. The desire for sexual relations, for children, for food, and so forth, are genuine, biological bequeathals from evolution; no amount of modern misdirection, intentional self-abnegation, religious devotion, or conscious "mind over matter" changes that.

As a species, human beings are sometimes seduced by the siren call of the Pleistocene savannah, and sometimes they indulge their free will—but all within a context set by natural selection. Moreover, any general theory of human action is, at best, going to be only generally true. Human beings are not billiard balls, all of whose actions can be precisely calculated and predicted. At best, we can come up with a formulation that explains the greatest possible variance in human activities, while also suggesting further avenues of inquiry.

Given the diversity of human behavior, any theory that is consistent with everything would have relatively limited power in explaining anything. It was precisely the great generality of the standard economics model that led us to reject it as the sole theoretical tool for explaining human behavior. Any theory that views children as simply another consumption good on a theoretical par with VCRs and BMWs does not, in our opinion, come close to identifying the basic mainspring of human behavior.

And this has been our goal: to suggest a mainspring, not to explain or predict every brief departure from perfect time keeping. In this chapter we shall briefly outline the main assumptions and the principal conclusions of our approach to the integration of evolution and economics. We shall also point toward those aspects of behavior that our model is least able to explain.

The Rational Progenitor

Our integration of economic and evolutionary theory is exceptionally simple in its formulation, yet dramatic in its implications. All that is required is to replace the utility function, used by economists to describe the ordering of individuals' preferences, by a new utility function that contains only one argument; namely, the number of potential descendants in some unspecified future generation. Both the traditional utility function, defined in terms of specific goods and services, and the more abstract one introduced by Gary Becker, defined in terms of a set of unspecified fundamental "commodities," lack any concrete statement about their contents, that is, what is valued and why.

In the end, both are only statements about the rationality and consistency of human behavior. This does not mean that economics as it is currently constituted is meaningless or incapable of making interesting statements about human behavior. The requirement of consistency provides restrictions on the range of behavior in which rational beings can engage, and Becker's assumption of a constant universal utility function has also contributed greatly. But instead of describing *what* rational individuals value, these restrictions only show *that* they act to achieve these values in an efficient manner.

In contrast, by eliminating everything from the utility function but fitness, we narrow the focus to the goal itself, as well as to how people accomplish this goal. Like any model, ours over-simplifies, but we hope that it—like any good model—leads to clarified thinking as well as a strong set of predictions about human behavior: Operating within the constraints of one's economic and social environment, each individual will attempt to maximize the contributions his or her genes make to future generations.

This argument is not altogether new. Indeed, the core principle of sociobiology, applied to the behavior of all living things—including human beings—is that selection will favor traits that maximize inclusive fitness. We have attempted to focus specifically on the implications of this approach for a wide-ranging economic analysis of human behavior. Our emphasis on "extended fitness" incorporates the population genetic concept of inclusive fitness, explicitly extending it "vertically" (noting that pay-offs may come in succeeding generations), as well as "horizontally" (including the non-descendant relatives emphasized by kin selection), and also adding a predicted role for accumulated wealth as both a contributor to and occasionally a substitute for reproductive success per se.

In maximizing their extended fitness, individuals face what can be thought of as a multi-step problem. They must maximize their net lifetime earnings, taking into consideration how expenditures on themselves will enhance their productivity. Such expenditures include food, housing, clothing, education, and medical services, as well as spending on activities that enhance reputation and thereby increase the number and quality of beneficial interactions with other persons, including potential mates. Investments in reputation are governed by the same logic that governs expenditures on maintenance. Spending on all these items should increase until the marginal returns from such spending are equal to their marginal costs. This will maximize net lifetime earnings.

Net lifetime earnings will be directed to activities that will directly or indirectly replicate one's genes. This includes enhancing one's inclusive fitness by providing aid to non-descendant relatives such as nieces and nephews. In addition, individuals will engage in a trade-off between quantity and quality of children, which is itself, an indirect strategy of gene replication. The parent sacrifices additional copies of its genes in the next generation in order to spend the resources to produce higher quality children who will be more successful in producing grand and great-grandchildren. The absolute number of genetic copies is reduced in the short-run for the sake of greater reproductive success in future generations.

Humans have options not available to other animals. Like animals they can invest in the quality of their offspring, that is, human capital, but in addition, people transmit other forms of wealth to their children. Providing gifts and inheritances of physical and financial capital to their children and other relatives is an indirect strategy for the propagation of the parents' genes. In attempting to maximize their long-run fitness, people must find the optimal trade-off not only between numbers of children and their quality but must also adjust these against the optimal amount of non-human capital transmissible to them. In so doing, parents are attempting to maximize what we have called their "extended fitness." Not surprisingly, these conditions coincide with the general conditions for maximization as developed by conventional economics. The only difference is that in our model, people are maximizing a meaningful biological commodity rather than an abstract, theoretical construct such as an unspecified utility function.

Put in the simplest terms, in a monogamous marriage, parents can maximize their extended fitness by investing in the number, quality, and physical capital of their children so as to maximize the reproductive resources available to those children.[1] This, in turn, is accomplished by maximizing the sum of total net wages: the wages of all children minus their maintenance and status-enhancing expenses, plus inherited wealth.[2] If we extend the analysis beyond children to include non-descendant relatives—as ultimately must be done—the prediction must also be modified by including the reproductive resources of their children in turn, appropriately weighted by the degree of genetic relationship.[3]

We believe that extended fitness holds the promise of moving economics from being a subjective science, concerned only with the formal logic of rational choice, to an objective science of human behavior. The conventional utility function of economic theory says nothing about what goods or services individuals will value or what the relationship between these values will be. Even in Becker's theory of the household production function, in which the utility function is defined in terms of fundamental human desires such as sex, food, shelter, children, and so forth, the exact list of these desires and their relationship to each other is unspecified.

By contrast, the theory of extended genetic fitness specifies only one value in the individual's utility function, namely, long-run fitness. Everything else is a means toward achieving this end, and belongs in a production function. Every person is seen as identical in his or her ultimate values. Differences in behavior are solely due to differences in the opportunities and constraints that confront each individual. These include all the particularities of sex, intelligence, physique, family, and environment which make individuals unique. Our theory predicts, as does Becker's, that similarly situated individuals will behave in the same way. The difference is that for Becker, this is an assumption supported by vague reference to humans having evolved in a common environment, while for us it is the inevitable result of individuals attempting to maximize their long-run fitness.

In our ideal, simplified system, differences in human behavior reflect differences in strategy and tactics used to achieve the same goal. In other words, when presented with a choice, individuals will prefer whatever most effectively enhances their extended fitness. This becomes a question not of values or preferences, but of efficiency. Theoretically, an external observer who possessed sufficient information about an individual's situation would be able to predict that individual's behavior. In practice however, this is difficult to achieve since the individual in question will generally have the best access to information relevant to his or her strategic decisions.

An important result of our analysis is that it provides a possible explanation for a paradox that has threatened to undermine the application of evolutionary theory to human behavior. The correlation between wealth, status and reproductive success has been well established for pre-industrial societies (Irons, 1979; Betzig, 1986). People sought wealth and power because it allowed them to have more children. With the advent of industrialization, all this has seemed to change. Not only did the correlation between wealth and fecundity appear to have substantially weakened, but men of immense wealth and power no longer appear to monopolize the reproductive potential of a large number of women.

Hitler and Stalin were more murderous and tyrannical than any emperor, sultan, or Inca king, but neither established harems. Even on a more modest scale, the wealthy men of modern industrial societies do not seem to enjoy access to as many women as did similar men in more traditional societies. As we already suggested, such differences are not necessarily as great as proposed by some anthropologists, since serial monogamy is a substitute for polygyny and children of adulterous relationships are difficult if not impossible to trace. Yet there is no denying that the fertility of the wealthiest countries is lower than that of poorer ones and moreover, within wealthy societies, there no longer appears the strong relationship between fertility and wealth that evolutionary theory might predict.

This paradox can be resolved in two ways: (1) by the prospect that human beings shift flexibly from parenting strategies characterized by the equivalent of r-selection among animals to something closer to a K-selection regime, and (2) by recognizing that as part of this shift, wealth—non-human capital—is a close substitute for numbers of children. Men or women who limit the number of offspring to whom they will bequeath non-human capital can, in the process, be doing as much or more to advance their long term fitness as those individuals who have more offspring, but provide fewer resources to each.

A fascinating question—one that we cannot address here but would seem to warrant attention—concerns the process whereby human beings presumably evolved the inclination to substitute the accumulation of wealth for the production of children. After all, in view of the comparatively weak-bodied nature of *Homo sapiens*, it seems clear that the evolutionary success of early human beings, and quite possibly that of other antecedent hominids, must have depended to a significant degree on access to tools and clothing, implements for cooking, fighting, and hunting, and so forth, as well as domesticated animals, not to mention the capacity to store quantities of food and other items for later use. All this could well have generated a deep-seated inclination toward accumulating "stuff" of all sorts, especially those likely to contribute to one's own success as well as to that of one's offspring and other relatives.

Ever since John Locke, the Western tradition of political philosophy has emphasized the importance of property as a cornerstone of the social contract between individuals and their governments. At least one current scholar argues that property rights are intrinsic to freedom itself, and that insufficient respect for such rights was fundamental to the failure of numerous tyrannies, including twentieth-century communism (Pipes, 1999). On the other hand, there is a competing tradition, readily traceable from Jean-Jacques Rousseau, arguing that private property rights are inimical to human freedom. Whatever philosophical tradition you accept, and the authors themselves are not in agreement, it seems likely that during the evolutionary history of our species, possessions have been intimately connected with success, both personal and reproductive. To be sure, possessions and possessiveness alone are unlikely to be favored by natural selection, and a single-minded, exclusive focus on wealth or property is sure to be maladaptive: a childless miser, for example, will not be an evolutionary success, but neither will a parent who fails to recognize the importance of bestowing adequate investment on his or her offspring.

Our concern for now is to suggest that—for good or ill—property has long been of intense interest to human beings, precisely because it is biologically relevant, and to propose that considerations of property, possessions, and wealth have thus become closely bound up with the deep-seated human tendency to maximize fitness—particularly via offspring and their descendants.

In any event, the strategy of wealth accumulation depends on institutions that protect property rights and allow owners of capital to pass on their property and its return to their heirs. If the political process is such that large accumulations of capital are always at risk of being appropriated, then the return on such capital accumulation will be low or even negative. In such an environment, only a fool would trust his or her genetic future to such a fragile vessel. Substantial capital accumulation would only be undertaken by those few with the power to secure their possessions. In such societies, capital would be scarce and the rate of economic growth very low. If, however, property rights could be secured, reproductive resources would be shifted from numbers of children to non-human capital whenever the return on the latter is higher than the return from the former. Fertility would decline and the economy would grow. As economists have long pointed out, sustained economic growth requires a legal environment that acknowledges and protects property rights to the factors of production.

In terms of theoretical models of human behavior, the theory of extended fitness has two major advantages: it is simple and it is powerful. By powerful, we mean that its assumptions lead to distinct predictions about human behavior that can be verified or disputed by empirical observation. To the extent that people act to maximize the reproductive resources available to those who carry copies of their genes, our theory is supported. To the extent that people engage in conduct that does not do this, it is refuted.

In a formal sense, it only takes one counter-example to refute any theory. By this standard, ours has been refuted in many specific instances, but so would every other meaningful hypothesis about human behavior. In general, the more powerful a theory in generating interesting hypotheses, the more often it will be contradicted. For example, the hypothesis that people act to maximize their utility is extremely weak. In fact, without further restrictions on the hypothesis, it is incapable of being refuted. Since no observed behavior is inconsistent with it, it is incapable of explaining anything. Only by making additional assumptions about the nature of preferences can economics generate interesting statements.

The usefulness of any theory is a combination of its power to generate refutable predictions, its simplicity, and the percentage of human behavior that it actually explains. Extended fitness may be the simplest theory that reconciles economics and evolutionary theory, but without more research and investigation, it is impossible to say precisely how much of human behavior it can explain. The vast bulk of human energy is devoted to the mundane but essential activities of economic production, broadly defined to include household production, courting, child rearing, and reputation and status-enhancing activities. All these either directly or indirectly enhance an individual's extended fitness.

Consistent Exceptions

Sometimes, behavior that appears to violate fitness maximization actually, on closer inspection, is revealed to be consistent with it. Although few such cases are as convincing as that of the "mother's brother" phenomenon, described earlier, there is good reason to look hard at any behavior—especially if relatively widespread—before concluding that it is simply a non-adaptive aberration. For example, a parent could conceivably commit infanticide if by doing so, the parent's ultimate genetic prospects are enhanced. There is the case of a South Carolina mother who infamously killed her two sons in 1994. She was a single parent, whose boyfriend evidently balked at uniting with her because of the burden of her pre-existing children ("Susan Smith," *Los Angeles Times*).

Suicide is another possible candidate, seemingly maladaptive in the extreme, and yet, at least one evolutionary analysis concluded that not uncommonly, suicide makes a kind of genetic sense. Thus, suicidal persons are often reproductively and/or romantically un-successful and/or their death appears to free resources that would otherwise be unavailable to their kin (de Catanzaro, 1991). How-ever, we would guess that a large proportion of such desperate acts are pathologic rather than adaptive, the result of faulty reasoning or gross misperceptions of reality due to biochemical imbalances that manifest as "depression."

Then there is adoption. Although stepchildren, as we have seen, are at substantial risk of abuse or neglect, adopted children are not. This is consistent with the fact that whereas stepchildren typically enter the non-biological parent's life as an often-unwanted add-on to a newly established mateship, adoption is eagerly desired by the adopting parents. In itself, however, this requires explanation.

First, we note that adoption is overwhelmingly a second choice; given the opportunity, the vast majority of people prefer to make their own children. Second, since human beings give birth to help-less young, there has been very little opportunity during human evo-lution for people to evolve a rigid child-recognition mechanism, of the sort that is well-known among other mammals and birds, for example, who otherwise run a substantial risk that their offspring might be misidentified (Beecher, 1992).

There are numerous reasons why adoption could be adaptive, especially during the vast historical period preceding modern times. To take just one example, our hunter-gatherer ancestors doubtless lived in small bands, in which there was a high probability that adults were related to any orphaned child. It could be that in a closely related band of monkeys or Pleistocene humans, adoption of a dead relative's offspring makes genetic sense. According to inclusive fit-ness theory, if it takes a certain amount of resources to bear and rear a child but only half that amount to rear another's child, then a fe-male would be indifferent between having a child of her own or rearing her sister's child. Depending on the exact ratio of the costs of bearing to rearing children, a female would be willing to adopt a sister's or even a more distant relative's child.

Add to this the possibility that by adopting an unrelated individual, adults might enhance their social reputation, thereby gaining a fitness pay-off via "indirect reciprocity."

An anthropological study of adoption in Oceania (where the practice has historically been quite common) found that adopters are significantly biased toward genetically related children, especially cousins and closer (Silk, 1990). Moreover, biological parents remain deeply concerned about the welfare of their adopted-out offspring. Even among those who take in the offspring of non-relatives, such behavior appears to substantially raise economic productivity by contributing to the family workforce, which in turn promises to increase the fitness of the adopters' genetic children. In such situations, therefore, adoption can have a genetically beneficial "Goldilocks Effect," helping to achieve optimally efficient family size by reducing those that are too large and increasing those that are too small.

Finally, it must be pointed out that when childless couples adopt a child, they are, in a sense, scratching a biological, evolutionary "itch," namely the deep-seated yearning to have the experience of being a parent (which is not necessarily the same as being a parent, genetically). As we have seen in other contexts, people are eager to achieve proximal satisfactions, which are themselves relatively hard-wired into the human psyche, and which under most circumstances, correlate with ultimate, evolutionary success. It is not surprising that even after having been disconnected from their ultimate genetic pay-off, such satisfactions are still sought.

Recall our earlier discussion of why people generally like to eat fat, why most of us consider sugar "sweet," or why, for example, post-menopausal women still enjoy sexual relations, as do men who have had vasectomies. A similar argument can explain the widespread use of contraception, which is explicitly intended to foil the enhancement of fitness.

Generally, we expect infertile marriages to experience a high frequency of divorce. After all, it is highly unlikely that both partners are infertile. It is interesting in this regard that "divorce" among gulls is highly correlated with reproductive success the preceding year: couples that produce offspring are significantly more likely to remain together the next year (Coulson, 1966). Among human be-ings, there is, in fact, a higher rate of divorce among infertile couples, but it is not universal (Becker, 1981, p. 224). In such cases, a proxi-mate mechanism (love between married couples) may often over-ride the factors that originally selected for that mechanism in the first place: love serves male-female bonding, which in turn serves genetic fitness, but is not indissolubly tied to it.

Male homosexuality is another behavior that has puzzled evolu-tionary theorists. If, as recent evidence suggests, there is a genetic basis to this behavior, then how could a "gene" for homosexuality have prospered? Its bearers should have substantially fewer chil-dren than heterosexuals, subjecting any genetic correlates to severe adverse selection. If, at the extreme, gay men produced no children, then the only vehicle for the transmission of such a genetic tendency would be their genetic relatives who happened to carry it. Although the possibility exists that homosexuality has been promoted via kin selection, there is no evidence that homosexuals contribute to higher-than-average reproductive success on the part of their relatives.

The possibility also exists that gay men father sufficient numbers of children to account for any genetic persistence. Thus, a prefer-ence for men does not render one incapable of heterosexual rela-tions. Bisexuality is a well-established phenomenon, as well as people "coming out" after a marital history that included reproduction. In traditional societies, particularly among the wealthy classes, father-ing of children was considered a duty to the family. Once accom-plished, the husband was free to seek his pleasure elsewhere.

It is noteworthy that regardless of the factors responsible for main-tenance of homosexuality, an examination of male and female ho-mosexuality strongly confirms the male-female difference in sexual proclivities already discussed. Thus, lesbian pairings are notable for their relatively low-key sexuality and tendency toward monogamy, whereas gay men (especially prior to the AIDS epidemic, but to some degree, even in spite of its devastating effects) are often renowned for their promiscuous, variety-seeking lifestyle. In both cases, les-bian and gay couples offer the opportunity for female and male sexual strategies to reveal themselves in comparatively pure form, uncon-strained by the compromises necessitated by heterosexual unions (Barash and Lipton, 1997).

It would be ironic if the sexual revolution of the late twentieth century undermined some of the biological conditions required for the persistence of homosexuality. "Coming out of the closet" may well be an act of moral courage, but to the extent that it encourages gays and lesbians not to have children, it may prove to be a form of genetic suicide for homosexuality itself.[4]

Another realm of seemingly maladaptive behavior involves the elderly. From the point of maximizing genetic fitness, an argument can be made that human beings live too long, with humans continuing to consume resources long after it makes reproductive sense to do so, when they are no longer either reproductive or involved in child rearing. Women often enter menopause in their late forties but can easily live into their late eighties and early nineties. Humans are unique in having such a prolonged post-reproductive existence.

First, note that there is nothing unnatural about senescence, the decline in fertility and increase in morbidity and mortality that accompany advancing age. As elucidated by George C. Williams (1957), senescence is a side effect of selection operating most intensely on genes that are beneficial early in one's life, with evolution favoring them, even if this means that there will be negative consequences at a later age. Also, if there occurred mutations with no benign effects but whose deleterious consequences only became manifest late in life, there would have been little pressure from natural selection to eliminate them from the gene pool. Over time, such mutations would have accumulated like junk in an attic, to surface only when the other sources of mortality have been diminished enough to allow the organism to reach an advanced age.

For almost all of human evolutionary history, very few people survived long enough to die of old age. But many people now live in an environment where degenerative diseases are common sources of mortality. This is a recent development, having occurred only in the last few hundred years, and so, human beings likely have not evolved to be able to cope with a large population living to prolonged old age.

Why is this important? Because it presents a potential test of the rational maximizer models of human behavior. Despite their seemingly anomalous situation, the elderly, no less than anyone else, should expend their efforts to maximize their genetic fitness. In particular, they should invest resources in maintaining their lives only so long as such continuation brings reproductive benefits greater than the alternative reproductive uses for these resources. From a genetic point of view, it is a mistake to spend large sums of money prolonging one's life for a few years when this money could help one's grandchildren. From the perspective of long-term fitness, one can live too long, especially with the advent of high-tech medical procedures. To some degree, the immense societal problem now posed by outrageous medical expenses incurred during the final few weeks of life can be seen as a tariff imposed on our biological inclinations by recently achieved cultural accomplishments. (A similar argument applies to controversies over euthanasia and the "right to die." In an unforgiving, non-technological environment, there would be little call for the services of a Dr. Kevorkian.)

For most of human history in most societies, the behavior of the elderly seems consistent with rational fitness maximization. Extended multi-generational families were the rule, in which surviving grandparents rendered important child-rearing aid to their children. It was not unusual for the grandmother to provide a great deal of the primary childcare as the mother was engaged in economic production; as we have seen, this has led to the so-called "grandmother hypothesis" for the evolution of menopause.

On the other hand it is difficult for the rational maximizer to explain the breakdown of the extended family. What, according to this view, are all those senior citizens doing in Florida, playing golf, canasta, and shuffleboard, when there are grandchildren needing their assistance? What are these grandparents doing sunning themselves in "God's waiting room" while their daughters and daughters-in-law are at the brink of exhaustion attempting to work at full-time careers while raising a family? Can anything explain this seeming disregard for the well being of one's descendants?

First, let us not exaggerate this type of behavior. Millions of grandparents provide a great deal of assistance in the form of both time and money to their grandchildren, even when they do not live together. And, from casual impressions, it seems that the less the grandparents have, the more they provide. The behavior that is particularly difficult to explain—and that, frankly, stumps us as well—is that of a small class of relatively affluent retirees. Perhaps, once their own children are independent, individuals can be seduced by those proximate satisfactions—leisure, comfort, "easy living"—that under non-technological conditions and shorter life spans correlated closely with extended fitness. If so, then maybe the gift (or curse) of consciousness further allowed them to evaluate their options and mentally project a gratifying lifestyle into the future, regardless of its fitness consequences: this is sometimes known as "planning for retirement."

On the other hand, there are ways in which such elderly self-indulgence might yet be consistent with our rational maximizer approach. Thus, upper income elderly are given incentives to move away from their children to avoid high income and estate taxation. Resources not spent on taxes can then be gifted to their children.

Secondly, we note that several aspects of modern Western society undermines the opportunity and to some extent the willingness of grandparents to provide direct aid in childrearing. Thus, imagine a family from Kansas City, whose children go to college some distance from home, and then accept jobs and begin raising their own families hundreds, even thousands of miles apart. Even if the grandparents elect to live near one such grown child, he or she might also relocate in the near future, making grandparenting more a matter of orchestrated visiting than of committed involvement. The "culprits," then, would be transportation, communication, and a social and economic system that encourages and sometimes even demands mobility by young adults.

Also involved is the decline in intact monogamous families. The reproductive interests of all adults are more or less similar in the household of an exclusively monogamous couple consisting of their children and one or more non-reproductive grandparents who have no other children. When the interests of the parents coincide so closely, as we have seen, they can be treated as having a single utility function. But although the grandparents' reproductive success depends on that of their grown children, their interests are not identical, if the grandparents have other children. In this case, they will maximize their extended fitness by the proper allocation of time and wealth among all their children and grandchildren. Despite this lack of full commitment to the offspring of any one of their children, however, grandparents can still be trusted to place a high value on their grandchildren as a whole.[5] But any disruption in exclusive monogamy will tend to undermine the aid that can be expected from grandparents.

Divorce and remarriage shuffle children among households. Children from different fathers and less often, different mothers reside in the same domicile. In such "distended families," in which the children in the household are not equally related to two sets of grandparents, emotional loyalties and financial obligations (as well as expectations) become confusing and awkward. When grandparents are not genetically related to all the children, some aid that they provide will necessarily accrue to the benefit of unrelated grandchildren. Whether in the form of labor or money, any aid to grandchildren allows parents to divert more assistance to other children. As a result, grandparents can get more genetic bang for their buck by preferentially aiding their children with intact families or by deferring aid to grandchildren until they are on their own.[6] This may, in fact, provide a clue as to why the elderly are willing to spend significant resources to extend their lives. The longer they live, the better able they are to ascertain which of their children and grandchildren would be the most reproductively productive recipients of their gifts and bequests. Not to mention their ability to "enforce" good behavior among their descendants, as Becker demonstrated in his "Rotten Kid" theorem.

Even if grandparents were willing to provide direct child-rearing assistance, the parent of the unrelated children may not be enthusiastic about receiving it. Given the favoritism grandparents are likely to show for their descendants, their presence in the household may be a mixed blessing for the unrelated children.

Flexible Maximizers

Our theory of extended fitness views human beings as rational, long-term maximizers of their genetic success in the same way that economics views them as rational maximizers of their utility. This assumes that human behavior is plastic enough to adapt to changing environments and circumstances, which is not unreasonable given that human beings are remarkably capable of modifying their behavior to adjust to different situations. Recall our earlier discussion of the Mukogodo people of Kenya, who bias their investment toward daughters over sons, in accord with the former's greater reproductive opportunity. There is no reason to think that this preference is "genetic," any more than is the preference of other, wealthier tribes for sons. Rather, human beings consistently reveal enough flexibility to modify their investment patterns in accord with their genetic interest, choosing patterns that maximize their fitness payoff in the light of prevailing circumstances.

As anthropologist William Irons (1979) has emphasized, people do not always consciously seek reproductive success but rather, in consciously striving for cultural success, they make reproductive success probable. In most cases, cultural success is adjusted to help achieve its biological counterpart.

An important part of this argument rests on the hypothesis that when environmental changes force a divergence between cultural and reproductive success, "members of the society gradually redefine their goals to make them correspond with those things which will increase the probability of a high inclusive fitness" (Irons, 1979, p.258). Culture and social structure is the unintended result of human behavior tracking the environment and maximizing inclusive fitness within the opportunities and constraints imposed.

Irons examined the correlation between wealth and reproductive success among the Turkmen of Persia. He found significantly higher fertility for the wealthier half of the population, particularly among males. In our approach, we follow a similar strategy. Like Irons, we do "not inquire into the proximate psychological mechanisms which cause people to consciously strive for things which have evolutionary consequences beyond their recognition" (Irons, 1979, p.258).

According to this approach, behavior that persists over many generations is unlikely to be maladaptive, although once again, we emphasize that adaptiveness, per se, may not be consciously striven for, or even acknowledged. Long before contact with Western technology, the Inuit igloo was a marvel of engineering with its highly efficient hemispheric shape, its tunnel entrance (now copied by the most advanced mountaineering tents) and movable entrance, which could be adjusted to admit just precisely the correct amount of air to be warmed by an oil lamp, with the heated air rising and escaping via another aperture at the top. Yet, with all its exquisite design, its designers, the early Inuit, expressly denied any basic knowledge of simple physical principles, including even the notion that hot air rises! Clearly, some process analogous to natural selection (in its results if not its mechanism) had produced a "fit" design without any consciousness of the subtle forces involved. It is at least possible that much of human behavior is like this: we construct remarkably complex and—for the most part—effective behavioral systems without necessarily knowing why, or even having tried to do so.

Although the Inuit did not concern themselves with whether hot air rises, igloos that were based on other principles undoubtedly produced cold occupants who were unenthusiastic about the design. Similarly, fitness-reducing behavior patterns are less likely to be successful and passed on to others, regardless of whether the participants had ever heard of Darwin, evolution, or economics. Just as igloos "behave" in a manner that maximizes their interior warmth, people, in short, have long been in the habit of behaving adaptively, whether they knew it or not.

Anthropologist William Durham (1979) emphasized that many cultural practices tend to be fitness-maximizing, not necessarily because people possess one or more genes for these practices, but because by a variety of mechanisms, people are drawn to prefer such activities. Thus, the normal socialization of children involves a large dose of "enlightened self-interest," whereby most people are preprogrammed to emulate behavior that is identifiably for their own good. Human beings are also inclined to achieve "satisfaction" in their lives, and "square wheels, crooked spears and sickly children are unlikely to provide much satisfaction" (Ruyle, 1977). And finally, cultural practices that promote biological success are likely to get themselves copied into many little heads, in turn to be promulgated in the future (not unlike the concept of "memes" developed by Richard Dawkins).

For an example of an adaptive cultural process, take the fact that New World indigenous people employ maize as a food staple. Maize is deficient, however, in the essential amino acids lysine and tryptophan, as well as the vitamin niacin (of which tryptophan is a chemical precursor). A population largely dependent on maize would probably develop the disease pellagra. However, treating maize with alkali and then cooking it causes an almost threefold increase in the available lysine, plus increases in tryptophan and in the ratios of other important nutrients. Alkali treatment is achieved in diverse ways, by different indigenous groups, most often by using ashes or lime; the crucial point is that these techniques have apparently been derived independently by virtually all societies relying on maize (Katz, 1974). Such cooking traditions are justified in different ways, but never by pointing to their effects on necessary amino acids!

Similarly, people invest in children and other relatives, and accumulate property and other wealth, only rarely pointing to their effects on fitness. An activity that appears on the surface to be a waste of resources may indirectly, through some hidden mechanism, advance one's genetic interest. And if this is not the case, the divergence is likely to be only temporary until actual behavior converges with whatever is evolutionarily optimal—or at least, more adaptive that non-adaptive.

We suspect that much of the behavior that characterizes modern society, and which appears at first glance to be maladaptive such as fertility limitation, may in fact prove to maximize reproductive success. In any event, it is not all or nothing. After a dramatic change in environment, we expect to see a range of responses. Some people will behave in more adaptive ways than others. It is entirely plausible that the ability to reason beyond proximate satisfactions toward ultimate ends should vary within the population. Those individuals who do not value children but only value sex, for instance, will be severely selected against when safe, affordable, and satisfying contraception becomes widely available.

People vary in intelligence and foresight. Since one function of conscious intelligence is to allow individuals to think beyond the proximate and to imagine the long-run consequences of their actions, those with higher intelligence typically respond to more distant goals. Although the man with limited foresight cannot "see" beyond the proximate goal of casual sex with a prostitute, the more intelligent man realizes that such sex has potentially great cost and does little or nothing to advance his long-term interests. Humans may well be a mixture of Pleistocene proximate gratifications and more general reproduction-enhancing inclinations. It is interesting that those individuals with the greatest intelligence, foresight and most of all, discipline tend to be the most financially successful in the modern world—although admittedly, such individuals are not always the most successful reproductively.

We admit that, at present, it is uncertain whether maximizing the total reproductive resources of one's children and close relatives is the best strategy for maximizing one's expected contributions to the gene pool in the long run. Some researchers, indeed, have concluded otherwise: For example, a cross-sectional study of the fertility of modern New Mexican men found that whereas parental investment raises the income of children, it does not increase the average child's fertility, which was interpreted as demonstrating that such behavior "maximizes the economic productivity of lineages at the expense of fitness" (Kaplan, et al., 1995, p. 325-6.)

It may be that such people are deceived by the lure of economic success and non-reproductive personal satisfactions, acting (at least in evolutionary terms) like moths drawn to a flame. If so, then if there is genetic diversity underpinning the diversity of such behavior, the latter would likely diminish in the next few hundred, or thousand, generations. Or it may be that these New Mexican men—along with much of human society in the aftermath of industrialization—are making an adaptive, flexible, tactical shift, analogous to the transition from an r-selection regime to one characterized by K-selection. If so, then once again it would take more than a few generations to assess whether such a shift is fitness enhancing in the evolutionary sense. (To be fair, a similar caveat must be applied to any demonstrations of positive correlations between cultural and biological success, and to which we referred in support of our approach. Only time—and more research—will tell.)

Our bets are on biology. After all, the earth supports a population of over five billion humans precisely because human investments in human and physical capital have gone far beyond the level suitable for the Pleistocene. We believe it more likely that the continued fall in fertility rates represents a rational adjustment to the increasing returns, over time, from investments in human quality and non-human capital.

We also suspect that recreational sex, for all its apparently non-reproductive component, can best be comprehended through the lens of fitness maximization. Despite the ready availability of contraceptives, we should not make the mistake of assuming that men who engage in promiscuous sex are engaging in totally non-adaptive behavior. Whereas the reproductive pay-off from extra-marital, pre-marital, and non-marital sex may not be what it once was, it is certainly not negligible. The return from this behavior may or may not justify its risks and costs, depending on the specifics of each opportunity. In any event, the continued existence of such behavior is not in itself evidence that men are currently behaving non-adaptively.

Insight into this problem comes from a study of the relationship between wealth and reproductive success among men in modern-day Quebec. The initial finding recalls the research on New Mexican men, described above: Wealthier men did not have more children. However, detailed analysis of the frequency of sexual intercourse and the number of partners experienced by different men enabled an estimate of the number of "potential conceptions" that would have been produced if birth control had not been used.

The results show a very strong correlation between the number of potential conceptions and male income, especially among unmarried men (Perusse, 1993). Women's preference for wealthy men also appeared to contribute substantially to this outcome, in which male striving for status and financial success is an adaptive counterpart to women's sexual preference. Although the ultimate reproductive consequences are currently skewed by the availability of birth control, both male and female behaviors reflect the persistence of underlying fitness-maximizing strategies.

We also have to be careful in making generalizations about long-run fertility in the middle of a demographic transformation. Declining overall fertility as a society's wealth increases does not imply that wealth and fertility are not correlated across members of that society. As Low states, concerning nineteenth-century Sweden, "I find it striking that, in a Western, late-marrying, monogamous, relatively egalitarian society, wealth differentials still promoted fertility differentials. When resources became constricted, family reproductive differentials shrank; but whenever possible, individuals (especially men) converted resources into children" (Low, 2000, 142).

Ecce Homo?

In writing this book, we have vacillated between hubris and humility, the former being inherent in any attempt to reformulate—or even to begin reformulating—so complex and widely-embracing a field as economics, not to mention the arrogance of even gesturing toward an alliance of such firmly grounded disciplines as economics and evolutionary biology. At the same time, one must be humble in the presence of so complex and contradictory a creature as *Homo sapiens*.

Winston Churchill once referred to Clement Atlee as "a humble man with much to be humble about." We hope that our humility, although explicit, is not too well deserved! Thus, we believe that evolutionary biology is "onto something" that will eventually allow social science to behold human beings as they are. In pointing toward that perception, we run risks of being unworthy of either of our parent disciplines: economics and evolutionary biology. But we would rather try and fall short than not try at all.

We have not presented the final word on this subject. Neither is it the first. It is likely to be controversial, however, not only because it threatens to undermine the self-congratulatory isolation that largely characterizes economics in particular (evolutionary theorists are less likely to feel defensive, since if anything, their perimeter of relevance is herein expanded).

In an integrated economic/evolutionary approach, economics brings the rigor of its analytics, its rich history of studying the conditions necessary for maximizing and efficient behavior. Evolutionary biology brings not only its link to the natural sciences and its ability to make concrete the economist's abstract concept of the utility function but also its emphasis on the strategic nature of behavior. While game theory was originated by economists, economics has traditionally assumed that consumer behavior is continuous, that is, that relatively small changes in income or relative prices cause similar small changes in behavior. Our approach makes no such assumption. The utility function is concerned only with extended genetic fitness; all the other biological, technical, and social factors which influence behavior are part of the household production function. This does not have to be stable or identical among individuals. Small changes in the environment can cause large changes in behavior as individuals shift their strategies. Small changes in relative prices can cause large changes in an individual's behavior. Economists assume that consumers are essentially passive, arranging the consumption basket to maximize utility. Even Becker, who has a far more active vision of consumer behavior, does this. We view consumers as being in a continuous struggle with other consumers in a battle over resources and mates. Economics has tended to emphasize the important role of human cooperation, while evolutionary biology has tended to emphasize conflict. By joining economics with biology we hope to strike a proper balance.

For many observers, an explicitly evolutionary view of human nature will appear unacceptably cold, even cynical. Others will simply resist any such analysis as "reductionistic," and thus, woefully inadequate. We would point out that traditional economic analysis, from Malthus to Milton Friedman, has never been especially "warm and fuzzy," but no less incisive for that. And as to reductionism, it is the driving force for most progress in science. We believe that evolution by natural selection, and its correlate of fitness maximization, fits this bill—without any grandiose expectations that under its aegis, all human behavior will be neatly "explained."

Others will object for religious or sentimental reasons, unable to abide the notion that human beings are subject to the same organizing principle of the natural world that underpins the behavior of other living things, from amoebas to zebras. In "The White-Tailed Hornet," Robert Frost captured some of the outrage that results from comparing (and thus, at some level, equating) human beings with animals:

> ...As long on earth
> As our comparisons were stoutly upward
> With gods and angels, we were men at least,
> But little lower than the gods and angels.
> But once comparisons were yielded downward,
> Once we began to see our images
> Reflected in the mud and even dust,
> 'Twas disillusion upon disillusion.
> We were lost piecemeal to the animals,
> Like people thrown out to delay the wolves.

On the other hand, the connectedness of all life forms—*Homo sapiens* included—can be seen as an ennobling vision, whereby the unity between hippo, hummingbird, halibut, hickory tree, and, yes, human being, is not cause for disillusionment, but rather, celebration. In the closing paragraph of *The Origin of Species*, Darwin wrote:

> It is interesting to contemplate a tangled bank, clothed with many plants of many kinds, with birds singing on the bushes, with various insects flitting about, and with worms crawling through the damp earth, and to reflect that these elaborately constructed forms, so different from each other, and dependent upon each other in so complex a manner, have all been produced by laws acting around us. ... Thus, from the war of nature, from famine and death, the most exalted object which we are capable of conceiving, namely, the production of the higher animals, directly follows. There is grandeur in this view of life ... that, whilst this planet has gone cycling on according to the fixed law of gravity, from so simple a beginning endless forms most beautiful and most wonderful have been, and are being evolved. (p. 373)

Finally, there is another perspective, independent of the virtues or perils of reductionism, indifferent to whether a fundamentally biological approach to human behavior is ennobling or degrading. In this perspective, the over-riding questions are simply "Does it work?" "Is it useful?" "Does it lead to interesting questions and satisfying answers?" And even, at the risk of infuriating many post-modernists, "Is it true?"

We think the answer to each of these questions is "Yes," and that even the inevitable failures to confirm will lead to sharper honing of the questions asked, a deeper understanding, and a more precise set of predictions. Thus, the ultimate—dare we say, "extended"?—test of this book is the speed with which it will be superseded.

Notes

1.   In the real world, this is only an approximation, since it does not take into account diseconomies of scale in the production of children by females as well as the effect

of investment in human capital on the wage rate of children and the cast of grandchildren.

2.   This condition is also true for non-monogamous mating. But in these cases the various sexual strategies adopted by men and women can, as we show in chapter 7, greatly complicate the analysis.

3.   Since nieces and nephews share only a quarter of an individual's genes while children share one half, it is generally genetically efficient for parents to focus all their reproductive effort on their own children. However, there are many circumstances where this is not true, such as when a niece or nephew has almost enough resources to afford a child. In this case, the genetic return from a gift to one's sibling's children would be very high.

4.   If there is a gene responsible for sexual orientation and if that gene were susceptible to mutation then it is theoretically possible that even if it is aggressively selected against, the gene for homosexuality may persist within the population at a stable rate. The losses due to the pressure of natural selection are constantly being offset by new mutations.

5.   Grandparents should be expected to show a preference for the children of their daughters over their sons, to the extent that there is any uncertainty in paternity. Therefore, a growth in sexual laxity and adultery will undermine the bonds between grandparents and their sons' children.

6.   Even in intact families, grandparents may be engaged in strategic games relative to the parents of their child's spouse. Each set of grandparents would wish to encourage the other set to make as large a contribution as possible to its child's family at the expense of the families of any other children.

Technical Appendix 1

N is number of children produced.
S is number of surviving children.
S_r is the survival rate of children.
C is the fixed cost of a child.
Q is the amount invested in quality of each child.
P is the full price of a child.
R is the reproductive resources of the parent.

Parents maximize S

1. $S = NS_r$

2. $S_r = f(Q)$ where $\dfrac{\partial S_r}{\partial Q} > 0$, $\dfrac{\partial^2 S_r}{\partial Q^2} < 0$

    subject to budget constraints

3. $R = NP$

4. $P = C + Q$

    Set up Lagrangian and take partial derivatives.

5. $S = Nf(Q) + \lambda(R - PN)$

6. $\dfrac{\partial S}{\partial N} = f(Q) - \lambda P = 0$

7. $\dfrac{\partial S}{\partial Q} = N\dfrac{\partial f(Q)}{\partial Q} - \lambda N \dfrac{\partial P}{\partial Q} = 0$

8. $\dfrac{\partial S}{\partial \lambda} = R - PN = 0$

    Substituting equation 6 into 7

9. $\dfrac{\partial f(Q)}{\partial Q} = \dfrac{f(Q)}{P} \dfrac{\partial P}{\partial Q}$

    Take partial derivative of P with respect to Q

10. $\dfrac{\partial P}{\partial Q} = 1$

Since $S_r = f(Q)$, substituting in equation 9 yields

11. $$\frac{\partial S_r}{\partial Q} = \frac{S_r}{P} = \frac{S_r}{C + Q}$$

Therefore, the optimal expenditure on quality occurs at the point at which a line drawn from the origin is tangent to the survival rate curve. Given the optimal expenditure on quality, Q^*, the number of children is simply,

12. $N = R/P^* = R/(C + Q^*)$
where $P^* = C + Q^*$

Technical Appendix 2

R_1 is total reproductive resources of children.
W is children's net wage.
Q is quantity of human capital invested in each child.
C is the fixed cost of a child.
P is total price of children.
R_o is reproductive assets of parent.
N is number of children.

Parent maximizes R_1

1. $R_1 = NW$

2. $W = h(Q)$ where

$$\frac{\partial W}{\partial Q} > 0, \quad \frac{\partial^2 W}{\partial Q^2} < 0$$

Subject to budget constraint

3. $R_o = PN$

4. $P = C + Q$

Set up Lagrangian and take partial derivatives.

5. $R_1 = Nh(Q) + \lambda(R_o - PN)$

6. $\dfrac{\partial R_1}{\partial N} = h(Q) - \lambda P = 0$

7. $\dfrac{\partial R_1}{\partial Q} = N\dfrac{\partial h(Q)}{\partial Q} - \lambda\dfrac{\partial P}{\partial Q}N$

8. $\dfrac{\partial R_1}{\partial \lambda} = R_o - PN = 0$

Substituting equation 6 into 7

9. $\dfrac{\partial h(Q)}{\partial Q} = \dfrac{h(Q)}{P}\dfrac{\partial P}{\partial Q}$

Take partial derivative of P with respect to Q

10. $\dfrac{\partial P}{\partial Q} = 1$

Substitute into equation 9

11. $\dfrac{\partial h(Q)}{\partial Q} = \dfrac{h(Q)}{P}$

Since $h(Q) = W$

12. $\dfrac{\partial h(Q)}{\partial Q} = \dfrac{W}{P} = \dfrac{W}{C+Q}$

Having solved for optimal investment in human capital, Q^*,

13. $N = \dfrac{R_o}{P^*}$ where $P^* = C+Q^*$

Technical Appendix 3

R_1 is total reproductive resources of children.
W is children's net wage.
Q is quantity of human capital invested in each child.
C is the fixed cost of a child.
P is price of each child.
I is amount of non-human capital bequeathed to children.
r is the return on non-human capital.
R_0 is parent's reproductive resources.

Parents Maximize R_1

1. $R_1 = NW + (1 + r)I$

2. $W = h(Q)$, where $\dfrac{\partial W}{\partial Q} > 0$, $\dfrac{\partial^2 W}{\partial Q^2} < 0$

Subject to budget constraint

3. $R_0 = I + PN$
   $P = C + Q$

Set up Lagrangian and take partial derivatives

4. $R_1 = Nh(Q) + (1 + r)I + \lambda (R_0 - PN - I)$

5. $\dfrac{\partial R_1}{\partial N} = h(Q) - \lambda P = 0$

6. $\dfrac{\partial R_1}{\partial Q} = N\dfrac{\partial h(Q)}{\partial Q} - \dfrac{\lambda \partial P N}{\partial Q} = 0$

7. $\dfrac{\partial R_1}{\partial I} = (1 + r) - \lambda = 0$

8. $\dfrac{\partial R_1}{\partial \lambda} = R_0 - PN - I = 0$

9. $\lambda = 1 + r$

247

Substitute equation 9 into equation 5

10. $\dfrac{W}{P} = \dfrac{h\,(Q)}{P} = 1 + r$

Substitute equation 9 into equation 6

11. $\dfrac{\partial\,h\,(Q)}{\partial\,Q} = (1 + r)\dfrac{\partial\,P}{\partial\,Q}$

taking partial derivative of P with respect to Q

12. $\dfrac{\partial\,h\,(Q)}{\partial\,Q} = 1 + r$

13. $W/P = \dfrac{\partial\,h\,(Q)}{\partial\,Q} = 1 + r$

Technical Appendix 4

R_1 is total reproductive resources of children.
W is children's net wage.
Q is quantity of human capital invested in each child.
N is number of children.
P_T is total price of producing all children.
I is amount of non-human capital bequeathed to children.
r is the rate of return on non-human capital.
R_O is the reproductive resources of the parent.
P is the price of the Nth child.

Parents Maximize

1. $R_1 = NW + (1 + r)I$

2. $W = h(Q)$

Subject to budget constraint

3. $R_O = I + P_T$
    $P_T = f(N) + QN$

Set up Lagrangian and take partial derivatives.

4. $R_1 = Nh(Q) + (1 + r)I + \lambda (R_O - P_T - I)$

5. $\dfrac{\partial R_1}{\partial N} = h(Q) - \lambda \dfrac{\partial P_T}{\partial N} = 0$

6. $\dfrac{\partial R_1}{\partial Q} = N\dfrac{\partial h(Q)}{\partial Q} - \lambda \dfrac{\partial P_T}{\partial Q} = 0$

7. $\dfrac{\partial R_1}{\partial I} = 1 + r - \lambda = 0$

8. $\dfrac{\partial R_1}{\partial \lambda} = R_O - P_T - I = 0$

9. $\lambda = 1 + r$

Substitute equation 9 into equation 5

10. $h(Q) = (1 + r) \dfrac{\partial P_T}{\partial N}$

Take partial derivative of P_T with respect to N

11. $\dfrac{\partial P_T}{\partial N} = \dfrac{\partial f(N)}{\partial N} + Q$

Substitute equation 11 into 10

12. $h(Q) = (1 + r) \dfrac{(\partial f(N) + Q)}{\partial N}$

Substitute equation 9 into equation 6

13. $N \dfrac{\partial h(Q)}{\partial Q} = (1 + r) \dfrac{\partial P_T}{\partial Q}$

Taking the derivative of P_T with respect to Q

14. $\dfrac{\partial P_T}{\partial Q} = N$

15. $\dfrac{\partial h(Q)}{\partial Q} = (1 + r)$

Since the price of the Nth child produced is the additional cost of producing that child,

16. $P = \dfrac{\partial f(N)}{\partial N} + Q$

Substitute equation 16 into 12

17. $h(Q)/P = 1 + r = W/P$

18. $W/P = 1 + r = \dfrac{\partial h(Q)}{\partial Q}$

Technical Appendix 5

Using the Cobb-Douglas production function, a popular type often employed by economists, the amount of net income, y, produced by any generation can be related to the quantity of physical capital, K, labor, L, and land, T. (Net income includes household production.)

1. $y = A \, K^{1-\beta-\alpha} T^{\alpha} L^{\beta}$

The quantity of labor is itself a function of the number of workers, N, and the total amount of human capital, Q. For this purpose, S is a constant.

2. $L = S \, N^{1-\lambda} Q^{\lambda}$, or

3. $L = S \, N \, \dfrac{(Q)^{\lambda}}{N}$

Equation 3 rewrites equation 2 in a form where the quantity of labor is directly proportional to the number of workers, where the efficiency of each worker is a function of the amount of human capital invested per worker.

Substituting equation 2 into equation 1 and adding the Lagrangian budget constraint produces

4. $y = A \, K^{1-\beta-\alpha} T^{\alpha} S^{\beta} N^{\beta-\lambda\beta} Q^{\lambda\beta} + \delta(R - P_K K - P_Q Q - P_N N)$

where P_Q is the price of one additional unit of capital, P_N is the cost of one additional worker holding total expenditure on quality constant, and P_K is the cost of an additional unit of physical capital.

Taking the partial derivative of net income with respect to each variable factor of production, we obtain,

5. $\dfrac{\partial y}{\partial K} = MP_K = A \, (1-\beta-\alpha) \, K^{-\beta-\alpha} T^{\alpha} S^{\beta} N^{\beta-\lambda\beta} Q^{\lambda\beta} - \delta P_K$

6. $\dfrac{\partial y}{\partial N} = MP_N = A \, K^{1-\beta-\alpha} T^{\alpha} S^{\beta}(\beta-\lambda\beta) \, N^{\beta-\lambda\beta-1} Q^{\lambda\beta} - \delta P_N$

7. $\dfrac{\partial y}{\partial Q} = MP_Q = A \, K^{1-\beta-\alpha} T^{\alpha} S^{\beta} \, N^{\beta-\lambda\beta} \, \lambda\beta \, Q^{\lambda\beta-1} - \delta P_Q$

8. $\dfrac{\partial y}{\partial T} = MP_T = A \, K^{1-\beta-\alpha} \, \alpha \, T^{\alpha-1} S^{\beta} \, N^{\beta-\lambda\beta} \, Q^{\lambda\beta}$

In equilibrium, the marginal product of every factor of production must be equal to its market price. Taking the ratio of the marginal products with respect to each other produces

9. $$\frac{MP_K}{MP_N} = \frac{(1-\beta-\propto)N}{K(\beta-\lambda\beta)} = \frac{P_K}{P_N}$$

10. $$\frac{N}{K} = \frac{(\beta-\lambda\beta)}{(1-\beta-\propto)}\frac{P_K}{P_N}$$

11. $$\frac{MP_K}{MP_Q} = \frac{(1-\beta-\propto)Q}{\lambda\beta K} = \frac{P_K}{P_Q}$$

12. $$\frac{Q}{K} = \frac{\lambda\beta}{(1-\beta-\propto)}\frac{P_K}{P_Q}$$

13. $$\frac{MP_N}{MP_Q} = \frac{(1-\lambda)Q}{\lambda N} = \frac{P_N}{P_Q}$$

14. $$\frac{Q}{N} = \frac{\lambda}{1-\lambda}\frac{P_N}{P_Q}$$

Since the variable factors of production last only one generation, in each generation, the amount of N,Q,and K available is determined by the net income, Y, of the parents. Net income is divided up among these three factors of production according to the equilibrium ratios described in equations 9, 11 and 13. (In addition, the cost of producing a worker of optimal quality, Q^* $(P_N + P_Q)$, is, in equilibrium, equal to the marginal product of the amount of labor a worker of that quality produces.) By properly defining the units of measure, we set the price of physical and human capital as equal to one dollar. To increase the labor force by one while leaving the total amount invested in human capital constant, requires an expenditure of C, the first term in the cost of producing a child of a given quality. In equilibrium, the ratio of the costs of producing each of the variable factors of production is equal to the ratio of their marginal products. Since land is fixed, there is no cost of producing it, but its rental price is equal to its marginal product. All the variable factors of production are assumed to last one generation or lifetime. For there to be growth in the economy, population, etc., net income must be greater than the cost of reproducing the current levels of population and physical and human capital.

When net income is just sufficient to reproduce them, the economy will stagnate. At this point, the marginal products of the variable factors of production may be less than their costs of production. The difference is made up by the return on land. Investors will accept negative returns because they have no alternative. Every investment, every strategy to transfer resources to the next generation produces a negative rate of return. In such a world, the only way for growth to occur is for there to be technological advances.

In the Cobb-Douglas production function, technological advances which are neutral, that is, do not favor any one factor of production, are represented by changes in the parameter A. An increase in A increases the marginal products of all factors equally and does not alter the equilibrium ratios of the factors of production. Because of this, variable A does not appear in equations 10, 12, or 14 above.

However, technological change does not have to be factor neutral. We argue that technological change, over the past several centuries, has had a disproportionate impact on the marginal product of investments in human capital. In the Cobb-Douglas production function, this could arise from a rise in both A and λ, the exponent that determines the efficiency of investment in human capital. From equation 14, it is apparent that an increase in λ will increase the equilibrium per capita investment in human capital. From equations 10 and 12, we can also show that a rise in λ will reduce the equilibrium ratio of population to physical capital and increase the ratio of human to physical capital.

Such technological change would occur if both A and λ were positive functions of all past investments in human capital.

15. $A_t = g(\int Q_{t-i})$

16. $\lambda_t = h(\int Q_{t-i})$

The rise in A over time represents the positive effect that past investments in human capital have on the productivity of all factors, while the rise in λ represents the disproportionate effect such investments have on increasing the return from current investments in human capital.

Bibliography

Abernethy, Virginia. "Optimism and Overpopulation." *Atlantic Monthly*. December 1994: 84+.

Alatalo, R.V., A. Carlson, A. Lundberg, and S. Olfstrand. "The Conflict Between Male Polygamy and Female Monogamy: The Case of the Pied Flycatcher Ficedula Hypoleuca." *American Naturalist*. 1981, 117: 738-753.

Alexander, Richard D. *The Biology of Moral Systems*. New York: Aldine de Gruyter, 1987.

—. *Darwinism and Human Affairs*. Seattle: University of Washington Press, 1979.

—. "Evolution and Culture." Chagnon and Irons, 59-78.

Anderson, A. "The Evolution of Sexes." *Science* 1992, 257: 324-326.

Anderson, J.G., H. S. Kaplan and J. B. Lancaster. "Paying for Children's College: the Paternal Investment Strategies of Albuquerque Men." Paper delivered to the Human Behavior and Evolution Society, University of Arizona, Tucson, 1997.

Appelbaum, Richard P. and William J. Chambliss, *Sociology*. New York: Harper Collins College Publishers, 1995.

Arutiunov, Sergei. quoted in *Update*, Center for Foreign Policy Development, Brown University, 1993,8: 6.

Axelrod, Robert. *The Evolution of Cooperation*. New York: Basic Books, Inc., 1984.

Bainton, Roland H. *The Reformation of the Sixteenth Century*. Boston: Beacon Press, 1952.

Baker, Robin R. and M. A. Bellis. *Human Sperm Competition*. London, UK: Chapman & Hall, 1995.

Barash, David P. "Predictive Sociobiology: Mate Selection in Damselfishes and Brood Defense in White-crowned Sparrows." in *Sociobiology: Beyond Nature/Nurture?* G. Barlow and J. Silverberg eds. Boulder CO: Westview Press, 1980.

—. *Sociobiology and Behavior*. New York: Elsevier, 1982.

—. *The Whisperings Within*. New York: Harper & Row, 1979.

—, and Judith Eve Lipton. *Making Sense of Sex*. Washington, D.C.: Island Press, 1997. (in paper as *Gender Gap*, New Brunswick, NJ: Transaction Publishers, 2001).

—, and Judith Eve Lipton. *The Myth of Monogamy*. New York: Henry Holt/ Times Books, 2002.

Barkow, Jerome H. "Beneath New Culture is Old Psychology: Gossip and Social Stratification," Barkow, Cosmides and Tooby, 627-637.

—, Leda Cosmides, John Tooby ed., *The Adapted Mind*. New York: Oxford University Press, 1992.

Bartlett, John. *Familiar Quotations*. 16th ed. Boston: Little, Brown and Co., 1992.

Bartley, W. W., III ed., *The Collected Works of F. A. Hayek, Vol. I, the Fatal Conceit*. Chicago: The University of Chicago Press, 1989.

Batten, Mary. *Sexual Strategies*. New York: G. P. Putnam's Sons, 1992.

Baumol, William J. *Economic Dynamics*, 2nd ed. New York: The Macmillan Company, 1967.

Beard, Mary and Michael Crawford. *Rome in the Late Republic*. Ithaca, NY: Cornell University Press, 1985.

Becker, Gary S. *Accounting for Tastes*. Cambridge, MA: Harvard University Press, 1996.

—. *The Economic Approach to Human Behavior*. Chicago: The University of Chicago Press, 1976.

—. *Economic Theory*. New York: Alfred A. Knopf, 1971.

—. *Human Capital*, 2nd ed. New York: Columbia University Press for the National Bureau of Economic Research, 1975.

—. *A Treatise on the Family*. Cambridge, MA: Harvard University Press, 1981.

—, and H. Gregg Lewis. "On the Interaction between the Quantity and Quality of Children." *Journal of Political Economy*. Vol. 81, No.2, Part II, March/April 1973: S279-S288.

Beecher, Michael D. "Successes and Failures of Parent-offspring Recognition in Animals." In *Kin Recognition*. P. G. Hepper, ed. Cambridge, UK: Cambridge University Press, 1992.

Bergstrom, Theodore C. "Economics in a Family Way." *Journal of Economic Literature*. Vol. XXXIV, Dec. 1996: 1903-1934.

Berté, Nancy A. "K'ekchi' Horticultural Labor Exchange: Productive and Reproductive Implications." Betzig, Borgerhoff Mulder, and Turke, 83-96.

Bertram, B. C. R. "Kin Selection in Lions and Evolution." in *Growing Points in Ethology*. P. P.G. Bateson and R. A. Hinde eds. New York:Cambridge University Press, 1978.

Betzig, Laura L. *Despotism and Differential Reproduction*. New York: Aldine Publishing Co., 1986.

—. "Mating and Parenting in Darwinian Perspective." Betzig, Borgerhoff Mulder and Turke, 3-20.

—. "Redistribution: Equity or Exploitation?" Betzig, Borgerhoff Mulder and Turke, 49-63.

—. "Sex, Succession and Stratification in the First Six Civilizations: How Powerful Men Reproduced, Passed Power to Their Sons, and Used Power to Defend Their Wealth, Women and Children." in *Social Stratification and Socioeconomic Inequality*, Vol. 1. Lee Ellis, ed. Westport, CT: Praeger, 1993.

—, Monique Borgerhoff Mulder and Paul Turke, eds. *Human Reproductive Behavior*. Cambridge: Cambridge University Press, 1988.

Birkhead, T. R. and A. P. Moller. "Female Control of Paternity." *Trends in Ecology and Evolution*. 1993,8: 100-103.

Bohannan, Paul. *Social Anthropology*. New York: Holt, Rinehart and Winston, 1963.

Boone, James L. III. "Parental Investment, Social Subordination, and Population Processes Among the 15th and 16th Century Portuguese Nobility." Betzig, Borgerhoff Mulder and Turke, 201-219.

—, and K.L. Kessler. "More Status or More Children." *Evolution and Human Behavior.* 1999, 20: 257-277.

Boorstin, Daniel J. *The Discoverers*. New York: Vintage Books, 1985.

Borgerhoff Mulder, M. "Reproductive Consequences of Sex-biased Inheritance." In *Comparative Socioecology of Mammals and Man.* V. Standen and R. Foley, eds. London, UK: Blackwell, 1988.

—. "Resources and Reproductive Success in Women, with an Example from the Kipsigis of Kenya." *Journal of Zoology*. 1987,213: 489-505.

Borgstrom, George. "The Numbers Force Us into a World Like None in History." *Smithsonian.* Vol. 7, No. 4, 1976, 70-77.

Boulding, Kenneth. *Conflict and Defense: A General Theory*. New York: Harper, 1962.

Brady, Gordon L. and Robert D. Tallison, ed. *On the Trail of Homo Economicus: Essays by Gordon Tullock*. Fairfax, VA: George Mason University Press, 1994.

Broom, Leonard, Philip Selznick and Dorothy H. Broom. *Essentials of Sociology*. 3rd ed. Itasca, IL: F. E. Peacock Publishers, Inc. 1984.

Brown, Donald E. *Human Universals*. New York: McGraw-Hill, Inc. 1991.

—, and Dana Hotra. "Are Prescriptively Monogamous Societies Effectively Monogamous?" Betzig, Borgerhoff Mulder and Turke, 153-159.

Buchanan, James M. *Economics: Between Predictive Science and Moral Philosophy*. College Station: Texas A&M University Press, 1987.

—. *The Economics and the Ethics of Constitutional Order*. Ann Arbor: The University of Michigan Press, 1994.

—. *Ethics and Economic Progress*. Norman, OK: The University of Oklahoma Press, 1994.

—, and Gordon Tullock. *The Calculus of Consent*. Ann Arbor: The University of Michigan Press, 1965.

Burns, George. *George Burns: in His Own Words*. H. Fagen, ed. New York: Carroll & Graf, 1996.

Buss, David M. *Evolutionary Psychology*. Boston, MA: Allyn & Bacon, 1999.

—. "Sex Differences in Human Mate Preferences: Evolutionary Hypotheses Tested in 37 Cultures." *Behavioral and Brain Sciences*. 1989,12: 1-14.

—, R. Larsen, D. Westen, and J. Semmelroth. "Sex Differences in Jealousy: Evolution, Physiology, and Psychology." *Psychological Science*. 1992,3: 251-255.

—, and D. P. Schmitt 1993. "Sexual Strategies Theory: an Evolutionary Perspective on Human Mating." *Psychological Review*. 1993,100: 204-232.

Caplan, Arthur L., ed. *The Sociobiology Debate*. New York: Harper & Row, 1978.

Carlson, Allan C. *Family Questions*. New Brunswick, NJ: Transaction Publishers, 1990.

Carter, Susan B. and Richard Sutch. "Myth of the Industrial Scrap Heap: A Revisionist View of Turn-of-the-Century American Retirement." *Journal of Economic History*. Vol. 56, No. 1, March, 1996:5-38.

Cartwright, Frederick F. *Disease and History*. New York: Dosset Press, 1991.

Chagnon, Napoleon A. "Is Reproductive Success Equal in Egalitarian Societies?" Chagnon and Irons, 374-401.

—. "Life Histories, Blood Revenge, and Warfare in a Tribal Population." *Science*. 1988,239: 985-991.

—. "Male Yanomamo Manipulations of Kinship Classifications of Female Kin for Reproductive Advantage." Betzig, Borgerhoff Mulder and Turke, 23-48.

—, and P. E. Bugos. "Kin Selection and Conflict: An Analysis of a Yanomamo Ax Fight." Chagnon and Irons, 213-237.

—, and William Irons, ed. *Evolutionary Biology and Human Social Behavior*. North Scituate, MA: Duxbury Press, 1979.

Chaliand, Gérard, ed. *The Art of War in World History*. Berkeley: University of California Press, 1994.

Chisholm, James S. "Toward a Developmental Evolutionary Ecology of Humans." MacDonald, 78-102.

Cipolla, Carlo M. *The Economic History of World Population*. 7th ed. Harmondsworth, Middlesex, England: Penguin Books Ltd., 1979.

Cody, Martin S. "A General Theory of Clutch Size." *Evolution*. 1966, 20: 174-184.

Cosmides, Leda and John Tooby. "Cognitive Adaptations for Social Exchange." Barkow, Cosmides and Tooby, 163-227.

—, John Tooby and Jerome H. Barkow. "Introduction: Evolutionary Psychology and Conceptual Integration." Barkow, Cosmides and Tooby, 3-15.

Coulson, J.C. "The Influence of the Pair-bond and Age on the Breeding Biology of the Killiwake Gull, *Rissa tridactyla*." *Journal of Animal Ecology*. 1966,35: 269-279.

Cowlishaw, G. and R. Mace. "Cross-cultural Patterns of Marriage and Inheritance: a Phylogenetic Approach." *Ethology and Sociobiology*. 1996,17: 87-98.

Crimmins, Eileen M. and Maria T. Pramaggiore. "Changing Health of the Older Working-Age Population and Retirement Patterns over Time." Ricardo-Campbell and Lazear, 132-161.

Croly, Herbert. *The Promise of American Life*. New York: Archon Books, 1963.

Cronk, L. "Group Selection's New Clothes." *Behavioral and Brain Sciences*. 1994, 17: 615-617.

Daly, Martin and Margo Wilson. *Homicide*. New York: Aldine de Gruyter, 1988.

—. "Violence Against Stepchildren." *Current Directions in Psychological Science*. 1996,5: 77-81.

—. "Whom are Newborn Babies Said to Resemble?" *Ethology and Sociobiology*. 1982,3: 69-78.

Darwin, Charles. *The Origin of Species*. New York: The Modern Library, (1859) 1960.

Davies, J. K. *Democracy and Classical Greece*. 2nd ed. Cambridge, MA: Harvard University Press, 1993.

Dawkins, Richard. *The Blind Watchmaker.* New York: W. W. Norton & Co., 1987.

—. *The Extended Phenotype.* New York: Oxford University Press, 1982.

—. *The Selfish Gene.* New York: Oxford University Press, 1989.

de Catanzaro, D. "Evolutionary Limits to Self-Preservation." *Ethology and Sociobiology.* 1992,12: 13-28.

Degler, Carl N. *In Search of Human Nature.* New York: Oxford University Press, 1991.

DeKay, W. T. "Grandparental Investment and the Uncertainty of Kinship." Paper delivered to the Human Behavior and Evolution Society, Santa Barbara, CA, 1995.

Dennett, Daniel C. *Darwin's Dangerous Idea.* New York: Simon & Schuster, 1995.

Dickemann, Mildred. "Female Infanticide and Reproductive Strategies of Stratified Human Societies." Chagnon and Irons, 321-368.

Dobzhansky, Theodosius. "Evolution in the Tropics." *American Scientist.* 1950,38: 209-221.

Dunbar, Robin I. M. "Darwinizing Man: A Commentary." Betzig, Borgerhoff Mulder and Turke, 161-169.

—. *Grooming, Gossip and the Evolution of Language.* Cambridge, MA:Harvard University Press, 1997.

Durham, William H. "Toward a Co-evolutionary Theory of Human Biology and Culture." Chagnon and Irons, 39-59.

Durkheim, Emile. *The Division of Labor in Society.* New York: The Free Press, 1965.

Ehrenreich, Barbara. *The Hearts of Men.* New York: Doubleday, 1984.

Ehrlich, Isaac. "Participation in Illegitimate Activities: A Theoretical and Empirical Investigation." *Journal of Political Economy.* Vol. 81, May/June, 1973: 521-565.

Einstein, Albert. *Cosmic Religion: With Other Opinions and Aphorisms.* New York: Covici-Friede, 1931.

Eisenstein, Elizabeth L. *The Printing Press as an Agent of Change.* Cambridge: Cambridge University Press, 1991.

Ellis, Bruce J. "The Evolution of Sexual Attraction: Evaluative Mechanisms in Women." Barkow, Cosmides, and Tooby, 267-287.

Elton, Edwin J. and Martin J. Gruber. *Modern Portfolio Theory and Investment Analysis,* 2nd ed. New York: John Wiley & Sons, 1984.

Essock-Vitale, Susan M. and Michael T. McGuire. "What 70 Million Years Hath Wrought: Sexual Histories and Reproductive Success of a Random Sample of American Women." Betzig, Borgerhoff Mulder, and Turke, 221-235.

Euler, H. A. and B. Weitzel. "Discriminatory Grandparental Solicitude as Reproductive Strategy." *Human Nature.* 1996,7: 39-59.

Evans-Pritchard, E. E. *Essays in Social Anthropology.* New York: The Free Press of Glencoe, Inc., 1963.

Feigelman, William, ed. *Sociology Full Circle: Contemporary Readings on Society,* 6th ed. Fort Worth: Harcourt Brace College Publishers, 1993.

Ferrill, Arthur. *The Origins of War*. London: Thames and Hudson, 1988.

Fisher, R.A. *The Genetical Theory of Natural Selecton*. Oxford, UK: Clarendon Press, 1930.

Fleming, Thomas. *The Politics of Human Nature*. New Brunswick, NJ: Transaction Books, 1988.

Forester, Colin and G.S.L. Tucker. *Economic Opportunity and White American Fertility Ratios 1800–1860* New Haven: Yale University Press, 1972.

Fox, Robin. "Kinship Categories as Natural Categories." Chagnon and Irons, 132-144.

Freeman, Derek. *Margaret Mead and Samoa: the Making and Unmaking of an Anthropological Myth*. Cambridge, MA: Harvard University Press, 1983.

Frey, R. G., ed. *Utility and Rights*. Minneapolis: University of Minnesota Press, 1984.

Friedman, Milton and L.J. Savage. "The Utility Analysis of Choices Involving Risk." *Journal of Political Economy*. Aug., 1948: 270-304.

Frost, Robert. "The White-Tailed Hornet." *Collected Poems of Robert Frost*. New York: Halcyon House, 1940.

Gandolfi, Anna Sachko and Laurence Miners. "Gender-Based Differences in Life Insurance Ownership." *Journal of Risk and Insurance*. Vol. 63, No. 4, Dec., 1996: 683-693.

Garrett, R. Atlantic Disasters: The Titanic and other Victims of the North Atlantic. London, UK: Buchan & Enright, 1986.

Garver, Eugene. *Machiavelli and the History of Prudence*. Madison, WI: The University of Wisconsin Press, 1987.

Gaulin, Steven J.C. and J. S. Boster. "Dowry as Female Competition. *American Anthropologist.*" 1990, 92: 994-1005.

—, D. H. McBurney and S. L. Brakeman-Wartell. "Matrilineal Biases in the Investment of Aunts and Uncles." *Human Nature*. 1997,8: 139-151.

Giddens, Anthony. *Introduction to Sociology*. New York: W. W. Norton & Co., 1991.

Goldin, Claudia and Hugh Rockoff, eds., *Strategic Factors in Nineteenth Century American Economic History*. Chicago: University of Chicago Press, 1992.

Grafen, Alan. "Biological Signals as Handicaps." *Journal of Theoretical Biology*. 1990,144: 517-546.

Grant, Michael. *The Founders of the Western World*. New York: Charles Scribner's Sons, 1991.

Gwynne, D.T. "Sexual Difference Theory: Mormon Crickets Show Role Reversal in Mate Choice." *Science*. 1981, 213: 779-780.

Haig, David. "Genetic Conflicts in Human Pregnancy." *Quarterly Review of Biology* 1993,68: 495-532.

Haines, Michael R. "The Population of the United States, 1790-1920." *NBER Working Paper Series on Historical Factors in Long Run Growth*. Paper No. 56, June, 1994.

Hamilton, William D. "The Genetical Evolution of Social Behavior. I and II." *Journal of Theoretical Biology*. 1964,7: 1-52.

—. "Sex Versus Non-Sex Versus Parasite." *Oikos*. 1980,35: 282-290.

Hardin, Garret. "The Tragedy of the Commons." *Science*. 1961,162: 1243-1248.

Harris, Marvin. *Culture, People, Nature*. 4th ed. New York:Harper & Row Publishers, 1985.

Hartung, John. "Polygyny and Inheritance of Wealth." *Current Anthropology*, Vol. 23, No. 1. February 1982, 1-12.

Hawthorne, Nathaniel. *The House of the Seven Gables*. New York: Dodd, Mead & Company, 1950.

Hayek, F. A. *The Counter-Revolution of Science*. London: The Free Press of Glencoe, 1964.

—. *Law, Legislation and Liberty*. Chicago: University of Chicago Press, 1973.

Heilbroner, Robert L. *The Worldly Philosophers*. 6th ed. New York: Simon & Schuster, Inc., 1986.

Henderson, James M. and Richard E. Quandt. *Microeconomic Theory*. New York: McGraw-Hill, 1958.

Herrnstein, Richard J. and Charles Murray. *The Bell Curve: Intelligence and Class Structure in American Life*. New York: Free Press, 1994.

Hill, Kim and A. M. Hurtado. "The Evolution of Premature Reproductive Senescence and Menopause in Human Females." *Human Nature*. 1991,2: 313-350.

Himmelfarb, Gertrude. *The De-Moralization of Society*. New York: Alfred A. Knopf, 1995.

Hirschleifer, Jack. "Economics from a Biological Viewpoint." *Journal of Law and Economics*. Vol. 20, No. 1, April, 1977:1-52.

—.   "The Expanding Domain of Economics." *American Economic Review*, Vol. 75, No. 6, December 1985: 53-68.

Holmes, Warren G. and Paul W. Sherman. "Kin Recognition in Animals." *American Scientist*. 1983, 71: 46-55.

Horgan, John. 1991. "In the Beginning." *Scientific American*. February, 1991, 264: 116-125.

—. "The New Social Darwinists." *Scientific American*. October 1995, 174-181.

Hrdy, S.B. *The Langurs of Abu*. Cambridge, MA: Harvard University Press, 1979.

Hume, David. *Writings on Economics*. Madison: The University of Wisconsin Press, 1970.

Hurst, L. and W. D. Hamilton. "Cytoplasmic Fusion and the Nature of the Sexes." *Proceedings of the Royal Society of London*. 1992,B. 247: 189-194.

Irons, William. "Cultural and Biological Success." Chagnon and Irons, 257-272.

—. "How Did Morality Evolve?" *Zygon*. Vol. 26, No. 1. March 1991: 49-89.

—. "Natural Selection, Adaptation, and Human Social Behavior." Chagnon and Irons, 4-39.

—. "Parental Behavior in Humans." Betzig, Borgerhoff Mulder, and Turke, 307-314.

Jaher, Frederic Cople, ed. *The Rich, the Well Born, and the Powerful*. Urbana: University of Illinois Press, 1973.

Jenni, Donald A. and G. Collier. "Polyandry in the American Jacana." *Auk.* 1972, 89: 743-765.

Johnson, Paul. *A History of Christianity.* New York: Atheneum, 1976.

Kaplan, Hillard S. "A Theory of Fertility and Parental Investment in Traditional and Modern Societies." *Yearbook of Physical Anthropology.* Vol. 39. 1996: 91-135.

—. Jane B. Lancaster, Sara E. Johnson, John A. Bock."Does Observed Fertility Maximize Fitness Among New Mexican Men?" *Human Nature.* Vol. 6, No. 4, 1995: 325-360.

Katz, P.L. "A Long-Term Approach to Foraging Optimization." *American Naturalist.* 1974,108: 758-782.

Keegan, John. *A History of Warfare.* New York: Alfred A. Knopf, 1993.

Kenrick, D. T. and R. C. Keefe. "Age Preferences in Mates Reflect Sex Differences in Reproductive Strategies." *Behavioral and Brain Sciences.* 1992,15: 75-133.

—. E.K. Sadalla, G. Groth, and M.R. Trost. "Evolution, Traits, and The Stages of Human Courtship: Quantifying the Parental Investment Model." *Journal of Personality.* 1990, 58: 97-116.

Kendrick, John W. *The Formation and Stocks of Total Capital.* New York: Columbia University Press for the National Bureau of Economic Research, 1976.

Keppie, Lawrence. *The Making of the Roman Army.* New York: Barnes & Noble Books, 1994.

Kinder, Hermann and Werner Hilgemann. *The Anchor Atlas of World History.* Vols. I & II. Garden City, NY: Anchor Books, 1974, 1978.

King, C.E. and W. W. Anderson. "Age-Specific Selection II, the Interaction Between r and K During Population Growth." *American Naturalist.* 1971,105: 137-156.

Klein, Peter G., ed. *The Collected Works of F. A. Hayek, Vol. 4, The Fortunes of Liberalism.* Chicago: The University of Chicago Press, 1992.

Kotlikoff, Laurence J. "The Relationship of Productivity to Age." Ricardo-Campbell and Lazear, 100-131.

Krebs, Dennis, Kathy Denton and Nancy C. Higgins. "On the Evolution of Self-Knowledge and Self-Deception." MacDonald, 103-139.

Krebs, J.R. and N.B. Davies ed., *Behavioural Ecology: An Evolutionary Approach.* 3rd ed. Oxford:Blackwell Scientific,1991.

Kroeber, Alfred. "The Superorganic." *American Anthropologist.* 1917,19: 23-51.

Kukathas, Chandran. *Hayek and Modern Liberalism.* Oxford: Clarendon Press, 1990.

Lack, David. *Ecological Adaptations for Breeding in Birds.* London, UK: Methuen, 1968.

Landsburg, Steven. *The Armchair Economist: Economics and Everyday Life.* New York: Free Press, 1993.

Lange, Oskar and Fred M. Taylor. *On the Economic Theory of Socialism.* Benjamin E. Lippincott, ed. Minneapolis: University of Minnesota Press, 1938; reprinted, New York: McGraw-Hill, 1964.

Lerner, Abba P. *The Economics of Control: Principles of Welfare Economics*. New York: Macmillan, 1944.

Lessels, Catherine. "The Evolution of Life Histories." Krebs and Davies, 32-65.

LeVine, R.A. "Gusii Sex Offenses: Study in Social Control." In *Forcible Rape: the Crime, the Victim, and the Offender*. D. Chappell, R. Geis and G. Geis, eds. New York: Columbia University Press, 1977.

Little, B.R. "Personal Projects Analysis: Trivial Pursuits, Magnificent Obsessions, and the Search for Coherence." in *Personality Psychology*, (ed: D. M. Buss and N. Cantor) New York: Springer-Verlag, 1989.

Low, Bobbi S. "Sexual Selection and Human Ornamentation." Chagnon and Irons, 462-487.

—. *Why Sex Matters*. Princeton, NJ: Princeton University Press, 2000.

MacArthur, Robert H. and Edward O. Wilson. *The Theory of Island Biogeography*. Princeton, NJ: Princeton University Press, 1966.

MacDonald, Kevin B., ed. *Sociobiological Perspectives on Human Development*. New York: Springer-Verlag, 1988.

Mace, R. "Biased Parental Investment and Reproductive Success in Gabbra Pastoralists." *Behavioral Ecology and Sociobiology*. 1996,38: 75-82.

Malliaris, A. G. and W. A. Brock. *Stochastic Methods in Economics and Finance*. Amsterdam: North Holland Publishing Co., 1982.

Mandeville, Bernard. *Fable of the Bees*. Oxford: The Clarendon Press, 1924.

Masters, Roger. *The Nature of Politics*. New Haven, CT: Yale University Press, 1989.

Maynard Smith, John. *Evolution and the Theory of Games*. Cambridge: Cambridge University Press, 1982.

—, and G. R. Price. "The Logic of Animal Conflict." *Nature*. Vol. 246. November 2, 1973, 15-18.

McEvedy, Colin and Richard Jones. *Atlas of World Population History*. Harmondsworth, Middlesex, England: Penguin Books Ltd., 1980.

McNeill, William H. *The Pursuit of Power*. Chicago: The University of Chicago Press, 1982.

Michael, Robert T. "Causation Among Socio-Economic Time Series." National Bureau of Economic Research, Working Paper No. 246, 1978.

Murdock, George P. *Ethnographic Atlas*. Pittsburg, PA: Pittsburgh University Press, 1967.

Murray, Charles. *Losing Ground*. New York: Basic Books, 1984.

Nanda, Serena. *Cultural Anthropology*. 5th ed. Belmont, CA: Wadsworth Publishing Co., 1994.

Nesse, Randolph M. and George C. Williams. *Why We get Sick*. New York: Times Books, 1994.

Neubauer, Peter B., M.D. and Alexander Neubauer. *Nature's Thumbprint*. Reading, MA: Addison-Wesley Publishing Co., Inc., 1990.

North, Douglass C. and Robert Paul Thomas. *The Rise of the Western World*. Cambridge: Cambridge University Press, 1973.

Nozick, Robert. *Anarchy, State, and Utopia*. New York: Basic Books, Inc., 1974.

Olson, Mancur. *The Rise and Decline of Nations*. New Haven, CT: Yale University Press, 1982.

Orians, Gordon H. "On the Evolution of Mating Systems in Birds and Mammals." *American Naturalist*. 1969,103: 589-603.

Owen, John B. *The Eighteenth Century 1714-1815*. New York: W.W. Norton and Company, 1976.

Pacey, Arnold. *Technology in World Civilization*. Cambridge, MA: The MIT Press, 1991.

Packard, Michael D. and Virginia P. Reno. "A Look at Very Early Retirees." Ricardo-Campbell and Lazear, 243-272.

Packer, Craig, D. Schell, and A. E. Pusey. "Why Lions Form Groups: Food is Not Enough." *American Naturalist*. 1990, 136: 1-19.

Palivos, Theodore. "Endogenous Fertility, Multiple Growth Paths, and Economic Convergence." *Journal of Economic Dynamics and Control*. 19 (1995): 1489-1510.

Parker,G., R. R. Baker and V. Smith. 1972. "The Origin and Evolution of Gamete Dimorphism and the Male-Female Phenomenon." *Journal of Theoretical Biology*. 1972,36: 529-552.

Perusse, Daniel. 1993. "Cultural and Reproductive Success in Industrial Societies: Testing the Relationship at the Proximate and Ultimate Levels." *Behavioral and Brain Sciences*. 1993,16: 267-283.

Philippi, Tom and Jon Seger. "Hedging One's Evolutionary Bets, Revisited." *Trends in Ecology and Evolution*. Vol. 4. 1989:41-44.

Pierotti-Cei, Lia. *Life in Italy During the Renaissance*. Milan: Liber, 1987.

Pipes, Richard. *Property and Freedom*. New York: Alfred A. Knopf, 1999.

Polachek, Solomon W. "Human Capital and the Gender Earnings Gap." *Out of the Margin*. Edith Kniper and Jolande Sap, eds. London and New York: Rutledge Press, 1995, 61-79.

Polanyi, Karl. *The Great Transformation*. Boston: Beacon Press, 1962.

Poly, Jean-Pierre and Eric Bournazel. *The Feudal Transformation*. New York: Holmes & Meier, 1991.

Posner, Richard A. *Economic Analysis of Law*. Boston: Little, Brown, 1973. 2nd edition, 1977.

—. *Sex and Reason*. Cambridge, MA: Harvard University Press, 1994.

Procacci, Giuliano. *History of the Italian People*. Harmondsworth, Middlesex, England: Penguin Books Ltd., 1978.

Quirk,James and Rubin Saposnik. *Introduction to General Equilibrium Theory and Welfare Economics*. New York: McGraw- Hill, 1968.

Radnitzky, Gerard and W. W. Bartley III, eds., *Evolutionary Epistemology, Rationality and the Sociology of Knowledge*. LaSalle, IL: Open Court, 1993.

Ransom, Roger L. And Richard Sutch. "The Decline of Retirement in the Years Before Social Security: U.S. Retirement Patterns, 1870-1940." Ricardo-Campbell and Lazear, 3-37.

Rawls, John. *A Theory of Justice*. Cambridge, MA: The Belknap Press of Harvard University Press, 1971.

Redondi, Pietro. *Galileo: Heretic*. Princeton, NJ: Princeton University Press, 1987.

Rees, Nigel, ed. *Cassell Dictionary of Humorous Quotations*, London: Cassell, 1998, 211.

Ricardo-Campbell, Rita and Edward P. Lazear, eds. *Issues in Contemporary Retirement*. Stanford, CA: Hoover Institution Press, 1988.

Rice, William. "Sexually Antagonistic Male Adaptation Triggered by Experimental Arrest of Female Evolution." *Nature*. 1996, 381: 232-234.

Ridley, Matt. *The Red Queen*. New York: Macmillan Publishing Co., 1993.

Robb, A.L. and J.B. Burbidge. "Consumption, Income and Retirement." Working Paper No. 87-17, Dept of Economics, McMaster University, Hamilton, Ontario, August, 1987.

Rosman, Abraham and Paula G. Rubel. *The Tapestry of Culture*, 5th ed. New York: McGraw-Hill, Inc., 1995.

Rousseau, Jean-Jacques. *The Second Discourse* 1750. (transl. P. Echler) New York: Collier, 1910.

Rozin, Paul. "The Evolution of Intelligence and Access to the Cognitive Unconscious." In J. M. Sprague and A. N. Epstein eds. *Progress in Psychobiology and Physiological Psychology*. New York: Academic Press, 1976.

Ruyle, E. E. Comment on "The Adaptive Significance of Cultural Behavior." *Human Ecology*. 1977, 5: 53-55.

Ryan, Michael. *The Tungara Frog*. Chicago: University of Chicago Press, 1985.

Samuelson, Paul A. and William D. Nordhaus. *Economics*. 12th ed. New York: McGraw Hill, 1985.

Saxe, John. "The Blind Men and the Elephant." *The Poetical Works of John Godfrey Saxe*. Houghton: Boston, 1892.

Segal, Nancy L. "Cooperation, Competition, and Altruism in Human Twinships: A Sociobiological Approach." MacDonald, 168-206.

Sen, Amartya K. "Rational Fools: A Critique of the Behavioral Foundations of Economic Theory." *Philosophy and Public Affairs*. Vol. 6, No. 4. Summer, 1977: 317-344.

Shepher, Joseph. "Mate Selection Among Second-Generation Kibbutz Adolescents and Adults: Incest Avoidance and Negative Imprinting." *Archives of Sexual Behavior*. 1971,1: 293-307.

Silk, Joan B. "Human Adoption in Evolutionary Perspective." *Human Nature*. 1990,1: 25-52.

Smith, Adam. *The Wealth of Nations*. Chicago: University of Chicago Press, 1976. (Orig. 1904)

Smith, Anthony D. *The Ethnic Origins of Nations*. Oxford, UK: Blackwell, 1991.

Smith, John Maynard. *Evolution and the Theory of Games*. Cambridge, UK: Cambridge University Press, 1982.

—. *Games, Sex and Evolution*. London, UK: Harvester, 1988.

Smith, Martin S., Bradley J. Kish, and Charles B. Crawford. "Inheritance of Wealth as Human Kin Investment." *Ethology and Sociobiology*. 1987,8: 171-182.

Sober, E. and D. S. Wilson. *Unto Others: the Evolution and Psychology of Unselfish Behavior*. Cambridge, MA: Harvard University Press, 1998.

Steckel, Richard H. "The Fertility Transition in the United States: Tests of Alternative Hypotheses." Goldin and Rockoff, 351-374.

Stephens, D.W. and J. R. Krebs. *Foraging Theory*. Princeton, NJ: Princeton University Press, 1986.

Stigler, George J. *Essays in the History of Economics*. Chicago: The University of Chicago Press, 1965.

—. *The Theory of Price*. 4th ed. New York: Macmillan Publishing Co., 1987.

—, and Gary S. Becker. "DeGustibus Non Est Disputandum." *American Economic Review*. March 1977: 76-90.

"Susan Smith Indicted in Death of Sons." *Los Angeles Times*. 13 Dec. 1994, Part A: 39.

Symons, Donald. "On the Use and Misuse of Darwinism in the Study of Human Behavior." Barkow, Cosmides, and Tooby, 137-159.

Thiessen, Delbert, R. K. Young, and R. Burroughs. "Lonely Hearts Advertisements Reflect Sexually Dimorphic Mating Strategies." *Ethology and Sociobiology*. 1993,14: 209-229.

Thornhill,Randy, S. W. Gangestad, and R. Comer. "Human Female Orgasm and Mate Fluctuating Asymmetry." *Animal Behaviour*. 1995,50: 1601-1615.

—,   and Nancy W. Thornhill. "Human Rape: An Evolutionary Analysis." *Ethology and Sociobiology*. 1983,4: 137-173.

Tiger, Lionel. "Biology, Psychology and Incorrect Assumptions of Cultural Relativism." Chagnon and Irons, 511-519.

Tooby, John and Leda Cosmides. "The Psychological Foundations of Culture." Barkow, Cosmides, and Tooby, 19-136.

Trivers, Robert L. 1971. "The Evolution of Reciprocal Altruism." *Quarterly Review of Biology* 1971,46: 35-57.

—. "Parent-Offspring Conflict." *American Zoologist*. 1974,14:249-264.

—. "Parental Investment and Sexual Selection." In *Sexual Selection and the Descent of Man*. ed. by B.Campbell. Chicago:Aldine, 1972.

—, and Dan E. Willard. "Natural Selection of Parental Ability to Vary the Sex Ratio of Offspring." *Science*. Vol. 179, January 1973: 90-92.

Tullock, Gordon. *The Economics of Nonhuman Societies*. Tucson, AZ: Pallas Press, 1994.

—. *The Economics of Wealth and Poverty*. New York: New York University Press, 1986.

—, and Richard B. McKenzie. *The New World of Economics*. Homewood, IL: Richard D. Irwin, Inc., 1985.

Tuma, Nancy Brandon and Gary D. Sandefur. "Trends in the Labor Force Activity of the Elderly in the United States, 1940-1980." Ricardo-Campbell and Lazear, 38-83.

Turke, Paul W. "Evolution and the Demand for Children." *Population and Development Review*.Vol. 15, No. 1, March 1989:61-90.

—. "Which Humans Behave Adaptively and Why Does It Matter?" *Ethology and Sociobiology*. 11, 1990: 305-339.

van den Berghe, Pierre. *Human Family Systems: An Evolutionary View*. New York: Elsevier, 1979.

Van Valen, Leigh. 1973. "A New Evolutionary Law." *Evolutionary Theory*. 1973,1: 1-30.

Varian, Hal R. *Microeconomic Analysis*, 3rd ed. New York: W. W. Norton & Co., 1992.

Veyne, Paul, ed. *A History of Private Life*. Cambridge, MA: The Belknap Press of Harvard University Press, 1987.

Voland, Eckart. "Differential Infant and Child Mortality in Evolutionary Perspective: Data from Late 17th to 19th Century, Ostfriesland (Germany)." Betzig, Borgerhoff Mulder, and Turke, 253-261.

von Mises, Ludwig. *Human Action*, 3rd revised ed. Chicago:Contemporary Books, Inc., 1966.

Weatherhead, P. and R. Robertson. "Offspring Quality and the Polygyny Threshold: 'the Sexy Son Hypothesis.'" *American Naturalist*. 1979,113: 201-208.

Westneat, David F., P. W. Sherman, and M. L. Morton. 1990. "The Ecology and Evolution of Extra-Pair Copulations in Birds." *Current Ornithology*. 1990,7: 330-369.

White, Leslie A. *The Science of Culture*. New York: Farrar, Straus & Giroux, 1969.

Wiederman, M. W. and E. R. Allgeier. "Gender Differences in Mate Selection Criteria: Sociobiological or Socioeconomic Explanation?" *Ethology and Sociobiology*. 1992,13: 115-124.

Williams, George C. *Adaptation and Natural Selection*. Princeton, NJ: Princeton University Press, 1966 &1974.

—. *Sex and Evolution*. Princeton, NJ: Princeton University Press, 1975.

—. "Pleiotropy, Natural Selection, and the Evolution of Senescence." *Evolution*. 1957,11: 398-411.

Willis, Robert J. "A New Approach to the Economic Theory of Fertility Behavior." *Journal of Political Economy*. Vol. 81, No. 2, Part II, March/April 1973: S14-S64.

Wilson, Edward O. "Biology and Anthropology: A Mutual Transformation?" Chagnon and Irons, 519-526.

—. *Consilience*. New York: Alfred A. Knopf, 1998.

—. *On Human Nature*. Cambridge, MA: Harvard University Press, 1978.

—. *Sociobiology, the New Synthesis*. Cambridge, MA: Harvard University Press, 1975.

Wilson, James Q. *The Moral Sense*. New York: The Free Press, 1993.

Wilson, Margo and Martin Daly. "The Man Who Mistook His Wife for a Chattel." Barkow, Cosmides, and Tooby, 289-322.

Wood, Gordon S. *The Radicalism of the American Revolution*. New York: Alfred A. Knopf, 1992.

World Population Prospects: The 1994 Revision. New York: United Nations, 1995.

Wright, Robert. *The Moral Animal*. New York: Pantheon Books, 1994.

Yasuba, Yasukichi. *Birthrate of the White Population in the United States, 1800–1860, and Economic Study*. Baltimore: John Hopkins, 1962.

Young, T.P. "Natural Die-offs of Large Mammals: Implications for Conservation." *Conservation Bioglogy*. 1993, 8: 410-418.

Zahavi, Amotz and A. Zahavi. *The Handicap Principle*. New York: Oxford University Press, 1996.

Index

(Note: Because certain terms and concepts such as natural sciences, human behavior, social sciences, physical sciences, anthropology, sociology, psychology, evolutionary biology, utility, and human capital appear throughout this book, they are not specifically indexed here.)

Printed in the United States
by Baker & Taylor Publisher Services

Printed in the United States
by Baker & Taylor Publisher Services